# Natural History of the Columbia River Gorge

ROBERT HOGFOSS

NATURAL HISTORY OF THE COLUMBIA RIVER GORGE



*iUniverse books may be ordered through booksellers or by contacting:*

*iUniverse*
*1663 Liberty Drive*
*Bloomington, IN 47403*
*www.iuniverse.com*
*844-349-9409*



*ISBN: 978-1-6632-4259-4 (sc)*
*ISBN: 978-1-6632-4260-0 (e)*

*Library of Congress Control Number: 2022913185*

*Print information available on the last page.*

*iUniverse rev. date: 08/18/2022*

***The hills have now become mountains, high on each side [and] rocky steep.***

Meriwether Lewis describing the Gorge
(Journal entry, April 9, 1806)

# CONTENTS

# ACKNOWLEDGEMENTS

The author thanks the many individuals who have reviewed and commented on drafts of various sections. The book is all the better for their input. Any errors or omissions in the text are solely those of the author.

Proceeds of sale of this book go in part to help support *The Friends of the Columbia Gorge* (www.gorgefriends.org), a non-profit group dedicated to help preserve and protect the Gorge.

# FOREWORD

This book provides a comprehensive introduction to the natural history of the Columbia River Gorge. It is not a field guide, but a history that tells the story of the Gorge. There are six chapters, discussing the following:

Rocks (geology)

Water (hydrology and geomorphology)

Weather (meteorology, fire and floods)

Plants (flora)

Animals (fauna), and

People (prehistory, history and current life)

Recommended reading is suggested at the beginning of each chapter, and additional information and reference is included in the text and chapter notes. The book is intended to be supplemented with use of field guides for those who want to learn more about geology, bird, plant and animal identification in the Gorge (e.g., *Wildflowers of the Columbia River Gorge*, by Russ Jolley, *Trees & Shrubs of the Pacific Northwest*, by Turner & Kuhlmann; *In Search of Ancient Oregon*, by Ellen Morris Bishop, etc.) An excellent collection of historic photographs of the Gorge is *Wild Beauty* (Oregon State Univ. Press 2008), by Terry Toedtemeier.

Taken together this information should help the reader understand how the Gorge was formed, what plant and animal life uses this place as habitat and how humans have lived here over time.

The Columbia River Gorge National Scenic Area encompasses 292,500 acres along either side of the Columbia River, beginning at the Sandy River about 17 miles east of Portland, Oregon, extending east another 85 miles to just beyond the Deschutes River. It is bounded by more than 50 peaks and high points, giving it a fjord-like appearance.

## *Please Leave No Trace*

*...of your visits to the Gorge. As the saying goes: "leave only footprints; take only pictures" (but go light on the footprints, too, OK?) Your actions and your thoughtfulness help preserve this unique landscape, and the varied life within it.*

## A Note About Maps

Many different maps of the Gorge are available. The Gorge Commission (GC) makes free maps of the Scenic Area available at many locations, including the GC/Forest Service offices in Hood River and White Salmon, Skamania Lodge, The Columbia Gorge Discovery Center & Museum, Multnomah Falls visitor center, Bonneville Dam, and other locations. You can also access maps on the GC's website (www.gorgecommission.org), some of which are interactive with GIS data and others that can be downloaded. The Forest Service also makes maps available, and there are many maps of specific focus out there (such as maps showing only roads, trails, vineyards and wineries, etc.). A large, detailed map of the Scenic Area showing topographic lines, trails and place names (printed on waterproof paper) is available for sale by National Geographic. That map can usually be purchased from most of the above locations, as well as bookstores and REI.

# COLOMBIA RIVER GORGE

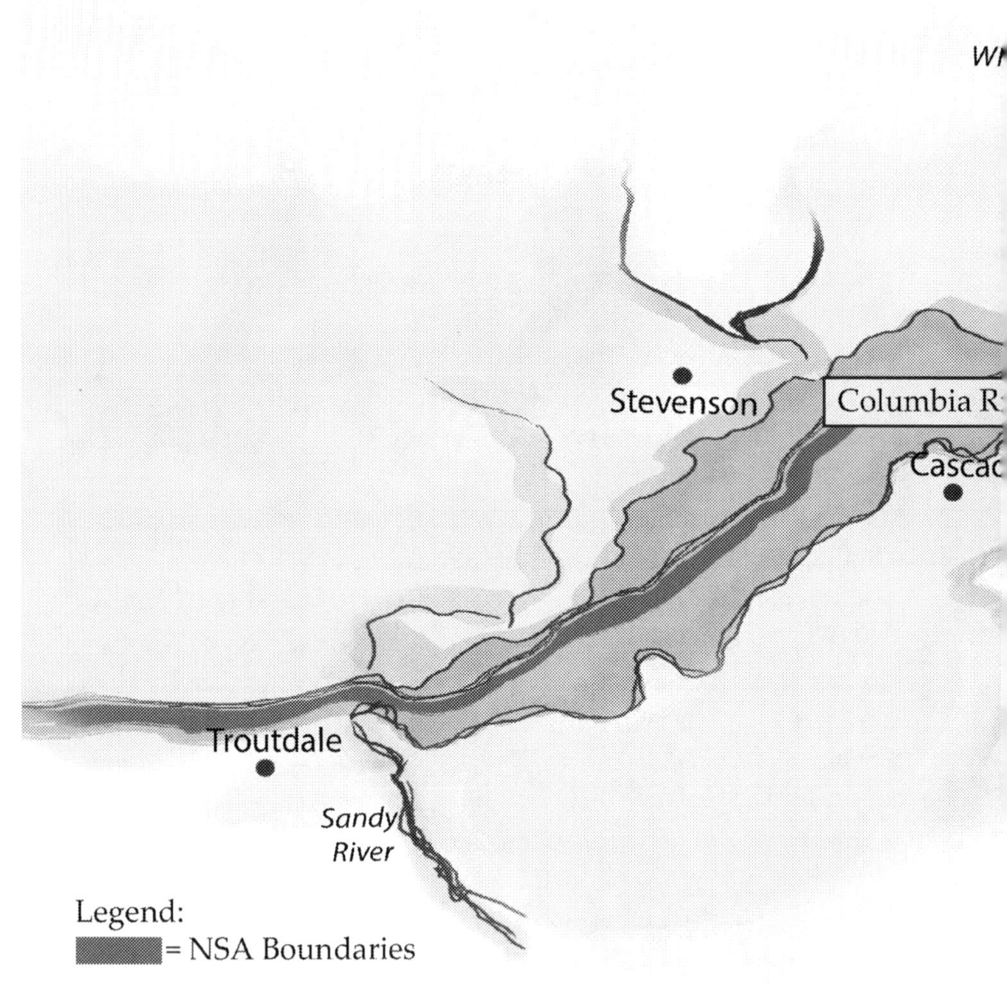

## TIONAL SCENIC AREA

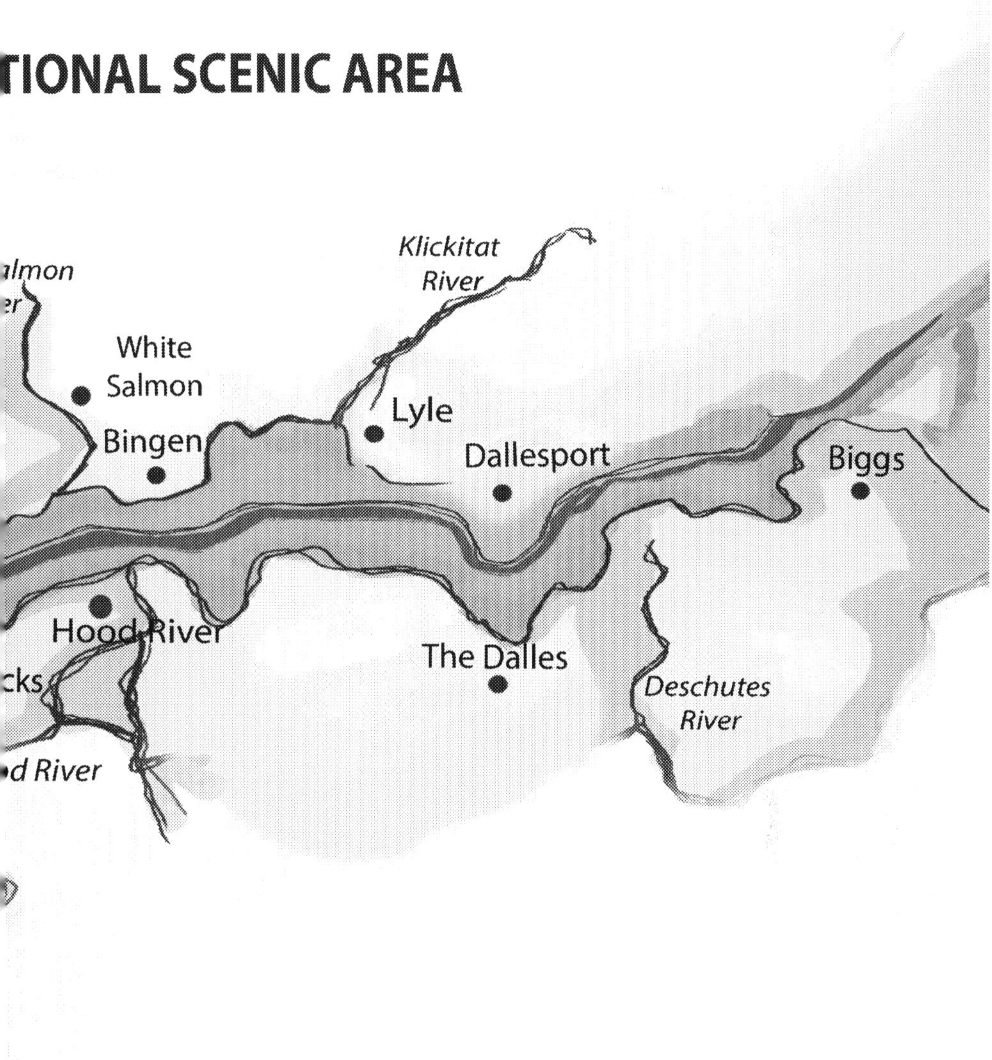

Klickitat River
lmon
White Salmon
Lyle
Bingen
Dallesport
Biggs
Hood River
The Dalles
cks
Deschutes River
d River

# PREFACE: NATURAL HISTORY

If you are reading this you are already curious about the natural world around you and about the history of place. I spent most of my youth asking questions about the natural world and history of place and studied everything I could about natural history in schools and in the field. The main thing I learned was that no single school or course taught an integrated knowledge about the natural world, and how people have lived in a given place over time. I learned that people inevitably gain that knowledge on their own, by listening and observing and learning, by living among others who have bits and pieces of such knowledge and learning from them, by finding mentors along the way.

I have had many mentors along the way. I meet new ones all the time. The best are those First Peoples and others who have lived in one place for a long time, who maintain traditional knowledge about the world around us and the history that has brought us to this place on this day. Natural history is more a way of life than an academic discipline, but it is a life filled with beauty and wisdom. It begins with an interest in learning about the world around us, and it never ends.

The Columbia River Gorge is a special place. It is likely that people have lived here continuously as long or longer than anywhere else in the Americas. Yet the Gorge remains wild, filled with beauty.

Although this book is intended to be a comprehensive introduction to the Gorge, it is inevitably just an introduction. There is a vast amount of information that resides in oral history, historical documents, books and articles about the Gorge. You are encouraged to pursue those resources (many referenced in the text or Chapter notes), and you are encouraged to get out and enjoy the Gorge itself. There is much to learn from this place and its natural history.

Robert Hogfoss 2022

# HOW TO BECOME A NATURALIST

Not that many generations ago we were all naturalists to varying degrees. Through much of the 1800s people in the United States still obtained the bulk of their food by hunting, catching, gathering or growing it. Many people worked out of doors, and everyone lived in houses that were more in contact with the environment than at present (no refrigeration, indoor plumbing or air conditioning). Life required a more immediate understanding of the natural environment than it does today.

Until a century ago most Americans still lived in rural environments. Sometime during the 1910s that ratio changed, with the majority of America's population moving to the cities (that same shift of majority population to the cities did not occur globally until 2007). At present, a majority of Americans live in cities. Only 1 in of 5 of us still live in rural environments.

Today we are a more urban people and our contact with the natural world is more occasional and recreational. We all nonetheless remain dependent on the natural world for sustenance, both physical and spiritual. Many of us still hearken to the out of doors and remain eager to learn more about the natural world around us. Many of us would love to become naturalists, if only in our local environments.

So how do you become a naturalist? The answer is this: spend as much time as possible out of doors, watch, listen and learn. Observe animals and birds when they move, then come back at different times to see how their sign changes (and mark the weather in your memory or notes). Watch and learn about the weather, the soil and the rocks. Learn the names of plants and animals and birds that live near you, and start to notice their habitats, habits and sounds. Notice the diurnal and nocturnal rhythms that occur in animal and bird movements. And at least every once in a while spend an entire day out of doors in one place, sitting quietly from dawn to dusk, absorbing all the activities of the natural world around you as the sun travels across the sky. Learn the movement and pattern of the sun, the moon and the stars.

Before long, you will start to recognize and anticipate the plants and animals as you move from habitat to habitat, from dawn to dusk, and from season to season. Before long you will remember that the natural world is also your world, and how *you* move through your habitat over the course of a day is *your* sign, marking you as either a part of that environment, a visitor or an intruder. Once you understand the natural rhythm of a given place and understand that you are a part of that rhythm, then you will have become a naturalist.

# CHAPTER I: ROCKS

## *(Geology)*

### Recommended Reading

*There are several good books on the geology of the Pacific Northwest, starting with Cascadia by Bates McKee (McGraw-Hill 1972). Geologic interpretation of the Northwest has advanced so markedly over the past 50 years, however, primarily in the area of plate tectonics, that most older texts are now outdated. In addition, the geology of the Gorge is unique even within the Pacific Northwest because of the local influence of basalt lava floods millions of years ago and the massive glacial floods at the end of the last Ice Age. Scott Burns, Professor Emeritus at Portland State University and former head of its Geology Department, has co-authored a comprehensive book on the Glacial (Bretz) Floods: Cataclysm on the Columbia, John Allen, Marjorie Burns and Scott Burns (Ooligan Press 2d rev. ed. 2009).*

*A recent overview of the geology of the Northwest more generally is Living with Thunder: Exploring the Geologic Past, Present and Future of Pacific Northwest Landscapes, by Ellen Morris Bishop (Oregon State Univ Press 2014). Another useful book by Ellen Morris Bishop is the elegantly comprehensive In Search of Ancient Oregon (Timber Press 8th Ed. 2016) which provides essential updates, as do the entirely revised Roadside Geology of Oregon and Roadside Geology of Washington by Marli Miller (Mountain Press 2d Ed. 2014). On geology generally, two books by Prof. Marcia Bjornerud provide a good overview: Reading the Rocks: Autobiography of the Earth (Perseus Books 2005) and Timefulness (Princeton Univ. Press 2018)*

# CHAPTER I

## *Rocks*

### (Geology)

THE GORGE IS an open, living textbook on geology. As you travel through the Gorge you can see examples of each geologic epoch that occurred here. Cuts for roads and railroads expose profiles of various geologic formations and the glacial floods that scoured the mountains along the banks of the Gorge and left their own massive profiles of geologic history for this place. The Gorge remains geologically active with many natural processes still occurring, including earthquakes, volcanoes, landslides and mudflows.

As noted in the *Timeline* included at the end of this book, the earth is 4.5 billion years old, but we can fast forward a good bit to begin the story of the Gorge as we know it today. As described further below, plate tectonics and subduction started the uplift that became the Cascade Mountains some 37 million years ago (although the current appearance of most volcanoes were formed less than 100,000 years ago). Beginning about 17 million years ago, in the *Miocene* geologic epoch, a series of large *basalt lava floods* covered what is now the Gorge (and much of eastern Oregon and Washington), followed by more volcanic eruptions between 2 to 5 million years ago. Then much more recently in geologic time, around 15,000 to

18,000 years ago, a series of glacial floods scoured the Gorge, caused by melting as the last Ice Age receded. Those glacial floods created the sharp relief we see on the sides of the Gorge today (*see* Chapter II.B for more discussion on the glacial floods).

In just the past few hundred years, there have been several large earthquakes and volcanic eruptions that affected the Gorge. In 1700 the most recent *Cascadia subduction zone* earthquake is estimated to have been an 8.7 to 9.2 event on the Richter scale. Most geologists believe that the Northwest is due for another Cascadia quake in the near future. In addition to earthquakes, Mount St. Helens had a massive volcanic eruption in 1980, and several smaller eruptions since then.

The concentration of high hills, cliffs, buttes, peaks and mountains along the Columbia River as it passes through the Cascade Mountain Range defines the Gorge. More than 50 distinct high points line the Columbia River through the Gorge, rising between 1,000 feet and nearly 5,000 feet above the level of the river over the course of only a few dozen miles, giving the Gorge its fjord-like appearance (see Section I.F below). Mt. Hood and Mt. Adams stand as sentinels just to the south and north of the Gorge, rising more than 11,0000 and 12,000 feet above the River, respectively. Mt. Hood and Mt. Adams are both active volcanoes, as are Mount St. Helens, Mount Rainier and Mt. Jefferson, which are all visible from many trails and viewpoints in the Gorge.

There are literally layers upon layers of dramatic geologic history laid out for us in the rocks of the Gorge, and that history is the foundation for all the other stories of wind, water, plants, animals and people.

## A. THE RISING LANDSCAPE: PLATE TECTONICS AND SUBDUCTION

It was not until this past generation that the scientific community began to fully accept what was previously considered to be a speculative theory about the earth, even though it had been part of many traditional creation stories around the world. The idea was that at one time all land mass on the planet was joined, then over time broke apart and spread into continents. Most of us can remember looking at puzzle pieces of maps of the earth when young, and readily recognizing that the continents fit together rather well. It took a bit longer for science to give formal credence to that observation.

The term *Pangea* dates to ancient Greece (meaning *whole earth*), but it was adopted by the German geologist Alfred Wegener in 1915 to refer to this concept of one land mass. Wegener proposed that there was once a *super continent* with all land mass connected, that subsequently drifted apart. Over the course of the 20th century scientists found evidence of this hypothesis in geologic and fossil records (similar rock features and similar fossil species found in different continents), in the current biological record and ultimately in DNA evidence.

By the mid to late 20th century the idea of *sea floor spreading* and of large *crustal plates* riding on the mantle of the earth that moved over time was generally accepted. It became understood that when crustal plates collided one plate would be forced below the other (*subduction*) and when that occurs the crust material typically becomes molten and releases energy upward, usually in the form of volcanic activity. Over the past 50 years scientists have learned much more about plate tectonics and subduction, but there are still many mysteries.

The current scientific opinion is that the North Pacific tectonic plate (which is really three inter-connected smaller plates, the largest of which is the San Juan plate) bumps up against the continental North American plate along the Northwest coast of America. As those plates collide the Pacific plate moves under the North American plate. This *Cascadia Subduction Zone* runs from the coast of northern California to an area off southern British Columbia.

Where tectonic plates collide, and subduction occurs, it creates earthquakes, landslides, volcanoes and uplift. All of those have occurred – and are still occurring – in and near the Gorge. Over time subduction has created the line of Cascade volcanoes and some of the other folds and rises in the landscape throughout the Gorge.

## B. BASALT LAVA FLOODS

Beginning about 17 million years ago – in the Miocene geologic epoch – and continuing for the next 12 million years a series of basalt lava floods occurred in the area that is now the Gorge. Most of these lava floods occurred in the first two million years, but they continued sporadically for another 10 million years. These lava floods were massive in scale: large cracks or fissures would open in long linear fashion on the surface, and then molten basalt would ooze out and spread horizontally over vast areas of what is now eastern Oregon and eastern Washington. Recent estimates are that these basalt lava floods likely spread at a brisk walking pace, around 3 to 5 miles per hour.

There were a large number of these basalt lava floods that occurred over that 12-million year period, and some of them were simply huge in scale, covering more than 77,000 square miles of eastern Washington and eastern Oregon. In some places the accumulated layers of this lava are more than 2,000 feet thick. Each basalt flood shows as a defined layer when viewed in profile, and since the Gorge itself creates that profile you can see what looks like layer cakes of multiple lava floods stacked on one another all through the Gorge. At several viewpoints on the east end of the Gorge you can also see how the last basalt floods left a perfectly flat terrain, except where affected by volcanism or uplift (the plateau to the southeast of The Dalles is a good example of level basalt flood remnants).

The basalt lava floods that occurred here represent the largest basalt floods found on the planet. There were hundreds of these basalt outpouring events during the Miocene, broken down generally into the Grand Rhond, Wanapum and Saddle Mountain formations. Most of the eastern and central Gorge is primarily comprised of the initial Grand Rhond formation (roughly up to Multnomah Falls), but just a bit further west Crown Point is comprised of the younger Wanapum formation, while the Bridal Veil Falls area is comprised of even younger Saddle Mountain basalt.

The chemical characteristics of the andesite and dacite that comprise the lava creating these basalt layers is such that when it cools it crystalizes, forming large *basalt columns*, typically six sided (but can be more or less). The rate at which the basalt cooled determined whether there would be columns and whether those columns would be large or small (slower rates of cooling result in larger columns). Where the lava encountered water as it was exuded the resulting rock became less consolidated, referred to as *entablature* (or if completely underwater it looked like and is referred to as *pillow basalt*). Compared to other rock, basalt weathers rather easily. As it does, it can oxidize out iron, explaining why some of the older basalt you see in the Gorge may be reddish in color.

Although the Columbia River began formation about 40 million years ago, it was during the Miocene geologic epoch that the river found its current location, sometimes blocked and sometimes channeled or moved north and west by the basalt floods.

## C. VOLCANISM AND UPLIFT

Primarily due to plate tectonics, volcanism along what is now the Cascade Mountain range began about 37 million years ago, with the most active period roughly 2 million years ago. As the ocean plates pressed against the continental plate and were pushed downward, they triggered melting of both crust and mantle material. Subducted material, once molten, produces upward pressure that finds release in volcanoes, geysers, hot springs, etc. Wherever tectonic plates collide the resulting rise of mountains or volcanoes occurs some distance inland from the point of contact. In this case, the tectonic plates are colliding just off the coast of Oregon and Washington, where the subduction occurs, while the Cascade Mountains rise well inland of the coast.

Most of the dozens of high peak volcanoes currently present along the Cascade Mountains north and south of the Gorge are quite recent in geologic timeframes, being roughly 100,000 years old or younger. We see the Cascade Mountains as the most recent and visible result of volcanism, but we can also see remnants of earlier volcanism in and near the Gorge, including evidence and remnants of older stratovolcanoes, shield volcanoes, lava domes, plugs, cinder cones and vents. For example, although Beacon Rock is a volcanic core about 56,000 years old, Rooster Rock across the river is part of the much older basalt floods that subsequently slid from Crown Point to its current location. Many older volcanic plugs and vents are found throughout the Gorge as well as in the Portland area.

The same geologic actions that lead to formation of volcanoes also often create vertical *uplift* of the surface rocks. Uplift can occur more slowly in association with plate tectonic movement and subduction, or more rapidly when associated with volcanic eruptions. Evidence of both is visible as you drive through the Gorge. Much of the rock in the Gorge was left *versant* – tilting generally downward at a 7-degree angle toward the south. As it turns out, this has significant effect on the creation and maintenance of waterfalls, as discussed in Chapter II.E.

As part of tectonic movement and uplift surface rock may become folded. When the rock is folded in a concave manner, with the layers dipping down toward each other in a "V" form, the formation is known as a *syncline.* Folds where the center presses upward in a convex or "A" form are referred to as *anticlines.* Anticlines present as ridges, while synclines present as valleys. The weight of the massive basalt lava floods also created synclines and anticlines as it caused the earth to sink in the Gorge.

There are a series of folded synclines and anticlines visible in the eastern Gorge (more easily seen there because of less vegetation screening the rocks). A classic and beautiful syncline is visible at Mosier, east of Hood River on the Oregon side of the Gorge (good views and photo opportunities are available across the river on Washington State Highway 14). Another classic syncline is across the river from Mosier and a bit east, known as Coyote Wall. A large anticline can be seen on either side of the river between Rowena viewpoint and Crates Point, and the Columbia Hills on the other side of the river (the "Ortley anticline").

The largest volcano to appear and erupt in the Pacific Northwest in recent geologic time was Mount Mazama – now Crater Lake – which occurred relatively recently, about 7,700 years ago. Mount Mazama was one of the larger volcanoes ever to erupt on the planet. Closer to the Gorge, Mount St. Helens had a major eruption on May 18, 1980. Mount Mazama and Mount St. Helens both affected the Gorge with significant ashfall, evidence of which can still be found along trails and in soils throughout the Gorge.

Mount St. Helens, Mt. Hood and Mt. Adams are all close by the Gorge, and all remain categorized as active volcanoes. Each of them had impacts on the Gorge in the past. They will again in the future.

## D. EARTHQUAKES AND LANDSLIDES

### The Cascadia Earthquake of 1700

Movement of tectonic plates and the resulting subduction causes earthquakes and landslides, in addition to uplift and volcanism. Earthquakes are also caused by fault lines in the crust slipping horizontally against or over each other. Earthquakes and landslides have both occurred frequently in the Gorge over time, including very recent times. The last Cascadia subduction zone earthquake that occurred in the Gorge is surprisingly well documented, both in the geologic record and in human records. That quake occurred in the year 1700, and was estimated to be very strong, between 8.7 and 9.2 on the Richter scale.

Through a remarkable combination of careful recordkeeping in Japan several hundred years ago and modern scientific investigation, it has been concluded that the 1700 Cascadia earthquake occurred around 9 p.m. local time on January 26, 1700 (which happened to be a Tuesday in our calendar). This precise dating was determined through analysis of detailed records kept by communities and Buddhist monasteries on the east coast of Japan at Honshu Island that carefully registered a major tsunami (16 feet high). The data related to the event was distinct from other earthquake events around the Pacific Rim in the same general timeframe. Other more local data in the Northwest confirmed that 1700 was the year of the last Cascadia event. That data came from various geological excavations, as well as from *dendrochronology*, or tree ring dating (which takes sample cores from trees to determine age – dead or fossilized trees can be cored and overlapped with more recent samples to extend the record far back in time).

The Cascadia subduction zone earthquake of 1700 left many visible effects in the Northwest and the Gorge, altering the landscape significantly.

### The Bridge of the Gods Landslide of 1450

Dendrochronology was also helpful in dating a series of four large landslides that occurred in the Gorge and that completely dammed the Columbia River long ago, creating the Cascades Rapids. These landslides came from Greenleaf and Table Mountains, and the evidence of their origin remains clear today (as shown by the sheered southern faces of these mountains, which can be seen from either I-84 or Highway 14). The resulting debris pushed the Columbia River southward, and the huge debris field – some five square miles – remains today. The slide debris field is bracketed by the Bridge of the Gods at Cascade Locks on the eastern end and by Bonneville Dam on the western end (the Army Corps of Engineers made use of the landslides to locate the dam).

Rock and soil from the landslides up to 200 feet high blocked the river and backed up the water as far upstream as the location of the John Day dam today, covering Celilo Rapids. The river eventually cut a new channel near the south bank of the landslide dam (scientists estimate it may have taken several years for erosion to cut a new channel). The new channel exposed a rapids that was created by the landslide debris. The new rapids became known as the Cascades Rapids (a name given by Lewis & Clark, then later applied to the Cascade Mountain range). The source of the large landslide field was obvious (Greenleaf and Table Mountains) but the date when the landslides occurred was initially unknown.

The first written speculation about the source of the large landslide came from Lewis & Clark, as noted in their journals during their downstream trip through the Gorge in 1805 and again in their 1806 return. On October 30, 1805, Clark noted in his journal entry that they observed the stumps of many dead trees in the River, *"giv[ing] every appearance of the rivers being damed up below from Some cause which I am not at this time acquainted with"* (original spelling). Lewis and Clark's journals described trees they encountered around the White Salmon River. Clark's entry for October 30 continued to note that they later came upon a bend in the river where there were numerous rocks in the channel. They referred to this as the Cascades Rapids. Clark noted this *"must be the Cause of the river daming up to such a distance above."*

Other pioneers and settlers commented on the presence of these partially fossilized trees over the years, referring to the trees left dead and stranded in the river as a "drowned" or "ghost" forest. Then in the early 1930s a Portland botanist by the name of Donald Lawrence undertook several studies of the trees in advance of the construction of the Bonneville Dam. Lawrence counted more than 3,000 dead trees in the river from the Cascades Rapids upstream almost as far as Celilo Falls.

Lawrence used dendrochronology (tree ring dating) and an early version of carbon-14 dating to estimate the years these trees died from floodwaters (and thus the date of the large landslides) to be between the years 1250 and 1560. That estimate was revised several decades later using improved radiocarbon dating techniques on some of the same tree core samples initially obtained by Lawrence. After this review, the year of the landslide was revised to be about 1450. It is likely that the 1450 landslide event that created the Bridge of the Gods and the Cascades Rapids was triggered by a large earthquake.

Other Landslide Events

Depending on the size and location of any given earthquake in or around the Gorge there may be dozens or hundreds of landslides resulting, ranging from relatively minor to topographical transformation. Another large landslide in prehistoric times caused part of the basalt block that forms Crown Point on the westside of the Gorge to slide down toward the river, leaving Rooster Rock as a remnant of that event (that landslide continues to move slowly downhill, as evidenced by the persistent cracks and slumps in the road leading down to the waterfalls from Crown Point). A landslide also created Crates Point west of The Dalles, where rock and soil from the northern side of Seven Mile Hill and Mount Ulka slumped down into the river.

When Mount St. Helens erupted on May 18, 1980 it began with a relatively small earthquake (around 5.0 on the Richter scale) that caused a massive landslide that broke off most of the north face of the mountain. The landslide, in turn, created a much larger opening vent which allowed a tremendous amount of ejecta, pumice and pyroclastic flow to be released. The landslide that occurred at the start of the 1980 Mount St. Helens eruption is estimated to have been the largest landslide in history, and it all but blocked the Columbia River downstream of the Gorge, halting navigation for months.

## E. SOILS

Soil is defined as the top layer of the earth's surface, comprised of particles of rock, minerals, silt, sand and organic material. Nearly all soil in the world has been transported to its current location by wind, water or earth movement; very little soil remains stationary at the location of its parent material. Millions of years of volcanic eruptions along the Cascade crest and thousands of years of floods down the Columbia River left soils comprised of volcanic ash, silt, sediment and gravel. Some of those floods deposited soil many hundreds of feet above the current level of the river. Sand and other minerals have also blown in by wind. Finally, organic material that has accumulated over thousands of years from dead trees and plants or animals that have decomposed all became part of the soil in the Gorge.

Ash, silt and sediment are types of *loess*, while soil containing more organic material is generally referred to as *loam*. On the west end of the Gorge, the soils are deep with loam from millennia of organic forest detritus. On the east side of the Gorge, where there is less precipitation and less vegetative material, organic material thins and the soils are typically more like loess from volcanic ash, sand, silt and gravel from floods, in contrast to the deep loam on the west side of the Gorge. You can see the deep organic duff along the roads or trails in the west end of the Gorge, and you can see sand and gravels exposed in the east end of the Gorge. Up until the 1970s, when roadside banks were stabilized, it was not uncommon for sand dunes to form along the highway east of The Dalles.

There are also *cryptogamic soils* on the eastern end of the Gorge, which appear as a crust between plants. Such soils are really interwoven filaments of cyanobacteria, the same that are found in lichens. Disturbances on such soils (footprints, tire tracks) remain for decades, and damage the environment used by local plants and animals. "Don't Bust the Crust" is a phrase used throughout the inland West to encourage care in walking around cryptogamic soils.

## F. MAJOR LANDFORMS IN THE GORGE PRESENT DAY

### Peaks and Highpoints

The following is a list of major landforms that line the Gorge, defined here as those points rising at least 1,000 feet above the river (up to nearly 5,000 feet). There are more than 50 of these high points between the Sandy River and the Deschutes River, and they are generally within 10 miles of the river, north or south. Not all of them are within the National Scenic Area boundaries, but the majority are, and all of them are recognizable to those driving through or hiking in the Gorge. This concentration of high points along the river is what gives the Gorge a distinctly fjord-like appearance. These highpoints can be located on any topographical map of the Gorge.

Also strikingly visible from the Gorge is the volcanic cone of Mount St. Helens (8,300') and the volcanic peaks of Mount Adams (12,280') and Mt. Hood (11,237'). From certain locations, you can also see Mt. Rainier (14,411'), Goat Rocks (8,184' at Gilbert Peak; 7,930' at Old Snowy) to the north, and Mt. Jefferson (10,495') to the south.

The most distinct points visible from either Interstate 84 or Highway 14 are noted by asterisk ("*"). Features less than 1,000' high but distinctive for other reasons are noted by brackets [ ]. These lists are not exhaustive, but they capture major high points.

*North Bank (WA), West to East*

31 peaks greater than 1000', of which 23 are > 2000' (8 of those are > 3000' plus 1 >4,000')

*Mt Norway (1,110')*
*Pohl's Hill (1,395')*
**Silver Star Mt (4,390')*
**Cape Horn (1,350')*
*Bob's Mt (2,110')*
*Archer Mt (2,020')*
*Three Corner Rock (3,550')*
**[Beacon Rock] (848')*
*Hamilton Mt (2,438')*
*Aldrich Butte (1,141')*
**Table Mt (3,417')*
*Sacagawea Rocks (2,145')*
**Red Rock Mt (avg 2,600')*

**Greenleaf Mt (3,422')*
*Rock Ck Butte (1,934')*
*Buck Mt (1,330')*
**Wind Mt (1,907')*
*Augspurger Mt (3,667')*
**Dog Mt (2,948')*
*Goat Pt (2,361')*
*Hauk Butte (2,600')*
*Shingle Mt (2,600')*
*Cook Hill Ridge (3,184')*
*Little Baldy (2,966')*
**Underwood Mt (2,755')*
*Nestor Pk (3,143')*
**Burdoin Mt (2,082')*
*Major Ck Ridge (2,112')*
*Windy Pt (1,069')*
**Stacker Butte (3,220')*
**Columbia Hills (avg 3,000')*
**Haystack Butte (2,798')*

<u>South Bank (OR), East to West</u>
21 peaks greater than 1000', of which 18 are > 2000' (with 4 of those > 3000' and 9 over 4000')

**Seven Mile Hill/Mt. Ulka (1,823')*
**McCall Point/Rowena (1,722')*
*Wasco Butte (2,345')*
*Sugarloaf (2,304')*
*Hood River Ridge/Mt (2,345')*
*Mitchell Pt (1,178')*
*Viento Ridge (2,800')*
**Mt Defiance (4,960')*
**Shellrock Mt (2,090')*

*Nick Eaton Ridge (avg 4,000')*
**Green Point Mt (4,737')*
**Tomlike Mt (4,549')*
**Chinindere Mt (4,673')*
**Indian Mt (4,800')*
**Tanner Butte (4,400')*
*Mt Talapus (3,865')*
*Palmer Pk (4,010')*
**Nesmith Pt (3,880')*
**Yeon Mt (3,200')*
**St Peters Dome (1,300')*
**Larch Mt/Sherrard Pt (4,056')*
*Lookout Pt (3,940')*
**[Rooster Rock] (less than 1,000')*
**[Crown Pt] (733')*

Watersheds and Rivers

There are numerous rivers and streams in the Scenic Area. Virtually all of them are steep and fast moving, due to the steep landforms that make up the Gorge. Many of the waters originate on the slopes of Mt. Hood or Mt. Adams. The rivers and streams in the Gorge all display the classic erosional style where over time a water course carves a V-shaped valley (in contrast to the U-shaped valleys formed by glaciers and the Gorge's form of an even more fjord-like shape caused by the glacial/Bretz floods).

As discussed in Chapter II, the rivers and streams that are tributary to the Gorge vary considerably from the westside to the eastside of the Cascade Mountains crest. Several of these rivers were dammed early in the 20th century, but two dams were removed in recent years (Marmot Dam on the Sandy River removed in 2007 and Condit Dam on the White Salmon River removed in 2011). In both cases native salmon and steelhead returned to those rivers within a year.

# CHAPTER NOTES

## Chapter I: Rocks (Geology)

1. In addition to the books noted in the list of Recommended Reading at the beginning of the Chapter, a good book to read for an overview of geology generally, with an even broader sense of scope (as suggested in the subtitle) is *Timefulness: How Thinking Like a Geologist Can Help Save the World*, by Marcia Bjornerud (Princeton Univ. Press 2018).
2. The earth has apparently formed supercontinent land masses several times, which then broke apart only to eventually reform. One such supercontinent that predated *Pangea* is referred to as *Rodinia* (Russian for "motherland").
3. *Volcanoes* exist just north and south of the Gorge. A system developed in 1980 for classification of the power of volcanic eruptions is called the "*Volcanic Explosivity Index*" (VEI). There are 8 levels on the VEI, with sub-numbering. Similar to the Richter scale used to measure earthquakes, each incremental increase on the VEI scale indicates a tenfold increase in magnitude. The eruption of the Yellowstone caldera around 640,000 years ago is estimated to have been a maximum VEI 8. Mount Mazama's eruption 7,700 years ago (now Crater Lake) is estimated to have been a VEI 7, and the 1980 eruption of Mount St. Helens is classified as a VEI 5.
4. *Basalt Lava Floods and the Yellowstone Hotspot*. Geologists currently believe that the massive basalt lava floods that created the layer cake appearance of the Gorge some 5 to 17 million years ago were triggered by what is currently referred to as the "Yellowstone Hot Spot." Now located under Yellowstone National Park, this hot spot is believed to be a five-mile vertical connection from the earth's mantle to the continental crust, venting magma to the surface over time. The hot spot/mantle has stayed in place as the continental plate drifts over it. Thus, the source of the current Yellowstone geologic activity was once under what is now the Gorge and eastern Oregon/Washington and caused the massive basalt lava floods that occurred here.
5. *Lake Bonneville Flood*. Just before the Lake Missoula glacial floods began a large body of water called Lake Bonneville filled what is now

the Salt Lake basin in Utah. The Lake breached containment near Red Rock Pass at the border of Utah/Idaho, with the resulting flood nearly twice as large as any of the many (forty to one hundred) Lake Missoula Flood events. Due to geographical restrictions, however, the Bonneville Flood event was much slower in discharge, only about 1/10th the flow of any individual Missoula Flood event. As a result, the Bonneville Flood took weeks to drain, while each Missoula Flood took only days. The Bonneville Flood primarily affected areas far upstream of the Gorge, such as Hells Canyon on the Snake River.

6. *Earthquakes and Landslides*. Donald Lawrence's perceptive explanations of the date and cause of the "drowned forest" of dead trees along the Columbia between Mosier and Cascade Locks was published as "*The Submerged Forest of the Columbia River Gorge," Geographical Review 26:4 (Oct. 1936) and "Bridge of the Gods Legend: Its Origin, History and Dating," Mazama 40:13 (1958).*
7. *Viewpoints and Photo Points*. The entire Gorge provides great views from almost any roadway, rail, water-craft or trail but there are several places accessible to vehicles that provide expansive views and excellent photo opportunities. Among those are the following:

## ON THE OREGON SIDE OF THE RIVER, FROM WEST TO EAST

*Women's Forum/Chanticleer Point* (off Highway 30) This is where the most iconic photos of the Gorge are taken, looking upstream (east) toward Crown Point and Beacon Rock.

*Larch Mountain/Sherrard Viewpoint* (Larch Mt. Rd, 14 miles off Highway 30) – a bit of a side trip, but worth it; picnic area and views of 5 mountains after a short trail (view of Mt. Hood, Jefferson, St. Helens, Adams and Rainier).

*Crown Point/Vista House* (off Highway 30) – just to the east of Women's Forum, closer views of Rooster Rock and Beacon Rock, but also some of the highest winds in the entire Gorge.

*Panorama Viewpoint*, Hood River (off Highway 35, about 3 miles from I-84) – good views of the Gorge and the Hood River Valley, restrooms and handicap accessible.

*Rowena Crest/Mark O. Hatfield Viewpoint (and tunnels along the Historic Highway nearby)* – dramatic views looking across the Columbia at the Wild & Scenic Klickitat River and the twin bridges of Lyle, and looking to the eastern end of the Gorge.

ON THE WASHINGTON SIDE OF
THE RIVER, EAST TO WEST

*Wishram Viewpoint* (pull off along Highway 14) – views of where Celilo Falls was located before being inundated by The Dalles dam.

*Rest Area just west of Lyle* (off Highway 14) – picnic area, restrooms and tremendous views downriver.

*Nancy Russell Viewpoint* – a stone walled amphitheater above Cape Horn (off Highway 14) with views upriver and across toward Multnomah Falls.

*Beacon Rock* – State Park with picnic area and restrooms, and a trail to the top of the landmark where Lewis & Clark camped and first recognized the influence of the Pacific tide.

*Cape Horn* – classic view of the western Gorge from the cliffs on Hwy 14, but limited parking and sharp drop-off.

8. *The Cascade Mountain Range* derives its name from the Cascades Rapids, which were called that by Lewis & Clark in 1805. Lewis & Clark referred to what is now known as the Cascade Mountain Range as "the Western Mountains." Naturalist David Douglas was the first to call them "the mountains by the Cascades [rapids]," which subsequently became known as the Cascade Mountains.

# CHAPTER II: WATER & ITS EFFECTS

## *(Hydrology & Geomorphology)*

**Recommended Reading**

*Standard texts on hydrology include Physical Hydrology by S. Lawrence Dingman (Prentice Hall 2001) and Applied Principles of Hydrology by John Manning (Prentice Hall 1996). There are several books and articles about the Missoula (or Bretz) glacial floods that carved the Gorge, including Cataclysms on the Columbia: the Great Missoula Floods by John Allen, Marjorie Burns and Scott Burns (Timber Press, 1987; 2d Ed. 2009 by Ooligan Press); and Bretz's Flood by John Soennichsen (Sasquatch Books 2008).*

*Good information on hydrology and hydrogeology of the Pacific Northwest can be found through the Army Corps of Engineers, Bonneville Power Administration, University of Washington, the U.S. Geological Survey, Oregon State University and the Pacific Northwest National Laboratory. All those entities have websites you can search (e.g., www.hydro.washington.edu)*

# CHAPTER II

## *Water & Its Effects*

### (Hydrology and Geomorphology)

THE COLUMBIA RIVER is one of the largest rivers in North America by both length and volume. The river is more than 1,200 miles long (1,242 miles) and it drains an area of more than one quarter million square miles (258,000 sq. mi.), roughly the size of Texas (268,000 sq. mi.) or France (248,000 sq. mi.). The watershed includes portions of seven states and British Columbia. The states that feed the Columbia include: Idaho, Montana, Nevada, Oregon, Utah, Washington and Wyoming. The river flow averages more than a quarter million cubic feet per second at its mouth where it empties to the Pacific Ocean. It is the largest river in North and South America that drains to the Pacific Ocean, and it generates a significant percentage of hydroelectric energy produced in the U.S.

The cliffs shaped by glacial (or Bretz) floods through the Gorge create dramatic waterfalls along this portion of the river. Before construction of mainstem dams there were also numerous rapids along the length of the river – especially in the Gorge – caused by the significant drop in elevation over the run of the river. The most significant rapids along the entire 1,242-mile-long river were in the Gorge itself. The combination and concentration of waterfalls and rapids in the Gorge have marked this as a unique place for thousands of years.

## A. ORIGINS OF THE COLUMBIA RIVER

The Columbia River has been a source of life to plants, animals and people in this region for millennia. Although the origins of the river go back many millions of years, the river moved northward to its present location during the Miocene geologic epoch (beginning some 17 million years ago). Over the course of the next 12 million years the river slowly carved its present course through hundreds of basalt lava floods that filled and flowed through the Gorge toward the Pacific Ocean (see Chapter I). Initially, the river was in a classic V shape, the result of years of erosion that formed a typical erosional river valley (like tributaries to the river still display). Then some 15,000 to 18,000 years ago (relatively recent in geologic time) a series of massive glacial floods carved out the walls of the river valley to create the Gorge as we find it today. When those floods ended, the Gorge had been transformed to a sharply defined U-shaped valley, more like those created by glaciers than by gradual erosion but even more rugged and fjord-like, having been more sharply carved than typically results from glacial flow alone.

## B. LAKE MISSOULA AND THE GLACIAL (BRETZ) FLOODS

In 1923 a young geologist named J Harlen Bretz published a scientific paper suggesting that a massive flood must have carved the "*channeled scablands*" of eastern Washington State (Bretz coined that term). By 1930 he concluded that the same flood must also have helped shape the Columbia River Gorge. Bretz was a true character. Born simply as Harley Bretz, he changed his name to J Harlen Bretz (no period after the "J") in college, to stand out. He started his career teaching high school biology in Seattle but got interested in geology and went back to the university and after obtaining a Ph.D he began studying the landforms of eastern Washington and Oregon.

Bretz's theory of a massive flood event shaping the Columbia basin was met with considerable skepticism by the geological academic establishment at the time. It took more than 40 years for his theory of a giant flood to be accepted, and then only after the first photos from the Landsat satellite in the 1970s clearly showed the course of floods that must have run down the basin at some point in the past.

Based on careful and prolonged fieldwork in eastern Washington Bretz concluded that a major flood must have coursed through the Columbia River basin, but he could not determine the source of such a flood. Another geologist working in Montana (Joseph Pardee) had been studying the evidence left by the last ice age, and eventually supplemented Bretz's theory by demonstrating that a series of ice dams formed as the last glaciers receded some 15,000 to 18,000 years ago. The ice dams formed near the Idaho and Montana border from the melting glaciers created a huge lake of meltwater and ice (called Lake Missoula by the scientific community). As the amount of water impounded in Lake Missoula grew the pressure finally burst through the ice dam, flooding into the Columbia Basin. The ice dam formed and breached again and again, each time resulting in a flood of ice and rock that scoured the Gorge.

Scientists estimate that the resulting floods were the largest in the history of earth, as massive quantities of water flowed westward repeatedly. As Lake Missoula emptied another ice dam would form and the process would begin again. Current estimates are that the ice dams formed and broke dozens of times over the course of several thousand years, with intervals of roughly 30 to 60 years between events. More than 40 separate floods came through the Gorge carrying ice and rock in walls of water up to 850 feet above current water levels at speeds estimated to have been 50 to 60 miles per hour. Where the river passes through the narrow Rowena Gap (by Lyle) you can see clearly how ice scoured the hillsides as it passed in each flood, leaving a sharp line between denuded basalt below and earth covered hillsides above. The flood waters that churned their way through the Gorge expanded again in the lower Willamette Valley between Portland and Eugene before finally draining to the ocean.

There are several places in the Gorge where you can see the effects of the floods as the waters poured through the Gorge. As noted above, the most notable view is at Rowena Gap, where the Gorge narrows between

Lyle, Washington and the Rowena Plateau viewpoint on the Oregon side of the river. The ice-filled flood waters forced their way through this narrow gap time and again, and in the process scraped away all soil and sediment, leaving only basalt on either side of the river. You can also see how the flood waters backed up before the Rowena Gap and then flowed onward as they passed through the Gorge. There are drifts of sediment at significant elevations just upstream of Rowena Gap (a dramatic one can be seen as you drive the two miles north on Washington State Highway 197 from The Dalles bridge to Highway 14; look slightly to the left about halfway up the hillside as you approach the T junction with Highway 14 and you can see a giant remnant of settled sediment that you will recognize as looking similar to a large mud puddle that has accumulated sediment ripples after a heavy rain).

Another relict of the Missoula floods you can see throughout the Gorge, especially on the east side where there is less vegetation, are glacial *erratics*. These are mostly granite or quartzite rocks and boulders (some quite large) that were carried in ice from the Rocky Mountains with the ice floods. The erratics settled out as the flow slowed and backed up while forcing its way through the Rowena Gap and other narrowings in the Gorge. When the ice floods reached the west end of the Gorge the floodwaters expanded into the Willamette Valley where more erratics settled out. These erratics often stand out noticeably from the more common basalt or other rock. The smaller erratics are typically rounded from being tumbled in the ice flows, while larger erratics were entrained in blocks of ice.

## C. CHARACTERISTICS OF THE MODERN COLUMBIA RIVER

The Columbia River begins in two natural (undammed) lakes in British Columbia (Columbia and Windermere lakes) at an elevation of roughly 2,690 feet above sea level. The river's 1,242 mile run to the sea is relatively steep, averaging a drop of 2.17 feet per mile, as compared to the Mississippi River's average drop of 0.65 feet per mile. Some stretches of the Columbia, especially in the Gorge, historically exceeded a 5 foot drop per mile prior to construction of dams. Such a steep run on a large river creates rapids, and the Columbia historically had numerous large rapids. Those rapids in turn created barriers for salmon and steelhead, where First Peoples gathered to fish.

The Army Corps of Engineers maintains a channel to a depth of 40 feet from the mouth of the river to Portland, and then 27 feet from Portland to Bonneville Dam. The remainder of the river through the Gorge is not dredged, but in some spots near The Dalles the river depth goes to more than 200 feet below the water surface.

The volume of water transported by the Columbia River varied greatly in historic times, from season to season and year to year. The average flow since records have been kept (through the present) has been roughly constant at 250,000 to 265,000 *cubic feet per second (cfs)* at the mouth of the river (one cubic foot of water equals 7.48 gallons). The highest flow ever recorded was in the spring of 1894, at roughly 1.25 million cfs (as measured at The Dalles), but that was before dams controlled the river's flow. Even with the dams, the flow during spring runoff often exceeds 350,000 to 400,000 cfs for several days each year in May or June. Lowest flows recorded before dams were as low as 50,000 cfs in the Gorge, and even with dams present flows drop below 100,000 cfs at times.

There are 14 primary tributaries to the Columbia River in the U.S. (defined here as those with more than 2,000 cfs average flow). Two of these primary tributaries are within the National Scenic Area (the Deschutes and Sandy rivers). Nine of the other primary tributaries are upstream of the Gorge and thus affect water volume through the National Scenic Area.

| *Columbia River Tributary* | *Average Flow (cfs)* | *Drainage Basin (sq. mi.)* |
|---|---|---|
| | | |
| Snake River | 56,900 | 107,500 |
| Willamette River | 37,400 | 11,460 |
| Kootenay River | 30,650 | 19,420 |
| Pend Oreille River | 26,430 | 25,800 |
| Cowlitz River | 9,140 | 2,586 |
| Spokane River | 7,900 | 6,680 |
| Lewis River | 6,125 | 1,046 |
| Deschutes River | 5,845 | 10,700 |
| Yakima River | 3,542 | 6,150 |
| Wenatchee River | 3,079 | 1,350 |

| | | |
|---|---|---|
| Okanogan River | 3,039 | 8,340 |
| Kettle River | 2,925 | 4,200 |
| Sandy River | 2,257 | 508 |
| John Day River | 2,060 | 8,010 |

SOURCE: BPA; USGS; UW Columbia Basin Research project

There are many smaller (less than 2,000 average cfs) tributaries to the Columbia River within the National Scenic Area, including the primary tributaries of the Klickitat, White Salmon, Hood, Little White Salmon and Wind rivers.

The relationship of drainage area to average runoff varies directly with whether a tributary is on the west side or the east side of the Gorge. West side rivers have a ratio of runoff or flow (as measured in cfs) to square mile of drainage that is as high as 4:1 or greater (e.g., the Willamette, Cowlitz, Lewis and Sandy rivers), while east side rivers may have a runoff to drainage ratio as low as 0.25:1 (e.g., the Deschutes, Okanogan and John Day rivers). Such large differences simply denote the significant change in annual precipitation from west side to east side locations relevant to the Cascade Mountain range, but also reflect differences in geography and watersheds, and associated changes in erosion rates, topography and vegetation.

## D. DAMS

The Army Corps of Engineers (COE) began building dams on the mainstem Columbia River in the 1930s, both to generate electricity and to provide irrigation for agriculture (and after major floods in 1948, the rationale of flood control was added). The first dam to span the mainstem Columbia River was Rock Island, far upstream from the Gorge. Begun in 1929, Rock Island became operational in 1933. The second dam on the river was Bonneville, located at the west end of the Gorge within the National Scenic Area boundaries, which became operational in 1938. The most massive dam on the River, the Grand Coulee, started construction in 1933 and became operational in 1942. The Dalles Dam began operation in 1957 on the east end of the Gorge also within the National Scenic Area boundaries. Once The Dalles dam came online, it essentially bracketed the Gorge between The Dalles dam and the Bonneville Dam in what the COE and the Bonneville Power Administration (BPA) refer to as either Lake Bonneville or the Bonneville Pool. The Columbia is still a formidable force of nature, however – not a series of pools – and it is only temporarily tamed.

Construction of dams created an immediate impact on fisheries in two ways: first by creating a barricade to migrating species, and second by flooding or washing out the gravel bars that serve as spawning grounds for fish. Both Bonneville Dam and The Dalles Dam were created with some allowance for fish passage at time of construction, but it was limited. In recent decades, the Army Corps of Engineers and Bonneville Power Administration have worked with tribes, state and local governments to enhance fish passage upstream as much as possible. Court orders and agreements among jurisdictions and the tribes require continued review and revision of fish management plans. The states also began experimenting in the 1950s with barging juvenile fish down river to supplement natural hatch, and those efforts continue.

The dams that have been built on the mainstem Columbia River are used for hydroelectric generation, irrigation and flood control. There are 14 dams on the mainstem of the river (3 in British Columbia, 7 in Washington; and 4 along the border of Washington/Oregon). There are another 15 dams on the Snake River (the major tributary to the Columbia), and more than 400 total dams on the Columbia River system, including all tributaries. A total of 31 dams on the Columbia system are managed by BPA. They provide more than 35% of all electric power for the Pacific Northwest, and transmit power to other states, including California.

When the Bonneville Dam was built it backed up the Columbia and washed out the Cascades Rapids. The Dalles Dam backed up the river even further and washed out Celilo Falls and the Narrows rapids, which together ran from ten to eleven miles above the location of The Dalles. The Narrows consisted of both the Upper (or Short) Narrows and the Lower (or Long) Narrows (also referred to as the "Ten Mile Rapids" and the "Five Mile Rapids," respectively, for their points of origin above The Dalles). All those rapids had been significant places of gathering, habitation and trading for thousands of years, due to the bountiful salmon fishing made possible by the rapids.

The location, elevation and first year of operation of the mainstem dams on the Columbia in the U.S. are summarized in the table below. The difference in elevation of water behind and below each dam varies from 43 feet (the Rock Island dam) to 334 feet (Grand Coulee). On average, there is about 70 to 100 feet of rise in water level at each dam on the mainstem of the Columbia River.

U.S. Dams on the Columbia River

| Name/Year of Operation | RIVER MILE | MAX POOL ELEV |
|---|---|---|
| *Grand Coulee (WA)/1942* | *597* | *1,290'* |
| *Chief Joseph (WA)/1955* | *545* | *956'* |
| *Wells (WA)/1967* | *516* | *781'* |
| *Rocky Reach (WA)1961* | *474* | *707'* |
| *Rock Island (WA)/1933* | *453* | *613'* |
| *Wanapum (WA)/1963* | *416* | *570'* |
| *Priest Rapids (WA)/1961* | *397* | *486'* |
| *McNary (WA/OR)/1954* | *292* | *357'* |
| *John Day (WA/OR)/1971* | *216* | *268'* |
| *The Dalles (WA/OR)/1960* | *192* | *160'* |
| *Bonneville (WA/OR)/1937* | *146* | *77'* |

Source: USGS; BPA; Univ of Wash., Columbia Basin Research, "Hydroelectric Information for Columbia River Projects" (2008).

There have been calls in recent years to remove four of the major dams on the Snake River upstream of the Gorge to preserve fish habitat and save certain runs. Some smaller dams in the system have already been removed for purposes of letting the river system return to a more natural state. Two dams removed in recent years within or near the National Scenic Area are the Marmot Dam on the Sandy River (removed in 2007) and the Condit Dam on the White Salmon River (removed in 2011). Both dams were roughly 100 years old (Marmot constructed in 1908 and Condit in 1913), yet within one year salmon and steelhead began returning to the rivers upstream of where the dams had been.

## Effects of Dams on Anadromous Fish (Salmon, Steelhead, Smelt & Lamprey)

Dams create major obstacles for *anadromous fish*, which are born in fresh water but migrate to the ocean for several years before returning to their home stream to spawn. Fish ladders are intended to allow adult salmon and steelhead to maneuver around dams on their upstream/return journey. Fish ladders can be effective depending on their design (sturgeon cannot climb fish ladders easily, so once a dam is built sturgeon become all but captive in the water below a dam).

While fish ladders can help adult salmon or steelhead and other anadromous fish return to the upstream reaches of the Columbia River to spawn, the initial trip downstream is far more difficult for the juvenile fish (and if a juvenile fish does not make it to the ocean in the first place, then the availability of a fish ladder for return is irrelevant). When salmon eggs (*roe*) hatch they are referred to as *fry*. When they grow large enough to begin their anadromous voyage to the ocean they are called *smolt* (or just juvenile fish). There are several ways juvenile anadromous fish can pass dams on their way downstream to the ocean: (1) pass through the hydroelectric generating turbines; (2) pass through the spillways used to release excess water; (3) get (intentionally) routed through pipes or channels built for juvenile fish as a bypass around both turbines and spillways; or (4) get barged or trucked around the dam. Mortality is high in the first two alternatives (turbines or spillways), and the bypass piping or channels could initially only accommodate a relatively small number of fish. As a result, barging of juvenile fish became a common way to avoid the highest rates of mortality at dams. Bypass screens and channels are being upgraded, but barging continues in use.

The State of Washington Department of Fisheries first tried barging juvenile anadromous fish in the Gorge in 1955. They loaded 200,000 juvenile Chinook Salmon onto a barge at the mouth of the Klickitat River and transported them past Bonneville Dam and then 165 miles downstream. The experiment worked well enough to be repeated. Over the decades there have been modifications to the barging program, but today the Army Corps of Engineers and associated entities barge millions of juvenile salmon and steelhead downstream through the Gorge every year. You can see the unique barges in the summer. Their design has changed over the years but now involves floating pens that minimize shock to the smolt and allow the young fish to sense the native waters while in transit.

As part of the U.S. Fish & Wildlife Service (F&WS), more than 70 National Fish Hatcheries (NFH) exist in the U.S., 5 of which are in the Gorge. Gorge hatcheries produce millions of salmonid juveniles annually that are either barged or released directly to the river. National Fish Hatcheries in the Gorge include Carson, Little White Salmon, Eagle Creek, Spring Creek and Willard. Together they release or transfer via barge more than 20 million salmon or steelhead annually. The FW&S and NFH work with the Treaty tribes in the Gorge to meet fishery management plans and tribal trust responsibilities.

## E. WATERFALLS

The Columbia River Gorge has the largest concentration of waterfalls in the U.S. (more than 70 named waterfalls within a short stretch of the western end of the National Scenic Area, and many more unnamed). Even a casual visitor to the Gorge, however, will see that most waterfalls in the Gorge are located on the south (Oregon) side of the river. The reason for this is found in the geological makeup of the area: the rock layers comprising the Gorge are generally tilted downward from the north to the south (due to the uplift and versant described in Chapter I).

As discussed in Chapter I, the various lava flows that make up the Gorge today look like a layer cake tilted to one side (typically 7-degrees downward toward the south). That image can be seen at many natural outcrops, road and railroad cuts. Due to the nature of the volcanic uplifting that occurred millions of years ago, and the weight of the basalt lava floods that gradually caused the landform to sink, the basalt layers were generally left in this downward slope toward the south. As the Missoula Floods cut through the Gorge, they cut through these layers of basalt, and in the process created cliffs that provide the structure for waterfalls. The stability of the cliffs varies from one side of the river to the other. On the south (Oregon) side, the rearward tilting layers were cut in such a manner to create a relatively sharp edge with the exposed layers angled upward, containing accumulated soil and debris between the layers. The rock walls of the layers remain intact even as the soil and debris between layers erodes. The result is a persistent edge at elevation that allows the formation of permanent waterfalls on the Oregon side.

On the other (north, or Washington) side of the river, the glacial floods created a forward tilting cut that allowed the soil, debris and rock between the layers to erode outward and downward. That process leads to landslides, slumps and mudflows instead of the kind of sharp relief required to create and maintain waterfalls. The process may also have been responsible in part for the massive landslide that entirely blocked the Columbia River in 1450, when a large portion of Greenleaf Mountain and Table Mountain slid into the water (which was likely triggered by a major earthquake, creating the Cascades Rapids). The process continues today, as small landslides and mudflows occur almost every winter along Highway 14 on the Washington side of the river (landslides also occur on the Oregon side, but many from other causes).

## Types of Waterfalls

The many waterfalls present in the Gorge today are classified for purposes of this book as either *perennial, seasonal, ephemeral* or *inundated* (see Chapter Notes for other forms of classification). The most significant *perennial* (year-round) waterfalls are fed both by rainfall and snow melt. The more significant perennial waterfalls are noted below. *Seasonal* waterfalls are those that are predictable and follow determined paths, but only appear when major rainfall or snowmelt occurs with the seasons, typically during the spring and early summer months. *Ephemeral* waterfalls occur only after snow melt in the spring or heavy rainfall occurring during any season, and they often follow varying pathways.

Some of the most dramatic waterfalls in the Gorge through historic and prehistoric times were associated with rapids and are in the last category, now *inundated* by the dams along the river. Such inundated falls include Celilo, the Narrows and the Cascades rapids.

Perennial Waterfalls in the Gorge

The most well-known waterfalls in the Gorge are those perennial waterfalls along Historic Highway 30 as it parallels Interstate 84 on the Oregon side of the river, between the Corbett and Ainsworth Exits off the Interstate (Exits 22 and 35, respectively). There is another exit off I-84 at Bridal Veil (Exit 28), which connects to Historic Highway 30. The only waterfall accessible directly from I-84 is Multnomah Falls (you use Exit 31 and park in a lot between the eastbound and westbound lanes of the freeway, then walk through an underpass to get to the Falls).

Visitors should use care in visiting any waterfall in the Gorge, because the trails are steep with sharp drop-offs, loose gravel and slippery footing.

The following perennial falls are those you encounter traveling east from Portland. Trails from these waterfalls lead uphill to other named and unnamed waterfalls and allow for interconnecting loops among the various falls. Again, exercise care – every year people get lost or injured on these steep trails. Also note that many trails remain closed following the large 2017 Eagle Creek wildfire. Check road and trail status before you go.

Beginning in 2022, time entry permits are required from May to September for driving Highway 30 along the waterfall route, from Crown Point to Ainsworth.

Latourell Falls

At 224 feet high, Latourell Falls is a single drop, plunge falls. It is located within Talbot State Park, where there is a parking area and picnic spots. Latourell is the closest of the Gorge waterfalls to Portland, on Oregon Historic Highway 30. You can hike a short but fairly level trail to get to the base of the falls, where the water plunges over an undercut basalt wall. A distinctive yellow powder lichen covers much of the upper basalt wall, thriving off the mist from the falling water.

There is another trail that takes you to Upper Latourell Falls and more views of the primary waterfall. The falls are named after Joseph Latourell, who was postmaster of the nearby Rooster Rock Post Office in 1887, which was on the railroad.

Shepherds Dell

This waterfall is about one mile east of Latourell on Highway 30. It is a two drop falls, totaling about 220 feet. The first drop is a plunge and the second is in a horsetail formation. The falls comes from Young's Creek. There is a short trail to the falls.

Bridal Veil Falls

The next waterfall along Historic Highway 30 going east from Portland is Bridal Veil Falls. The Falls is 120 feet high and is designated a State Scenic Viewpoint. It has a parking area, picnic area and restrooms set among large trees. There are two trails that lead to both the bottom and the top of the Falls. Bridal Veil is accessed from either I-84 at Exit 28 or at Milepost 28 on the Historic Highway 30, that parallels the Interstate.

In 1886 the Bridal Veil Timber Company built a flume that brought logs to the site of the falls where a sawmill was powered by the creek. Private land was purchased by the State in the 1970s and 1980s to provide the visitor area. Bridal Falls gets nearly a quarter million visitors per year.

Wahkeena Falls

Wahkeena is a 242 foot cascading waterfall with several drops (meaning it runs over the rock face in more than one run, rather than plunging off a single face). The name is taken from a Yakama word meaning beautiful. There is a short (two tenths of a mile) trail to the falls from the parking area. The trail goes further but becomes steep and slippery.

Multnomah Falls

At 620 feet and with two drops, this is the highest and most well-known waterfall in the Gorge. It is also one of the closest to Portland. It has a visitor center and a large parking lot. As a result, it is the most visited point in the entire Gorge, with more than two million visitors per year. Access to the falls is either from Exit 31 off I-84 (in either direction) or on Historic Highway 30 at Milepost 31. Benson Bridge (built in 1914) spans the pool between the two drops. The bridge is about a quarter mile walk up from the Lodge, which was built in 1925. The Lodge has a restaurant, a gift shop and a U.S. Forest Service interpretative center.

The falls sometimes freezes for a few days in late winter. The area was at risk of burning during the Eagle Creek fire of 2017 (some large trees around the Falls did burn), but fire crews kept the Lodge from catching fire.

As noted, more than two million people visit Multnomah Falls every year, and it is in danger of being loved to death. Shuttle buses and carpool services have been established in recent years, but the parking lot off the freeway frequently becomes full early in the day during the summer, and Route 30 becomes a traffic jam. In the near future it will likely become necessary to close Highway 30 to private traffic, relying on shuttle buses and emergency vehicles to access the falls, as done in a number of National Parks. The Historic Highway would remain open for bikes and hikers with such a change.

## Oneonta Falls

After Multnomah Falls, Oneonta Falls is the next named waterfall going east on Highway 30. There are several waterfalls along Oneonta Creek, set back upstream from the road. There are trails leading to and past the falls. The most well-known of the falls is a 100-foot single plunge drop, typically reached by walking up the creek at low water, but that can be hazardous due to slippery rocks and large logs left by flood flows along the water course.

The Falls is named after Oneonta, New York, because the photographer Carleton Watkins from Oneonta was the first to photograph the Falls around 1849. Watkins took many of the classic early photos of the Gorge.

Several wildflowers unique to the Gorge can be found near Oneonta Falls, and it has been designated as a botanical area by the State of Oregon. Oneonta has received such intense visitor days in recent years, however, that the botanical species present there are in danger of being lost. Please do not pick flowers or native plants at Oneonta (or anywhere else in the Gorge!), and time your visits so you can be there when it is not overcrowded. It is a much better experience then.

*At the time of this writing, Oneonta Falls remains completely closed to public access (with large cyclone fencing at the mouth of the falls between the walls of the gorge) because the Eagle Creek Fire of 2017 left so many hazard trees in and along the creek.*

## Horsetail/Ponytail Falls

Horsetail is a beautiful single drop plunge waterfall about 192 feet in height. Aptly named, it looks like a thick horse tail coming off the rocks. It falls into a small pool right off Highway 30 and the adjacent parking area.

A steep trail to the left of the falls leads up to Ponytail Falls above Horsetail, where you can walk behind the waterfall. From there the trail continues and connects to the upper Oneonta Falls trail. That trail is quite steep with sharp drop-offs, however, so use care.

### Seasonal Waterfalls

Seasonal waterfalls appear at the same location throughout the Gorge and its backcountry, usually in late winter or spring. Many, if not most, of them are unnamed. One of the more spectacular ones is just to the east of Crown Point (only some 25 to 30 miles from downtown Portland). This waterfall manifests in the winter and during spring runoff, and follows a graceful curve seen from I-84 before dropping hundreds of feet, often into mist. Several similar seasonal waterfalls can be seen along I-84 between Crown Point and Multnomah Falls, and others all the way to The Dalles. A few dramatic seasonal falls are along State Highway 14 in Washington between Bingen and Lyle.

### Ephemeral Waterfalls

More numerous than perennial or seasonal waterfalls, but less frequent, ephemeral waterfalls by definition appear only occasionally. They are not officially named and not entirely predictable in location. But you can find them every spring, or after any major rain or snow melt event, somewhere in the Gorge. They may only last for a few hours or days, but they are well worth stopping to watch when you encounter them.

### Inundated Waterfalls

Without question, the most famous waterfalls since the creation of the Gorge now lie within this *inundated* category. These are the waterfalls that provided sustenance and social gathering for thousands of years, by creating barriers to salmon and other fish in migration that allowed humans to catch and preserve large amounts of food resources.

## Celilo Falls

Now inundated but located near present day Wishram, Washington and Celilo Village, Oregon, Celilo Falls narrowed the river from nearly a mile in width to less than 200 feet. The falls dropped the river roughly 20 to 40 feet, depending on the season and runoff. In spring the high runoff could completely inundate the falls, although the passage was still dangerous. In fall with lower flows the drop could be steeper with more rocks exposed. Lewis & Clark passed Celilo in late fall of 1805 and found the rapids challenging. In contrast, when the Hudson Bay naturalist and fur agent David Thompson encountered Celilo in 1811, it was in July, and he found the rapids passable but fast. At high water during spring runoff, as much as one million cubic feet of water passed Celilo Falls every second.

## The Narrows

Not far below Celilo another daunting set of rapids began, collectively known as "The Narrows." The first rapids, known variously as the "Upper," "Short" or "Ten Mile" Rapids (beginning about 10 miles upstream of The Dalles), ran for about one mile with the river narrowing in places to no more than 150 feet, dropping some 20 feet. Below that run the "Lower" or "Long" Narrows began (also referred to as "Five Mile Rapids" for its distance upstream of The Dalles). The Long Narrows ran for three to four miles and dropped another 15 feet. The Long Narrows ended with a feature referred to as "the Big Eddy," which overlaid a deep hole and often created whirlpools.

## Three Mile Rapids

A final set of rapids began about three miles above The Dalles settlement, known as "Three Mile Rapids." The tail end of this rapids is still visible below the The Dalles dam and bridge.

Taken together, Celilo Falls, The Narrows and Three Mile rapids were considerably vexing to watercraft and a common practice was to portage. Collectively the rapids were called "*the dalles*" by early French-Canadian trappers, referring to the layers of rock creating disturbance in the river.

In total, the run of the River from Celilo through the Narrows presented a narrowing of the river and a drop of 60 to 80 feet. Celilo Falls and the Narrows were both inundated in 1957 when The Dalles dam was completed, although the features are still there, and will undoubtedly outlive the dams (see notes).

Cascades Rapids

As discussed in Chapter I, a massive landslide in 1450 completely blocked the Columbia River at the current location of the Bonneville Dam. When the force of water eventually broke through the landslide the residual rockfall created the Cascades Rapids (so named by Lewis & Clark). First Peoples in the Gorge remember when the landslide of 1450 occurred, as it is described in stories regarding the Bridge of the Gods that was created. Lewis & Clark were intrigued by the presence of a "ghost forest" of trees in the river upstream of the Cascade Rapids. They correctly concluded that the river must have been completely blocked at some time in the past. The Cascade Rapids had a drop of about 20 feet. The rapids was inundated in 1938 when the Bonneville Dam began operation.

## F. WILD AND SCENIC RIVERS

The National Wild & Scenic Rivers Act was signed into law in 1968 (16 U.S.C. 1271), to preserve natural, free flowing waterways around the country. Some 50 years later, the Act has protected nearly 13,000 miles on 209 rivers in 40 states across the U.S. At present, segments of 5 rivers within the National Scenic Area have Wild & Scenic River status: 2 in Washington and 3 in Oregon. The Wild & Scenic Rivers Act designates portions of rivers as either "wild," "scenic," "recreational" or some combination of those categories. In all cases but to varying degrees such rivers are protected from further development.

The two Wild & Scenic Rivers in Washington State that flow into the National Scenic Area are the Klickitat River and the Little White Salmon River. In Oregon, portions of three rivers with Wild & Scenic status enter the Columbia in the Gorge: the Deschutes River, Hood River and the Sandy River.

> Klickitat River (WA) The Klickitat River runs 96 miles from Mt. Adams to its confluence with the Columbia River just west of Lyle, Washington. The river runs at a steep pitch, averaging a drop of 26 feet per mile (compared to the 2.17 foot per mile drop on the Columbia). The 10.8 mile stretch of the Klickitat from the Columbia upstream to Wheeler Creek (near Pitt, Washington) was given "wild and scenic" status on November 17, 1986 as part of the Gorge National Scenic Area Act. The Klickitat Trail runs along the east bank of the river for about 15 miles upstream from the Columbia, paralleled by Washington State Highway 142 (there is a parking area and trailhead at the junction of Washington State Highway 14 and Highway 142, just west of Lyle, Washington). The trail provides access for both hikers and bikes. This portion of the Klickitat River is a gathering place for Bald Eagles in the winter, and there are several places where traditional dip net fishing is still practiced by members of the Treaty Tribes, especially near Fisher Bridge (which crosses a Class

5+ rapids). The river is popular for fishing, kayaking, rafting and birdwatching, in addition to hiking and biking. Six distinct runs of Chinook, Coho and Steelhead salmonids use the Klickitat River.

White Salmon River (WA) Like the Klickitat, the headwaters of the White Salmon River are on the southern slope of Mt. Adams. Also like the Klickitat, the Little White Salmon River was granted Wild & Scenic status as part of the National Scenic Area Act on November 17, 1986, with a subsequent addition in 2005. The White Salmon enters the Columbia River downstream of the Klickitat across from Hood River, passing under Washington State Highway 14. The river is currently designated Wild & Scenic for about 28 miles upstream from the Columbia to the confluence of Buck Creek near BZ Corners. The river is popular for whitewater kayaking and rafting. The White Salmon is a very steep river, dropping an average of 50 feet per mile, providing numerous Class 3 rapids and at least one Class 5 waterfall that is frequently run.

Deschutes River (OR) The Deschutes River at 252 miles long is the largest tributary to the Columbia River within the National Scenic Area boundaries. There are three separate sections of the river with Wild & Scenic status (31 miles designated as "scenic" and 143 miles designated as "recreational"). The last 100 miles of the river are known as the "lower Deschutes" and contain various wildlife and recreation opportunities. The Deschutes River State Recreation Area (off I-84 at Exit 97) has camping, hiking and mountain biking opportunities. The river has cultural significance and is popular for both whitewater rafting and fishing. There is an established population of Bighorn Sheep in the lower Deschutes.

Hood River (East Fork) (OR) A run of 13.5 miles of the East Fork of the Hood River was designated as Wild & Scenic in 2009. That run goes from near the Mt. Hood Meadows ski area along Highway 35 downstream to the Forest Service boundary. There are several Forest Service trails in this area.

Sandy River (OR) About 25 miles of the Sandy River were designated as Wild & Scenic in 1988. The river was called the Quicksand River by Lewis & Clark in 1805 because of the extensive sand and silt deposits found at the junction with the Columbia that year. The river is popular for recreation and fishing. There are several park areas at the mouth and along the river, including trails to the Elliptical Bird Blind created as part of the Confluence Project.

The Wild and Scenic Rivers Act is an important statute for helping to preserve wild rivers and their resources from development, but only one quarter of one percent of our nation's rivers are in such protected status. In contrast, some 17% to 20% of our river miles are impounded by dams (more than 75,000 large dams on 600 rivers nationwide).

# CHAPTER NOTES

## Chapter II: Water & Its Effects (Hydrology and Geomorphology)

1. *Bretz and the Glacial Floods*. In the book *Cataclysms on the Columbia* (see Recommended Reading at the beginning of this Chapter) the authors detail the difficulties Bretz had in trying to persuade the scientific community about his glacial flood theory. He wrote 4 background papers between 1923 and 1925 but did not fully discuss his theory of a flood because he still could not account for a source of such enormous floodwaters. Another geologist (Joseph Pardee) had the explanation for that but did not present it until 1940. Even then it took several more decades for the academic establishment to recognize the facts. Dramatic facts they were, making evident that the glacial (Bretz) floods carried 10 times the amount of water of all rivers on earth.
2. *Ancient Cataclysmic Floods*. Professor Scott Burns points out in the book noted above that there is evidence of other cataclysmic floods preceding the Bretz floods, at least as far back as 700,000 years ago.
3. *Scientists refer to the Last Glacial Maximum* (LGM) as occurring about 25,000 years ago, when the most recent glaciation period reached its southernmost extent in western North America. As the glaciers began to recede the meltwaters led to the Bretz floods some 15,000 to 18,000 years ago. The last glaciation fully receded to current boundaries about 11,700 years ago.
4. *Witness to Glacial Floods*. It is likely that First Peoples were present to witness the glacial/Bretz floods, and just as likely that the floods and their aftermath had a dramatic impact on those people surviving the events. It would have been an incredible sight to witness flood waters carrying ice and rock roll up hundreds of feet above the current river level though the Gorge.
5. *Waterfalls* are even more unique than snowflakes or fingerprints: not only are no two alike, but each individual waterfall appears different at different times. There have been various attempts to classify waterfall types over the years. Two of the more durable methods are: (1) by shape; and (2) by volume and characteristics of discharge. The first method usually provides a list of about 10 or more different shapes, such as:

*plunge; horsetail; fan; punchbowl; block; tiered; segmented; cascade; chute; scree; slide and ribbon*, or more (there are variations on this list). The second method was propounded by Alexander Beisel in 1980, and provides a formula to classify falls by volume and other characteristics, rating categories from 0.1 to 10.0. You need considerable information about flow, height, etc. to use the formula, however, and there is some controversy associated with the method. For purposes of this book, a more simple approach uses only 4 groupings: *perennial; seasonal; ephemeral and inundated*, more of a common sense method (by the way, the author's family is from Norway, and his surname means "High Waterfall" in Norwegian…which is not further classified).

6. *Characteristics of the Cascades Rapids*. Lewis & Clark found the Cascades Rapids to be quite vexing, as a "*verry Considerable rapid at which place the waves are remarkably high…water passing with great velocity forming and boiling in a most horriablle manner, with a fall of about 20 feet.*" (Journal entry, October 30, 1805). They portaged around the rapids, as did others.
7. *Development of Dams on the Columbia* was all but inevitable, as urban and commercial development progressed along the river. As part of the New Deal in the 1930s, Congress authorized regional commissions to pursue development of hydroelectric resources. The Northwest Regional Planning Commission was formed as a result, in 1934. That led to funding for both the Bonneville Dam and the Grand Coulee Dam (completed in 1938 and 1942, respectively). The Bonneville Project Act of 1937 led to creation of the Bonneville Power Administration (BPA) in 1940. BPA's priority was to provide "*electric energy to public bodies and cooperatives,*" on a not-for-profit basis. Within just a few years more than 30 public utilities were formed in Oregon, Washington and Idaho, providing electricity to urban and rural areas throughout the Columbia Basin. By the 1970s it was becoming clear that the construction of so many dams on the Columbia had adverse effects on fish, salmon and steelhead in particular. The Northwest Power Act of 1980 directed BPA to correct damage done to native fish runs.

8. *Information on Average Flow and Hydro Uses* can be found in The Columbia River System: Inside Story, prepared jointly by BPA, COE and the Bureau of Reclamation (1984, 2d Ed. 2001).
9. *Confirmation that Celilo Falls and The Narrows Still Exist.* The Army Corps of Engineers recently conducted sonar surveys of the bed of the Columbia River from The Dalles Dam upstream to Celilo, to determine whether there was any truth to long lingering rumors that the Corps blasted Celilo prior to flooding. The surveys showed conclusively – with stunning detail – that the Falls and The Narrows are still intact, only temporarily inundated by the dams. Oregon Public Broadcasting has a video story about these surveys (found at YouTube under the title "Is Celilo Falls Still Intact?"). There is also a map of the entire Columbia River bottom that shows in detail the river bottom through the Gorge, at www.usa.fisermap.org/depth-map/columbia-river/

# CHAPTER III: WEATHER & ITS EFFECTS

## *(Meteorology, Fires & Floods)*

**Recommended Reading**

*A good introduction to meteorology is Meteorology Today by Donald Ahrens (Brooks/Cole Publishing, 2009 or the 12th Ed. of the same as an ebook by Henson & Ahrens (CENGAGE 2020). A more scientific background is provided in Fundamentals of Weather & Climate by Robin McIlveen (Oxford Univ. Press, 2010). A good overview of the risks posed by climate change is Field Notes from a Catastrophe: Man, Nature & Climate Change by Elizabeth Kolbert (Bloomsbury, 2015). Cliff Maas describes and explains The Weather of the Pacific Northwest in detail (Univ. of Washington Press 2015).*

*The history of forest fires generally is discussed by Stephen Pyne in Fire in America (Univ. of Washington Press 1997), as is a more specific Fire Ecology of Pacific Northwest Forests, by James Agee (Island Press 1996). Timothy Egan describes the devastating fires that burned through the Northwest and the West in the early 1900s in The Big Burn (Houghton Mifflin 2011). The Vanport flood of 1948 is fully examined in Vanport, by Manly Maben (Oregon Historical Society 1987).*

# CHAPTER III

## *Weather & Its Effects*

### (Meteorology, Fires and Floods)

WIND AND PRECIPITATION are the meteorological variables we experience most directly in the Gorge. Wind is usually the most dramatic of the variables. The wind here is strong, at times very strong (gusts often exceed hurricane velocity – 74 mph plus – at Crown Point on the west end of the Gorge). Strong winds can also run in both directions, from the east as well as from the west. Rainfall is the next most noticeable weather phenomenon you will experience in the Gorge. Annual precipitation can vary by more than 60 inches from one end of the Gorge to the other, with only about 60 miles separating those extremes.

As a general rule, annual precipitation increases by roughly one inch per mile from Portland to the middle of the Gorge (the Cascade Crest, near Cascade Locks), then decreases at a rate of roughly one and one-half inch per mile from Cascade Locks to the eastern end of the Gorge (east of the Deschutes River). The average annual precipitation at Cascade Locks is 77 inches per year, while the east end of the Gorge (past the Deschutes River) annually averages only around 8 to 10 inches per year. Temperature also varies from one end of the Gorge to the other, although not as dramatically as wind or precipitation. Summer temperatures on the east side often exceed 100 degrees, while that high is less common on the west side. Similarly, the east side has more days below freezing and more snow than the west side, with only about 60 miles separating them.

The effects of these differences in wind, precipitation and temperature manifest in other phenomena such as fires and floods.

> *NOTE: the weather can change often and suddenly in the Gorge. Even on short outings, be aware that you may encounter strong winds, rain or snow, and bright sun (especially on the east side). Be prepared.*

## A. GORGE WIND: OROGRAPHIC INFLUENCES AND PRESSURE GRADIENTS

The Gorge channels wind like water. Unlike the fresh water of the Columbia River, however, which runs in only one direction (from the mountains to the sea), the winds in the Gorge can run strong in both directions: upstream ("west winds" blowing from the west) and downstream ("east winds" blowing from the east). When the *East Wind* runs it typically brings higher temperatures and lower humidity if in late summer or fall, or cold winds and ice if in winter, all the way to Portland. The East Wind occurs most often in late summer to fall, and in winter. It is one of the more significant effects of weather in the Gorge.

There are different kinds of wind at work in the Gorge, which you will quickly learn if you spend any time here. The East Winds here are dramatic, but the prevailing winds are from the west and they can also be very strong. The factors that cause East Winds and the prevailing west winds are completely different: one is largely topographic (orographic) and the other is due primarily to changes in pressure gradient systems.

### Prevailing West Winds: Topographic (or Orographic)

The Gorge is located around 45 degrees north in latitude. As with all locations at middle latitudes in the northern hemisphere of the planet (between roughly 35 and 65 degrees north of the equator) the prevailing winds in the Gorge are *westerlies*, meaning that winds generally move from the west (usually from the southwest at our location) eastward. In lower latitudes (between 35 degrees and the equator) the prevailing winds are referred to as *trade winds*, which reverse flow and run primarily from east to west. There are actually five bands of *prevailing winds* on earth that switch direction at roughly similar latitudes both north and south of the equator. At the poles (north and south) the prevailing winds again turn and are known in the northern hemisphere as *polar easterlies*.

Because of its position in the middle latitudes, the default wind flow in the Gorge is from the west. The major topography bounding the Gorge, being the chain of the Cascade Mountain range running north and south, is a feature that intercepts and compresses the prevailing wind and accentuates the westerly flow, often strongly, both through the Gorge and at mountain peaks and passes. This effect is known as a *topographic (or orographic)* flow of wind. Much like water flowing through a narrowing rapids, the prevailing westerlies build speed as they funnel through the Gorge or compress at peaks and passes. Just as the speed of water in a rapids or the speed of wind at any mountain pass will be greater than before that constriction, the wind speed in the Gorge itself is greatly increased from what is experienced at the same elevation further east or west of the Gorge. Storms carried by the prevailing winds off the Pacific Ocean bring increased winds generally, but those are further accentuated in the Gorge. So, prevailing winds in the Gorge are westerly, and topographical or orographic effects increase wind speed within the Gorge itself.

### East Winds: Pressure Gradient Flow

Winds in the Gorge can reverse flow at times, often dramatically. When the East Wind runs it often carries changes in temperature and humidity that are more stark than what is typically associated with the westerlies, bringing hotter and more dry air from the high desert plateau east of the Gorge to the westside in the late summer and fall, or cold winds and ice in the winter. The effect is striking, even in Portland. It is not latitude or topography that causes East Winds to blow, it is the influence of regional weather systems. East Winds are primarily caused by meteorological pressure gradients that occur routinely year after year. Such localized and predictable pressure gradients create *foehn winds*, forcing winds downslope (or eastward in the Gorge). Other examples of foehn winds include the

Santa Ana winds in southern California and the Diablo winds in northern California.

On the entire planet, high-pressure and low-pressure systems are constantly forming and moving with the jet stream and prevailing winds. High pressure is usually associated with clear and dry weather, while low pressure is usually associated with clouds and precipitation. Just as water flows downhill and topography affects the speed of wind as it flows across constricted or compressed terrain, so high-pressure systems tend to create or accelerate wind toward the nearest low-pressure system. The closer the space between a high-pressure and low-pressure boundary the greater the pressure gradient, and thus the greater the speed of wind from the high toward the low. Pressure gradients are depicted in isobars just like topographical isobars, where the closer together (or tighter) the isobar lines are, the steeper is the terrain. Similarly, when the isobars between high-pressure and low-pressure systems are close or tight the greater is the speed of wind.

When high-pressure weather systems establish themselves on the east side of the Gorge in eastern Oregon and Washington with a low-pressure system to the west, those systems are often separated by the relatively narrow width of the Cascade Mountain range. As a result, the pressure differential is steep as East Winds pour westerly through the Gorge. Because the Cascade Mountain range contains both the high-pressure and low-pressure systems on either side of it, the East Winds are accentuated by the topography of the Gorge itself, further increasing their velocity. East Winds are largely a seasonal phenomenon. Although they can occur any time of the year they most frequently occur in the late summer through early winter when conditions are right. As discussed further below, East Winds occurring in September have influenced the growth of the largest wildfires over time in the Gorge.

## B. EASTSIDE-WESTSIDE: WEATHER NORMS AND EXTREMES

### Wind

In the Columbia River Gorge strong winds are common and very high winds are frequent. The Gorge is always more windy than other locations near it. Hood River and the eastern Gorge have become world famous as windsurfing and kite boarding destinations because of the highly reliable winds. Both the prevailing west winds and the pressure gradient East Wind are strongest at their respective downwind ends of the Gorge, because the winds compresses and accelerate as they move through the middle of the Gorge. Thus, west winds are stronger at Hood River and The Dalles than in the middle of the Gorge, and East Winds are stronger at Crown Point than further upstream.

Extremes of wind speed in the Gorge are especially frequent at certain locations. When the East Wind runs, wind gusts at Crown Point on the western end of the Gorge frequently exceed 50 to 70 mph, and sometimes higher. Strong west winds also can reach high speeds in the eastern Gorge near Hood River and The Dalles, although usually not as strong as measured at Crown Point. When the East Wind runs it typically begins at The Dalles as a gentle breeze (just like a large bowl of water poured at the head of a sluice, the flow starts slowly). By the time it reaches Hood River the East Wind is already strong, and it gets much stronger before it reaches the west end of the Gorge.

#### Lenticular Clouds (Cloud Caps) and Other Wind Effects

Another effect of the strong winds associated with the Gorge occurs not in the Gorge itself but over high mountain peaks to the north and south. Wind compresses and accelerates speed in the Gorge and over mountain passes and peaks. In the latter case strong winds over peaks can create unusual cloud patterns called *lenticular clouds* or *cloud caps*. These usually appear over the top of Mt. Hood or Mt. Adams as saucer like shapes, even when the skies are otherwise clear. At times they can repeat going downwind, in a series of saucer like clouds. They occur when the rapidly rising wind over the peak squeezes out moisture which shows as cloud, then as the wind descends on the other side of the peak the temperature warms above the dew point and cloud formation ends. Lenticulars are fascinating to see but avoided by aviators because they warn of very high winds aloft.

Other wind related effects you can see in the Gorge are *krummholz* trees or shrubs (stunted and contorted by high wind) and *flag* or *banner trees* (trees not reduced in height but shaped by constant winds so that the branches extend downwind noticeably). Both effects are discussed in the section on "Trees and Shrubs" in Chapter IV (Plants).

## Precipitation

Unlike the steady presence of wind (whether from the west or the east), the striking attribute of precipitation in the Gorge is significant change between the west end and the east end of the Gorge. Annual rainfall can vary by more than 60 inches from the center of the Gorge at Cascade Locks to the east end of the Gorge near the Deschutes River (over the course of only some 60 miles). As noted in the previous section, the prevailing wind and weather in the Gorge comes from the west, and as weather systems move up and over the Cascade Range the atmosphere compresses water content, resulting in increasing rainfall as clouds move toward the Cascade crest. The amount of precipitation reaches a maximum in the Gorge around Cascade Locks, in line with the crest of the Cascade Mountains. Then having lost considerable moisture the precipitation tapers off even more rapidly as the clouds (now depleted of moisture) continue moving eastward.

As a rule of thumb, average annual precipitation *increases* by roughly one inch per mile from Portland to Cascade Locks. Then from Cascades Locks moving further eastward, average annual precipitation *decreases* even more sharply, by roughly one and one-half inch per mile to the Deschutes River and east end of the Gorge.

## Temperature

Due to the Cascade Mountain range's effect in wringing moisture out of weather systems as they move east there are usually fewer clouds and less precipitation east of the Cascade crest than on the west side. The west end of the Gorge is more often partly or fully cloudy than the east end. With more sunshine on the east side, the temperature in the summer is typically higher than on the west side and exceeds 100 degrees several times a year. The opposite occurs in the winter, as clear night skies allow ground temperature to cool, making the east side typically cooler than the west side, with more nights below freezing.

## Seasons

Yes, the Gorge has seasons. It is sometimes said that one could wake up on the west side of the Cascade Mountains any time of the year and find the same conditions: temperature in the mid-50s, light rain and surrounded by green coniferous trees. In other words, not much difference among seasons. Not so in the Gorge. The significant precipitation and temperature differential between the west and east ends of the Gorge accentuates seasonal differences. The east side is always hotter in the summer than the west side, and there is always some snow and ice on the east side in the winter (snow or ice storms occur far less frequently on the west side).

The west end of the Gorge has more cloudy days on average over the course of the year than does the east end of the Gorge. There are many times during the year where it may be cloudy or rainy in Portland and throughout the westside of the Gorge, but sunny and clear on the eastside. The clouds often clear and the sun often comes out around milepost 50 near Wyeth on Interstate 84. Thunderstorms are infrequent in the Gorge, but they do occur, usually associated with high temperatures aiding cumulus cloud formation.

Interstate 84 and Highway 14 are often closed on the east side of the Gorge for some periods of time in the winter due to snow, ice or landslides, while both roads typically remain open further west. Multnomah Falls often becomes partially covered in ice in late winter, even when Portland is not as cold. Finally, because there are more hardwood trees in the middle of the Gorge and eastward there are more autumn colors to be seen there in the Fall.

## C. FIRE OCCURRENCE AND NATURAL FIRE HISTORY

Fire has always been a natural part of the environment in the Gorge. In prehistoric and historic times fires were as frequent as floods here. Both were predictable seasonal events. Despite major human efforts over the past century, there is no management system as effective at preventing or controlling fires as dams are effective in managing seasonal floods. Fire remains a force of nature that is easier to predict than to control. Despite a hundred years of fire suppression efforts, fire remains a significant part of life in the Gorge and elsewhere in the West. That was made evident, once again, with the catastrophic Eagle Creek fire of 2017 in the Gorge.

All wildfire is influenced by three primary factors: fuel, weather, and topography. Each of those factors present themselves in large fashion in the Gorge. Simply put, the heavier the fuel loading (trees, shrubs or grass), the steeper the slope or the more dry or windy the weather, the more severe will be the fire. In the Gorge, there is heavy fuel loading on the west side and extensive flammable grasslands in the east. The slopes are steep and the wind is almost always present. In other words, any fire start in the Gorge has the potential to become large quickly.

Large fires tend to determine their own boundaries, and until there is a significant change in fuel, weather or topography, suppression efforts are of limited utility. That seems like an obvious observation, but it was largely ignored for one hundred years in fire suppression efforts. The mission of the early Forest Service was both to protect federal forests from fire and to re-forest logged areas. Those goals led to creation of the "10 a.m. policy" in 1935, where the Forest Service endeavored to extinguish all fire (regardless of size or location) by 10 a.m. the day following discovery. By the 1970s this approach required a huge budget yet failed to reduce risk because aggressive suppression actually increased fuel loading in some areas that could have been allowed to burn naturally.

Fire History and Natural Fire Rotation

The change in weather and vegetation from the west side to the east side of the Gorge correspondingly results in annual change in fire incidence and behavior. The natural fire rotation (meaning natural frequency and size of wildfires) on the west side of the Cascade Range in the Gorge area has been estimated to be between 350 and 700 years, meaning that historically the natural vegetation of the west side Doug-Fir/Hemlock ecosystem typically saw large fires in a given location only rarely, but when fire did occur it was typically very large and stand replacing. In contrast, the natural fire rotation of the Ponderosa Pine/White Oak ecosystem typical of the east side of the Gorge was historically as short as 7 to 11 years. Fires occurred more frequently on the eastside but those fires were typically smaller and produced relatively less damage.

Fire incidence and risk change from one end of the Gorge to the other due to changes in vegetation (fuel) type, and through fuel moisture trends. The type of small herbs and shrubs and more widely spaced trees on the east side dry out more quickly than the dense undergrowth and large diameter woody debris associated with the west side. While a pile of pine needles and small twigs (those less than one quarter inch diameter) can become dry and combustible within a few hours after rain, west side woody debris, much of which is over three inches in diameter, can take one thousand hours (more than forty days) of dry weather to become at risk of fire. As a result, fire frequency on the east side of the Gorge typically peaks in July and August (the hottest months) while fire frequency on the west side increases later, in September, when the larger woody debris has more fully dried.

On both the east and west ends of the Gorge wind greatly influences fire spread and effects. East Winds often occur in fall, especially September when large fuels are most dry. The historical record shows that the most extreme west side fires have occurred in September, associated with both the drying of large diameter woody fuel and high winds. The largest fires in the history of the Gorge began in September, pushed by East Winds and fueled by dry and dense forest fuels on the west end of the Gorge. The Yacolt Burn of 1902 and the Eagle Creek Fire of 2017 both began in the first week of September (both fires also began in Eagle Creek, both jumped the Columbia River and both were started by teenage boys – burning a wasp nest in 1902 and lighting smoke bombs in 2017). The Yacolt Burn consumed more than a quarter million acres, while the Eagle Creek fire of 2017 burned nearly 50,000 acres. (*Large fires* are currently defined as those more than 100 acres in timber or 300 acres in grassland; *Mega-Fires* – a term only recently needed – are those that exceed 100,000 acres in size.)

In short, fires on the west side of the Cascade Mountains occur on average less frequently than on the east side but typically become larger in size and create more damage, while fires on the east side occur more frequently but typically remain smaller. That historical fact is changing in recent years for both the west side and the east side as climate change and increasing population in wooded areas has extended fire season and increased both the frequency and size of fires generally, with the potential for large fires occurring well beyond what used to be thought of as traditional fire season.

## Fire Management and Policy

In the first decade of the 1900s several million acres of forest land burned across Montana, Idaho, Oregon and Washington. One of those catastrophic fires was the Yacolt Burn in 1902, which burned more a quarter million acres, including portions of the Gorge and Southwestern Washington. The fires were fanned by dry weather and high winds, but also fueled by large areas of logging slash. The Forest Service increased its fire prevention and fire suppression efforts after those devastating early fires, and as noted above in 1935 the Forest Service declared a "10 a.m. policy" to extinguish all fire starts regardless of size, location or risk.

The 10 a.m. policy initiated a long and expensive program of fire suppression by the Forest Service and other agencies. By the 1970s it became increasingly clear that such aggressive fire suppression was priming the forests for more catastrophic fires. Under natural fire conditions, fuel reduction is accomplished by relatively frequent small fires that make catastrophic fires less likely to occur. The 10 a.m. policy affected natural fire frequency in many forest systems and allowed fuel loadings to build over time.

An added complication to the overly aggressive fire suppression policy was the prevalence of generally lax land use policies. A lack of land use restrictions allowed homes and vacation properties to be built in the middle of forested areas, expanding the *wildland-urban interface*, with little to no defensive fire perimeters. Even as fire management agencies tried to establish natural fire policies they still had to protect human life and structures in the wildland-urban interface. As a result, a fire that may otherwise be allowed to burn to more defensible points (often with relatively little damage to the ecosystem) must be fought to protect isolated structures in the wildland-urban interface.

Federal, state and local governments now expressly encourage (and in some places require) private landowners to establish *defensible space* or *defensible fire perimeters* (including, among other things: the use of fire-resistant building materials such as brick, concrete, metal or stone for walls and roofs, and clearance or reduction of vegetative materials for at least 100 feet around structures). These efforts, either done voluntarily or through revised local land use laws, could help reduce risk of fire in the Gorge.

In recent years various land management agencies, state and local communities have worked to reduce fire danger through a combination of efforts: prescribed burning, select or partial cut logging or mechanical treatment of fuel accumulations. The Bureau of Land Management recently began a massive effort in the Great Basin (including areas just east of the National Scenic Area but within the Columbia River corridor) to establish fuel breaks along roads and rights-of-way.

As noted at the beginning of this section, large fires tend to determine their own boundaries. No matter how many resources are directed at a large fire there is little chance of containing it until there is a significant change in fuel, topography or weather. The Eagle Creek fire of 2017 only allowed limited suppression efforts because of the steep slopes and extreme fire behavior, but also because much of the area on fire was in protected land status. As a result (a positive result in the larger scheme of things) the fire burned in natural patterns, leaving mosaics of burned and unburned areas in stark contrast to the rectangular and sharp-edged clear cuts left by logging and the burning of logging slash. You can see *unburned islands (or refugia)* on the hills where the 2017 fire burned, consisting of remnant vegetation untouched by the fire. Those areas are key to providing habitat for animals that survived the fire, and as a base for repopulation and new colonization of various plant species.

Large Fires in or Near the Gorge in Recent Years

In addition to the Eagle Creek fire in 2017, several other large fires in or near the National Scenic Area have occurred in recent years, including the following:

> 2006: *The Bluegrass Fire* burned significant acreage along the north and east flanks of Mt. Hood.
>
> 2008: *The Gnarl Ridge fire* was started by lightning on August 7, 2008 on the northeast side of Mt. Hood, and grew to 3,200 acres.
>
> 2009: A fire near Mosier began on August 28, growing to 800 acres.
>
> 2011: *The Dollar Lake fire*, on the north flank of Mt. Hood, was started by lightning strikes on August 26, 2011 and grew to 6,200 acres.
>
> 2012: *The Cascade Creek fire* started from lightning strikes on Crofton Ridge on Mt. Adams on September 8, 2012, and burned roughly 20,000 acres. That fire was the largest on Mt. Adams since "the Great Conflagration Fire" of 1885, which burned some 17,000 acres.
>
> 2014: *The Rowena fire* started on August 5, 2014 and burned more than 2,600 acres, driven by strong west winds greater than 35 mph. The fire started east of Hood River, near the Rowena viewpoint, and burned to the western outskirts of The Dalles. It was believed to be human caused.
>
> 2015: *The Cougar Creek Complex fire* on Mt. Adams started by lightning on August 10 and ultimately burned roughly 53,000 acres, including large areas of insect damaged forest.

2017: *The Eagle Creek fire* in the center of the Gorge, which began on September 2, burned more than 48,000 acres.

The large fires on Mt. Adams and the north or east slopes of Mt. Hood were started by lightning, ignited in late August. The 2017 Eagle Creek fire was ignited by humans, started in the first week of September (like the Yacolt Burn in 1902).

## D. FLOODS, EROSION AND MUDFLOWS

Floods are a natural phenomenon in the Pacific Northwest generally, and the Gorge specifically, caused by a combination of factors: the amount and timing of precipitation, snowpack accumulation in mountains, temperature, snowmelt and runoff rates. As discussed in Chapter II, the Gorge has seen catastrophic flood events over geologic time, as the immense glacial meltwater floods helped create the Gorge as we find it today. These glacial or Bretz floods are believed to have been the largest floods of water ever to occur on the planet, occurring multiple times between some 15,000 to 18,000 years ago.

In recorded history, the highest flow on the Columbia River – before any dams were constructed – occurred in 1894, when a flow of 1.25 million cubic feet per second (cfs) was measured at The Dalles. The second highest flow in recorded history was the flood that began on May 31, 1948, which inundated the city of Vanport in north Portland (a city that was built rapidly in lowland areas to house workers building ships during WWII) and resulted in the deaths of more than a dozen people. The Vanport flood occurred when the Bonneville Dam was in place, but neither The Dalles Dam nor the John Day Dam were present to help restrain the floodwaters and Canada had not controlled floodwaters on its dams. The event was caused by record snowpack and an early spring (meaning rapid snowmelt) followed by another sudden melt in May combined with heavy rains. The flow from the 1948 flood measured 1.01 million cfs on May 31, then maintained a flow of about 900,000 cfs for three weeks in June (note: the third highest flood level measured on the Columbia occurred in 1876, when 1 million cfs was recorded at The Dalles). The 1948 flood at

Vanport was a tragedy for reasons well beyond the water levels (see Notes below). The flood did illustrate, however, that preservation of lowlands and wetlands is at least as important as dams in controlling flood waters.

The Columbia River is currently controlled by a series of 14 mainstem dams along its 1,242 mile stretch (and more than 400 dams within the entire drainage area), thus large scale flooding rarely occurs any more. Tributary streams do flood frequently, however, impacting the river with mud and debris, as can be seen annually at both the Sandy River and Hood River deltas.

## E. THE WATER CYCLE

The *water* (or *hydrologic*) *cycle* is a concept that has relevance to hydrology, climatology and even geology. It refers to the continuous movement of water from the surface of the earth (rivers, lakes, oceans) to the atmosphere (humidity, clouds, storms) and back to the surface and sub-surface of the earth (rain, snow, groundwater and water entrained in rocks). The water cycle is a significant component of weather on earth, and it has relevance to the Gorge.

The amount of water in the Columbia River at any given time as it passes through the Gorge varied considerably in historic and prehistoric times. After construction of the dams, flow has been controlled so that it typically carries about 250,000 cfs through the Gorge (but even with dams that flow can vary from 100,000 to 400,000 cfs, depending on annual precipitation and snowmelt in the Columbia River Basin).

Climate change is having a major effect on water cycles worldwide. In essence, increased global temperature has increased rates of both evaporation and precipitation. One might think that should not necessarily be a bad development (more rainfall), until you realize that prevailing winds move evaporated water downwind so increased precipitation often falls in another location than where evaporation occurred. On a global scale this is already having significant effects on agriculture and potable water supplies, creating both droughts and flooding in areas where drought and floods did not previously occur. On a local level we are already seeing increased drought and increased fire risk in the American West, including the eastside of the Gorge.

## F. CLIMATE CHANGE

Humans have affected the environment in major ways over the last several hundred years, especially from the middle of the 20$^{th}$ Century onward. Our impacts began with early agriculture but first became noticeable around the time of the Industrial Revolution in the 1700s. Effects became more significant as we began burning coal and other fossil fuels at an increasing pace, and simultaneously began cutting down increasingly large forested areas on the planet. The change in global climate is now well documented, and most Americans have gradually come to recognize that climate change is real, that the temperature of the planet is warming and that the effect is largely caused by human action.

Some skeptics remain, but as unusual or extreme weather events continue to occur at an alarming rate, most people now accept the reality of the situation. As the saying goes: *climate is like your personality, while weather is like your mood.* Your mood (the weather) may change often, sometimes dramatically, but your personality usually stays the same. If your personality (or the climate as a whole) *does* begin to change, it usually signals some serious underlying concern.

Our most recent geologic epoch has been designated as the *Holocene,* which began at the end of the last ice age, around 11,700 years ago. Many climate scientists have now proclaimed that a new geologic epoch has begun, called the *Anthropocene,* marking the point where human activity has affected natural processes on the earth as a whole. The delineator of these geologic epochs has been tentatively pegged at 1950, so if you were born before that date, you were born in the Holocene. After that date, you are a child of the Anthropocene. Either way, we are now all living in the Anthropocene.

The impacts of climate change on the Gorge are many, and already occurring. The hydrologic cycle of the Pacific Northwest will generally change with increased heat and variations in the amount and duration of precipitation, likely resulting in warmer temperatures and extended periods of drought. Those changes could affect water availability for plants, animals and people, and result in larger and more frequent forest fires.

There are things we can do as visitors or residents in the Gorge to help alleviate the impact of climate change, such as limiting use of fossil fuel fired transportation (carpool, take shuttle busses, hike, bike or use alternative energy vehicles and alternative energy resources), and encourage others to do the same.

# CHAPTER NOTES

## Chapter III: Weather and Its Effects (Meteorology, Fire & Floods)

1. *Causes of Wind Direction and Speed*. As Cliff Maas points out (see his book reference in the introduction), strong west winds in the Gorge can also be affected by 'sea breeze' pressure changes, beyond just orographic concentration of wind through the narrowing Gorge. But the larger themes remain.
2. *When Windy Isn't Windy*. *Viento* means windy in Spanish, and Viento State Park west of Hood River (Exit 56 off Interstate 84) is in a very windy location. But the name of the park came from three railroad employees who bought the land over a century ago with plans to develop it. The named their enterprise, and the area, using the first two letters of each of their last names: *Vi*llard, *En*dicott and *To*llman.
3. *Precipitation variation in the Gorge*. Portland, at Milepost (MP) zero, gets an average of 37" of precipitation per year. Troutdale, near MP 17 where the National Scenic Area begins receives 45" per year on average. Cascade Locks in line with the crest of the Cascade Mountains at MP 44 averages 77" per year. Hood River at MP 66 averages 31", The Dalles at MP 87 averages 15" and by the east end of the National Scenic Area, beyond the Deschutes River around MP 100 the average annual precipitation is only about 8" per year.
4. *Establishment of the Forest Service and Fire Suppression Policy*. The U.S. Forest Service was created in 1905. A series of National Forests (NF) were set aside by the federal government, portions of two within the boundaries of the National Scenic Area: the Mt Hood NF (which began as the Bull Run Forest Preserve in 1892 then absorbed parts of the Oregon NF and the Cascade NF in 1908, and eventually became the Mt Hood NF in 1924); and the Gifford Pinchot NF (initially part of the Mt. Rainier Forest Reserve, created in 1887, then becoming the Columbia NF in 1908 and eventually the Gifford Pinchot NF in 1949). Organized fire suppression by the Forest Service did not begin until the 1930s. The aggressive 10 a.m. policy was adopted in 1935

(put out all fires no matter the size or location by 10 a.m. the day following discovery).

5. *Forest Fire Behavior* is now fairly well understood and can be modeled by fuel type and fire regime. Heavy fuel loadings left from decades of fire suppression combined with climate change impacts show that fire behavior is becoming more intense in many areas of the west, including the Gorge.
6. *Fire History*. The estimates on natural fire rotation for the National Forests partly overlapping the Scenic Area are based on studies for the Forest Service conducted by the author in the early 1980s.
7. *"Confine, Contain, Control" Fire Management Policies*. Fire prevention and planning became an art as the beneficial effects of fire became better understood. Fire management policies now include *confine, contain and control* strategies. "Confine" connotes monitoring, either from air or observers on ground, with such observations potentially moving the fire response to a more aggressive level. "Contain" involves the establishment of fire lines using hand tools, bulldozers or natural features, and can be either "direct" (along the edge of the fire) or "indirect" (leaving some unburned area between the fire line and the fire). "Control" is the most aggressive strategy, where once a fire is contained crews continue to work to extinguish all remaining fire and embers in the burn area. Most large fires, including the 2017 Eagle Creek fire, are difficult to fully control before the seasons change. For that reason, several smokes and hotspots re-appeared in the Eagle Creek fire boundaries the following spring.
8. *Modified Fire Policies* were first put in place in the early 1970s at the Sequoia National Park in California, followed by similar "*confine-contain-control*" policies in other land management locations, including federal lands in the Northwest.
9. *Mega-Fire*. Defined for the U.S. (by the Boise Interagency Fire Center) as wildfires larger than 100,000 acres, mega-fires have become increasingly common in the West. There were some extremely large fires historically, before the term was coined, such as the Yacolt Burn of 1902 (a quarter million acres, including part of the Gorge) and the Yellowstone fires in 1988 (burning 1.2 million acres, 36% of the Park), but they were infrequent. Mega-fires are caused by a century

of fire exclusion, increased human activity in fire prone areas and, perhaps most significantly, climate change. Scientists predicted that climate change would eventually result in increasing large fires, but the occurrence has come decades ahead of prediction. The 2018 Camp Fire in northern California and the 2021 Bootleg Fire in Oregon may be only the beginning of increased mega-fire.

10. *Climate change* is already affecting the Gorge. Source specific impacts have been studied for several years, including impacts to air quality from coal burning electric utility generation facilities and large combined animal feeding lot (CAFO) activities in eastern Oregon. Portland General Electric's Boardman coal plant is scheduled to be closed in the near future, and there are plans to limit the CAFOs. The Friends of the Columbia Gorge and others are also working to preclude or limit train traffic through the Gorge that carries coal or oil, as both pose significant risk in the event of an incident.
11. *The Tragedy of the Vanport Flood* went beyond the water levels. The Kaiser Shipyards encouraged workers to come to Portland at the beginning of WWII to help build ships for the war effort. Some 40,000 people came, many from the American South. Although there were jobs at the shipyards there was insufficient housing. With no help from the City of Portland, Kaiser quickly built temporary housing just north of the City boundary in the floodplain south of the Columbia River (the area that is now Delta Park and the Portland International Raceway). The housing area was separated from the river by dikes from 15' to 25' high, which were collapsed or over-topped by the flood. After the war many people moved on, but almost half stayed, making Vanport the second largest city in Oregon but where many residents had no jobs and inadequate housing. When the 1948 flood came nearly all of the 18,500 people remaining in Vanport were left homeless, and many of them were African-American. The challenge of finding housing and jobs became even more difficult after the flood. The Vanport flood and the social impacts associated with it remain uncomfortable memories for the State of Oregon and the City of Portland.

# CHAPTER IV: PLANTS

## *(Flora)*

### Recommended Reading

*The classic plant reference book for the Northwest (including the Gorge) is Hitchcock & Cronquist's Flora of the Pacific Northwest (Univ. of Wash. Press; first published in 1973, with a 2d Edition issued in 2018). The best and most practical field guide for flowering plants in the Gorge is Russ Jolley's Wildflowers of the Columbia Gorge (Oregon Historical Society Press 1988) (the book is currently out of print, but used copies are available from Powell's Book and elsewhere). Another good book on wildflowers in the Gorge is Wildflowers of the Pacific Northwest, by Mark Turner & Phyllis Gustafson (Timber Press 2006). As to trees, Stephen Arno's new edition of Northwest Trees (Mountaineers Press 2020) is a wonderful narrative classic, and the more recent Trees & Shrubs of the Pacific Northwest is very thorough, by Turner and Kuhlman (Timber Press 2014), as is David Sibley's Guide to Trees (Knopf 2009). Jerry Franklin has published numerous articles on trees of the Northwest, and all his works are recommended. A recent field guide to mushrooms is Mushrooms of the Pacific Northwest, by Trudell and Ammirati (Timber Press 2009), which has good color photos and keys. Entangled Life by Merlin Sheldrake (Random House, 2020) presents fascinating insights to fungi generally.*

# CHAPTER IV

## *Plants*

### (**Flora**)

PLANTS IN THE Gorge change from west to east primarily due to the significant changes in annual precipitation, and to the change in soils. On the westside the Douglas-fir, Grand Fir, Hemlock and Cedar trees stand thick and tall, interspersed with various hardwoods and a lush understory. Around Hood River the overstory becomes dominated by more sparsely spaced Ponderosa Pine and Oregon White Oak. On the eastern end of the Gorge, near The Dalles, trees give way to Juniper, Big Sagebrush, Antelope Bitterbrush, Grey Rabbitbrush and bunchgrasses that stretch eastward for hundreds of miles across the high desert plateau.

The plants of the Columbia River Gorge use a wide range of ecological niches over a range of some 80 miles between the Sandy River and the Deschutes River. Habitats run from the moist (*mesic*) to dry (*xeric*) ends of the spectrum. Annual precipitation in the middle of the Gorge averages around 77 inches per year (near Cascade Locks on the River, which is in line with the crest of the Cascade Mountains), while the eastside annual precipitation can be as low as 8 inches per year (near Wishram and Biggs). Those extremes are only about 60 miles apart. The Gorge offers rich volcanic soils for plant growth, supplemented on the west side by deep vegetative duff. There are also rocky, sandy and streamside (*riparian*) habitats to exploit. Plants in the Gorge also find a wide range of temperature and light conditions, stretching from near sea level to almost 5,000 feet in elevation (*montane conditions*). Trees and shrubs, and most smaller plants, typically must adapt to high wind conditions, but micro-habitats are tucked among the valleys and rocks throughout the Gorge providing shelter to those smaller plants that need protection. Some trees and shrubs at either high elevation or high wind exposure become stunted, or *krummholz*.

You can find nearly 100 species of trees and shrubs in the Gorge (many of the shrubs flower and some produce fruit in the spring and summer), and more than 700 species of native plants and flowers. There are more than a dozen flowering plants that are *endemic* to the Gorge, meaning they are found nowhere else on earth.

## Photosynthesis

Photosynthesis is the process that is key to the existence of all trees and shrubs and flowering plants, by which plants convert the light energy in sunshine into chemical energy for food, stored as sugar. Using only water and carbon dioxide, photosynthesis provides food for plants, which in turn provide food for almost all other life on earth, by means of the food chain that begins with plants and moves through larger and larger animals. Photosynthetic plants also produce oxygen (after using or *fixing* the carbon obtained through carbon dioxide uptake during the process of photosynthesis). Photosynthesis is key to virtually all life on earth.

Not all plants use photosynthesis, however. Some algae (lichens) and some fungi (mushrooms) obtain their energy and necessary nutrients through other processes, where sunlight is not directly required.

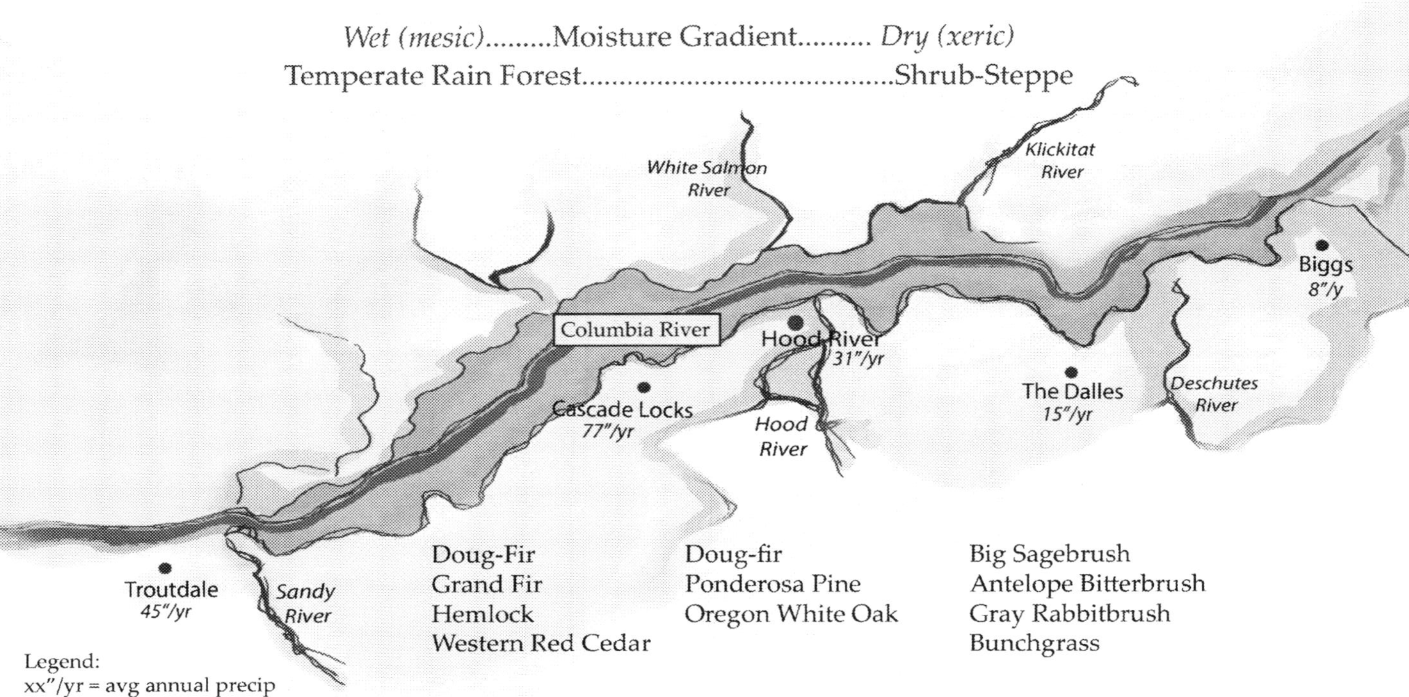
COLOMBIA RIVER GORGE NATIONAL SCENIC AREA
NATIVE PLANT HABITATS & ECOTYPES
Wet (mesic).........Moisture Gradient.......... Dry (xeric)
Temperate Rain Forest........................................Shrub-Steppe
White Salmon River
Klickitat River
Biggs 8"/y
Columbia River
Hood River 31"/yr
The Dalles 15"/yr
Deschutes River
Cascade Locks 77"/yr
Hood River
Troutdale 45"/yr
Sandy River
Doug-Fir
Grand Fir
Hemlock
Western Red Cedar
Doug-fir
Ponderosa Pine
Oregon White Oak
Big Sagebrush
Antelope Bitterbrush
Gray Rabbitbrush
Bunchgrass
Legend:
xx"/yr = avg annual precip
= NSA Boundaries
Graphic concept by Lisa Appel

Examples of all these types of plants are found in the Gorge.

Succession, Climax and Species Diversity

The terms *succession* and *climax* are often heard in discussions about trees and plants in the Northwest and the Gorge. Generally speaking, succession refers to the natural replacement of plant species in a given area over time, while climax refers to a relatively stable or mature plant community in a given place. As an example, after major disturbances such as fire, flood or wind, *pioneer* species will first appear (such as certain grasses, fireweed, vine maple or aspen), which take advantage of full sunshine and little competition (as well as nitrogen and other nutrients left as a result of fires). Over time, as the pioneer species help create new habitat and soils, other (*successional or seral*) species will invade, increasingly more tolerant of shade as they develop beneath existing species. Eventually, one or more species will overtop other competing overstory species, and then reduce competition by occupying the canopy and sunlight (even while allowing more shade tolerant understory species to grow below it). This then becomes a *climax* community…at least for a while.

Succession was first recognized and described not by a scientist or modern academic, but by Henry David Thoreau. The concept (and reality) is more observational and common sense than academic, although there are many fascinating scientific studies on succession. The concept of climax plant communities (especially trees) is also often the subject of much discussion, but climax communities are not the inevitable natural state of all ecosystems, or necessarily the most stable. In many ecosystems, including much of the Gorge, frequent physical disturbances (wind, fire and flood) may occur before climax plant communities appear, or become well-established.

*Species diversity* is another concept important to understanding plant (and animal) communities. Ecosystems with more diverse species generally tend to be more stable, as the variety of species will have differing resistance to disturbances (insect, disease, wind or fire). Diversity also tends to increase with succession, although some climax communities may inhibit diversity by one or just a few species occupying much of the habitat. Ecosystem diversity is often described in terms of *richness* and *evenness.* There is considerable research on these issues, the most current published in a variety of journals (search any of the topics for the latest observations and findings).

All these concepts are important to understanding plant communities, and they should help you make your own observations during your visits to the Gorge.

## Taxonomical Nomenclature

As global explorations began in the 1500s, the naturalists accompanying many of those voyages tried to describe the new plant and animal species they encountered. Since there were no national or international agreements on how to name things a variety of naming systems developed. Often the same organism was given many names, especially by horticulturists that domesticated foreign flora for medicinal, agricultural or horticultural purposes. By the 1700s, much of the scientific community had begun to use Latin as a common language in their naming practices, but there was still no uniform taxonomical nomenclature to make sense out of all the new discoveries. As more and more new plants and animals were introduced to the scientific community, there was growing confusion over distinguishing and comparing these specimens.

In the early 1700s, a Swedish scientist named Carl Linnaeus recognized the problem in using various names for the same plant and animal specimens. Linnaeus proposed a new system of *binomial nomenclature*, using Latin, where all specimens would be classified by a general type (*genus*) and an individual characteristic (*species*). Linnaeus' own name already had a Latin form due to the fact that his father (also a Swedish botanist) changed his name when he applied to college – adopting as his new name the Swedish word for Linden tree, in Latin form. After being granted nobility by the King of Sweden later in life, Linnaeus (the son) often went by a further Latinate version of his name: Carolus von Linne (see notes).

Linne's now famous *System Naturae* was published in 1735, and had enough of an impact that it went through twelve editions. It proposed to assign all plants and animals with a taxonomical nomenclature based on genus and species. That system remains in use today. The Linnaean naming system is efficient; it allows scientists and lay people to identify and compare plants or animals from different locations, based on physical attributes as well as demonstrable genetic relationships (Linnaeus grouped as species those individuals, even if presenting varying appearance, that could produce fertile progeny). Science further "split" or "lumped" species based on additional information about organisms and their relationships among other organisms. Thus, a wolf and a coyote and a dog are all in the *Canis* genus, but split in species classification (even though interbreeding can occur), with the wolf classified as *Canis lupus* while the coyote is *Canis latrans* and dogs are *Canis familiaris*. On the other hand, scientists used to distinguish two different woodpeckers across America as Red-shafted and Yellow-shafted Flickers, but they are now lumped as a single Northern Flicker species precisely because they did interbreed. The system is not perfect, and genetic analysis now offers more precision in identification and classification, but the Linnaean system of binomial nomenclature remains both in use and useful worldwide.

The Linnaean system is useful as you learn about the natural world because there are so many different common names for plants and animals, even in a local area. For example, someone may tell you about some beautiful sunflowers you should see in the spring in the eastern Gorge, but another person may refer to the same plants as Balsamroot (the latter is prevalent and showy here, but true sunflowers are also present, as are other yellow large-blossomed flowers). All plants and animals referred to in this book use the Linnaean naming system for reference, along with common and local names as appropriate. Many of the Linnaean species names for plants and animals in the Gorge reference Lewis & Clark or one of the early naturalists (Menzies, Douglas, Nuttall, Suksdorf), as they were the first Euro-Americans to describe the species.

## A. TREES AND SHRUBS

There is no bright line definition that distinguishes a tree from a shrub, but most foresters and botanists agree that shrubs are "tree-like" plants with woody stems (usually multiple) that typically do not exceed 15 to 20 feet in height. The Gorge abounds with both trees and shrubs, and the exception often becomes the norm here, with some plants normally presenting as shrubs becoming trees in this environment, and at the higher and more windswept elevations, some trees presenting in shrub form (*krummholz*).

In general, the forested areas of the Gorge include dense stands of both trees and shrubs.

Forest ecosystems in the Gorge begin in the west in the dense and productive *Doug Fir-Hemlock-Grand Fir* ecotype, which transforms east of the Cascade crest to a *Ponderosa Pine-Oregon White Oak* ecotype, and then becomes a *Shrub-Steppe* environment further east, immediately adjacent to the high desert of Oregon and the southern plateau of Washington. Average annual precipitation on the westside of the Gorge (at Cascade Locks) is 77 inches per year, while it is only about 8 inches per year on the eastside (at Wishram), with those extremes only about 60 miles apart.

There are *coniferous* (or evergreen) trees with needles and *deciduous* trees (those that lose leaves in the winter). Even coniferous trees lose needles, but only about 20% per year on average, allowing the tree to remain green throughout the year. Individual conifer needles usually live for only about 3 to 5 years, but the trees continually replace them (note the accumulation of dry needles beneath conifers from gradual replacement). There is also a *deciduous evergreen* in the Gorge, as well as some *non-native (introduced)* trees.

> *NOTE: This book only lists a few trees and shrubs the typical visitor or resident is most likely to encounter in travels through the Gorge. It does not list all species. Other books and guides noted in the Chapter heading and Notes provide additional information.*

Coniferous Trees: Predominantly Westside (*but may be found throughout the Gorge*)

> Douglas-fir (*Psuedotsuga menziesii*) is the most common and well-known tree in the Pacific Northwest, including the Gorge. Doug-fir is truly a regional tree, found nowhere else in North America. Four other species of the *Psuedotsuga* genus exist in the world (3 in China, 1 in Japan), but they are not widespread even where present. The tree is so prevalent in the Gorge that it deserves special discussion here.

Doug-fir is taxonomically unusual. It took botanists decades to agree on how to classify the tree. Archibald Menzies, the naturalist on George Vancouver's expedition to the Northwest in the 1790s first described Doug-fir when he encountered it on what is now Vancouver Island in Canada. Menzies could not decide whether the tree was a pine, a fir, a spruce or a hemlock. He initially called it a pine and sent samples back to England (unfortunately, the specimens did not survive). About a decade later, Lewis & Clark collected specimens from the same type of tree and called them a fir. Then in the 1820s and 1830s David Douglas collected specimens from the Gorge and sent them back to England for further examination and propagation.

For several more years botanists went back and forth in deciding how to classify and name this unusual tree. A French botanist (Carriere) eventually coined the new genus name *Psuedotsuga*, which became commonly known as the Douglas Fir (or Doug-fir), even though the tree is neither a "false hemlock" or a "fir" as both the Latin and common names suggest. It is unlike other coniferous trees, appropriately given its own genus.

Doug-fir is tolerant of shade and a variety of soils, allowing it to occupy a wide variety of ecotones throughout its range. It grows up to 300 feet tall and can live up to 1,000 years. It is a relatively hard softwood that grows to great heights with straight trunks, making it ideal for use as lumber and firewood. Traditional peoples made use of Doug-fir wood and used the leaves and inner bark for tea and medicinal purposes.

A distinguishing characteristic of Doug-fir is that the relatively small cones have three-pronged bracts that protrude from between the scales of the cones. The needles on Doug-fir are about 1" long, and the cones range between about 3" to 6" in length.

Western Hemlock (*Tsuga heterophylla*) is often found intermixed with Doug-fir or other conifer stands. The tree is distinguished by its drooping branches and a drooping leader at the top of the tree, and by its numerous small cones (smaller than Doug-fir cones). Both the needles and the cones are only 1" or less in length. Western Hemlock does not grow as large or live as long as Doug-fir, but it is very opportunistic and will fill open spaces in the forest caused by fire, wind throw or other damage. The Mountain Hemlock (*Tsuga mertensiana*) grows at higher elevations, often in shortened and windswept shape at timberline. That effect is known as *krummholz*, which due to the strong and persistent winds in the Gorge can make various conifers grow in shortened and windswept forms even at lower elevations. Mountain Hemlock needles are short like Western, but the cones are longer, up to 3" long.

Grand Fir (*Abies grandis*) is also often found in the Doug-fir Hemlock zone. It is distinguished from the other conifers by its cones that stand upright on the branches (like all true firs) and by the fact that the tree's branches usually extend all the way to the ground. It has flat, blunt needles about 1" to 2" long. Grand fir is more shade tolerant than Doug-fir, so it is also often found in the understory, waiting for an opportunity to overtop its cohorts.

Western Red Cedar (*Thuja plicata*) has great cultural and historic significance in the Pacific Northwest, used for everything from canoes to houses, baskets, clothing and furniture. A member of the Cypress family, Western Red Cedar can grow to more than 10 feet in diameter and over 200 feet tall. The tree prefers moist sites (at least 30 inches of precipitation a year) and can live to a thousand years. The aromatic, reddish-brown bark comes off in long strips, the needles are small and scale-like and the cones are small (less than one-half inch diameter).

<u>Coniferous Trees:</u> <u>Predominantly Eastside</u> (*but may be found throughout the Gorge*)

<u>Ponderosa Pine</u> *(<u>Pinus</u> <u>ponderosa</u>)* is the dominant tree on the east side of the Gorge, and the quintessential tree of the American West. The tree is drought tolerant and grows widely spaced, up to 150 feet tall in the Gorge. The bark is an orange red, appearing in thick plates. Needles are 5" to 8" long, in groups of 3, and the cones are usually 3" to 5" long. It is a distinctive tree hard to miss. David Douglas named the tree Ponderosa because of its "ponderous" appearance.

<u>Western White Pine</u> *(<u>Pinus</u> <u>monticola</u>)* is less numerous than Ponderosa Pine in the Gorge, but easy to distinguish. It does not grow as tall as Ponderosa and it is a less '"ponderous" tree overall. The needles are shorter than Ponderosa (about 1.5" to 4" long), in bundles of 5, and the bark is light gray with smaller scales. White Pine cones are long, from 6" to 10".

<u>Lodgepole Pine</u> *(<u>Pinus contorta</u>)* is less tall than Ponderosa or White Pine, usually only growing from 35 to 50 tall (but can grow higher in ideal sites), and it is not as long lived. Its needles are short (2" to 3", often curved at the tip) in bundles of 2, and its cones are small (2" to 3") and tightly closed. The cones are *serotinous,* meaning that they open only in response to certain environmental conditions, typically fire. Lodgepole is a pioneer species that is shade intolerant and quickly occupies a site after fire. Lodgepole grows readily in poor sites, like old lava fields. Young trees were indeed used as lodge poles for tipis.

Whitebark Pine *(Pinus albicaulis)* lives only at higher elevations, up to timberline. It can grow up to 50 feet tall but is usually less tall, appearing in a sturdy shape, often *krummholz* (wind-blown) at higher elevation. The needles are about 3" long, in bundles of 5. The bark is light gray (hence the name "whitebark"). The cones are 2" to 3.5" long, with tightly held seeds. The tree is a *keystone species* due to its importance to the ecology of higher elevation ecotones. Its cones provide a food source for various bird and mammal species. In late 2020 the tree was proposed to be added to the Endangered Species List due to widespread impacts from pine beetles and fungus, both linked to climate change.

Western Juniper *(Juniperus occidentalis)* is usually found on the eastern end of the Gorge at middle elevations where it can grow from 15 to 25 feet high. It typically grows in rocky areas where it does not have to compete with other tree species. The bark is a shaggy reddish brown, and the needles are short, scale-like and evergreen. The cones are small, blueish and look like berries. In recent years, Western Juniper has been encroaching on areas historically occupied by Big Sagebrush. The tree has a difficult time regenerating (from seed) after fire.

Common Juniper *(Juniperus communis)* is found on the eastern end of the Gorge and also at higher elevations of the Gorge. Smaller than Western Juniper and presenting more as a shrub than a tree, Common Juniper grows from 3 to 10 feet high, often windswept. Other than size and form, the tree has similar bark, needles and cones to Western Juniper.

Deciduous Trees: Found throughout the Gorge *(more prevalent where noted)*

Big Leaf Maple *(Acer macrophyllum)* is America's largest maple tree with the largest leaves (6" to 12" long, with long stems and deeply cut lobes). The trees can grow to nearly 100 feet tall in the Gorge. The tree is relatively shade tolerant (but not as much as Vine Maple). It is usually found along waterways or riparian habitat. Although present throughout the Gorge, it is most prevalent on the west side. Their robust hanging clusters of greenish flowers are easy to notice in the Spring.

Red Alder *(Alnus rubra)* There are several Alder tree species in the Gorge (Red, White and Slide or Tag Alder), but the most common is Red Alder. The tree can grow up to 60 or 80 feet here, with diameters greater than 10". The leaves are fairly large, 2" to 6" in length. The bark of alder trees is gray and generally smooth, but often has lichen and moss growing on it. The wood does not split cleanly for woodworking or firewood, but it has a distinctive smell when burned and is often used to smoke salmon, steelhead or other foods. It is also a beautiful wood for furniture. Red Alder is most pervasive on the westside and can be seen easily along Interstate 84 on the west end of the Gorge.

Oregon White Oak *(Quercus garryana)* (also known as Garry Oak or just Oregon Oak) is a significant component of the forest ecosystem in the eastern Gorge. The bark is gray and furrowed, and the leaves are 2" to 5" long, deeply lobed. Nicholas Garry was the Deputy Governor of the Hudson Bay Company in the 1820s and 1830s. Garry Oak's range is from the Willamette Valley through the Gorge and along the east side of the Cascades from northern Oregon to Southern Washington. The northernmost reach of Oregon Oak ends at the eastern end of the Gorge. In the Willamette Valley and elsewhere where fire was frequent (natural or man caused) the tree grew in a spreading open form and usually reached an old age. The tree can grow to as high as 80 feet and can be 300 to 400 years old. Acorns from White Oak were a foodstuff for traditional peoples.

Pacific Dogwood *(Cornus nuttallii)* is a tree that adapts to the understory of westside conifers and maples, growing from 10' to 60' tall. The leaves are arranged oppositely and about 4" in length. It produces attractive white flowers in the early spring, which stand out against surrounding green conifer trees where it is typically found. On their return trip through the Gorge on April 5, 1806, Meriwether Lewis correctly concluded that Pacific Dogwood was a different species than the Dogwoods found on the east coast. Some years later naturalist David Douglas suggested that the east coast and west coast dogwoods really are the same species. In the 1830s, naturalist Thomas Nuttall settled the discussion, concluding that Pacific Dogwood is indeed distinct from its east coast version, in part because Pacific Dogwood flowers are larger than the Dogwood variety common in the Eastern U.S. The taxonomic name for Pacific Dogwood recognizes Nuttall (with a nod to Lewis for his initial assessment).

Cottonwood *(Populus trichocarpa)* (also known as Western or Black Cottonwood) is native to the western U.S. and most prevalent on the west side of the Gorge in lowland and riparian areas. The trees have deeply furrowed gray bark and triangular leaves about 2" to 6" long. They are fast growing and shade intolerant, but do not have long lifespans (both because they can be overgrown by conifers and because the wood is soft and susceptible to injury or disease). Cottonwood can grow to over 150 feet. There are extensive stands of Cottonwood along Interstate 84 on the western end of the Gorge, and the fluffy seeds in spring (derivation of the name "cotton" wood) are abundant on roads and lowland trails.

Willow *(Salix species)* is found throughout the Gorge (both west side and east side) in riparian habitat (along rivers, streams and wetlands). There are more than 400 species of willow and there are several species in the Gorge, so it is most useful to generalize for this overview to describe willow generically (apologies to the willow specialists). Virtually all willows have elongated *lanceolate* leaves, with slender branches hanging down in a pendulous manner. Willow trees bend with the wind and take root readily when cut or burned. The leaves are typically bright lime green in spring.

Deciduous Evergreen Trees

Western Larch *(Larix occidentalis)* is a *deciduous evergreen,* meaning that although it has needles, all the needles drop in winter after first turning a golden yellow in fall. The tree grows tall (up to 260') and narrow with a pyramidal top. The needles are short (about 1.5") and in bundles of more than 5. Cones are small (1"). Larch can grow old (more than 500 years) and is valued for its timber and as firewood (it splits cleanly). It is sometimes called "Tamarack," but that name properly applies to a different, smaller *Larix* species on the east coast.

Non-Native (Introduced) Trees

Many non-native trees and shrubs have been introduced to the Gorge over the past hundred plus years for horticultural reasons. Some escape, become acclimated to the Gorge environment and are now fairly common. Some of these non-native trees are invasive and generally considered to be undesirable competition for native species. They occupy space, change the plant community, alter the soil chemistry and shade out native plants, suppressing their growth. But they are here, and it helps to be able to identify them in comparison to native trees.

Lombardy (or Black) Poplar *(Populus nigra)* Native to southern Europe, introduced to the U.S. for use as windbreaks. The tree is fast growing and narrow, and can reach 80' or 100' tall in the Gorge. The wood has few uses, and the trees are not long lived. They spread by extensive root systems that can adversely affect water sources and other plants. You can see long rows of them along fence lines, serving as wind breaks. They have distinctly triangular-shaped leaves.

Russian Olive *(Elaeagnus augustifolia)* is native to southern Russia and central Asia, introduced to the U.S. in the late 1800s as a drought resistant large shrub/small tree to act as a wind break or stabilize stream banks. Once established, Russian Olive trees spread rapidly, to the exclusion of native species. They grow from 10' to 30' tall in the Gorge in a spreading fashion and are found almost exclusively on the eastside. The leaves have a silvery appearance and the fruit has an olive shape. The flowers are fragrant in the spring.

Black Locust *(Robinia pseudoacacia)* is native to the American Southeast (principally Appalachia) but has been introduced all over the U.S. and abroad. A hardwood resistant to rot, the tree was brought to the Gorge by early settlers on the Oregon Trail for use as a shade tree and for making fenceposts. It is an early successional species, growing best in sunlight and adapted to dry soils (this makes it more common on the eastside). It grows from 40' to 80' tall in the Gorge and has long pendants of fragrant white flowers in early spring. The leaves are pinnately compound, and the branches often have thorns.

Common Shrubs and Bushes: Found throughout the Gorge

Vine Maple *(Acer circinatum)* is the most common understory shrub species on the westside, also present on the east side where conditions allow (usually along streams). It grows as multiple stems in a spreading form. It is shade tolerant but when it takes root in an opening it can assume tree form and grow up to 25 feet high. The leaves are roundish, about 1" to 4" across, and have 5 to 7 lobes, each of which ends in a point. The leaves are a bright yellow green in spring, which contrasts starkly with other trees and shrubs around it. The deciduous leaves turn bright red or gold in the fall. Vine Maple sprouts readily after any disruption (fire, flood, wind or volcano – reappearing rapidly after the Mount St. Helens eruption).

Black Huckleberry (*Vaccinium membranaceum*) produces highly prized native berries. It grows at elevation (around 2,000') primarily in the west-central Gorge, from 2 to 5 feet high. Huckleberry flowers in mid-summer and produces edible berries by late summer/early fall. Red Huckleberry is also present in the Gorge. Both were used extensively by First Peoples.

Ocean Spray (*Holodiscus discolor*) is a showy shrub that grows up to 13 feet high, with white blossoms that hang in a spray fashion. The plant blooms from late spring through mid-summer, mostly in the west and central portion. It is visible from several roadways in the Gorge.

Mock Orange (*Philadelphus lewisii*) is a large shrub (member of the Hydrangea Family) that can be found throughout the Gorge but is most common on the east side and grows from 4 to 10 feet high. The shrub has fragrant white blossoms that show from late spring through mid-summer. Meriwether Lewis identified the plant on the Lewis & Clark return trip in 1806.

Big Sagebrush (*Artemisia tridentata*) grows on the eastern end of the Gorge from The Dalles eastward. It has greenish gray leaves that are pleasantly pungent. The bush usually grows from 2 to 4 feet high but can get as large as 8 feet tall. It flowers in late summer to early autumn and can live more than 50 years. It is slowly being encroached upon by Western Juniper.

Rabbitbrush (*Chryothamnus var.*) is a shrub on the eastern end of the Gorge (The Dalles eastward) with yellow flowers blooming late in season. The shrub grows from a few feet tall up to 6 feet high. There are gray and green rabbitbrush present (the latter has a more flattened top to the floral display).

Antelope Bitterbrush (*Purshia tridentata)* is another common eastside shrub, growing from 3 to 8 feet tall. It is darker green than Sagebrush and has more dense branches. It blooms throughout the spring with cream-colored flowers. It is an important resource for birds and wildlife in the shrub-steppe environment.

Devil's Club (*Oplopanax horridus*) is relatively common on the westside of the Gorge but can be present in wet, shaded sites further toward the central and eastside. It is a formidable plant, all but impossible to walk through, growing up to 10 feet high with large leaves up to 14" across. The plant has spines along the entire stalk and bristles on the underside of leaves. It is impressive to see, but uncomfortable to approach (note the Latin species name). Devil's Club is abundant on the winding road leading down from Crown Point to the waterfalls. The plant has traditional medicinal and body painting uses (the latter as ash from burned stems).

Wild Rose (Nootka and Prairie) There are at least two species of wild rose in the Gorge: Nootka Rose (*Rosa nutkana*) can be found throughout, but Prairie or Wood Rose (*Rosa woodsii*) is more confined to the eastside. Both species grow from about 2 feet up to 6 feet high or higher. Nootka Rose usually grows in thickets while Prairie Rose often grows as isolated groups of plants. Both plants have light red to pink flowers, 5-petaled and about 1.5" across. The stems have thorns. Both plants produce rosehips (favored by deer and good for tea).

Non-Native (Introduced) Shrubs and Bushes

Himalayan Blackberry (*Rubus bifrons*) is the most common introduced Blackberry in the Gorge. Leaves have 5 leaflets, and the stems can grow 30" long with stout prickles. It often forms impenetrable thickets in disturbed areas and roadsides – crowding out native plants. They are a favorite of berry pickers when in fruit. Evergreen Blackberry *(Rubus laciniatus)* is another problematic introduced species. Both species are considered noxious weeds in the region.

Scotch Broom (*Cytisus scoparius*) Like other introduced trees and shrubs, Scotch Broom was initially thought to help prevent erosion. Unfortunately, the plant spread far beyond its intended areas and has become an invasive labeled as "noxious" by both Oregon and Washington. The shrub grows from 3 to 9 feet high in a spreading form, with bright yellow flowers that bloom through summer. It often appears in the median along Interstate 84 through the Gorge, until it can be rooted out again.

<u>A Note on Poison Oak</u>

*Poison Oak (<u>Rhus</u> <u>diversiloba</u>, also classified as <u>Toxicodendron</u> <u>diversilobum</u>) is native to and relatively common in the Gorge. It can cause skin irritation and rash (dermatitis) ranging from bothersome to severe. The leaves can range in color from green to blackish purple, and often appear waxy. It can grow as an individual plant, in thick groupings or as a vine, and it often reaches large shrub size. Poison Oak contains the same toxin (urushiol) found in Poison Ivy and Poison Sumac. Some people are more sensitive to the toxin than others, but most people have some sensitivity to the plant (and your sensitivity can change over time). Poison oak leaves grow in groups of 3 (sometimes other odd numbers like 5 or 7) with individual leaves from 1.5" to 4" long, usually with slight lobes. The plant is deciduous; its leaves change color (usually red) and drop in the fall. Note that the leafless stems retain toxic qualities through the winter.*

## B. FLOWERING PLANTS

The Gorge comes alive with wildflowers in the spring and early summer. The bloom generally begins on the east side, but flowering plants can be found somewhere in the Gorge in all but the coldest winter months here (December through February). Even during the winter – often times especially in the winter – you can find lichens and mosses blooming. There are more than 750 species of native flowering plants in the Gorge (more than another 150 introduced). Since this *<u>Natural History</u>* is presented in an overview format, it only describes a few representative plants the visitor or resident is most likely to notice in the Gorge. The reader is strongly encouraged to get a copy of either Russ Jolley's or the Turner & Gustafson book on flowering plants (and for those botanists among you, the Hitchcock & Cronquist one volume plant guide will be a must). One of the various tree guides noted in the Chapter heading is also recommended, as well as the Trudell mushroom guide for mycologists. Some of the more commonly encountered plants are noted below, along with some suggestions for times and places to see them.

PLEASE DO NOT PICK WILDFLOWERS or NATIVE PLANTS!

Although they may appear abundant, each year their habitat shrinks. The cumulative impact of millions of visitors to the Gorge every year adds up over time. If you pick a flower you will interrupt its flowering cycle and ability to produce seeds. Enjoy the flowers and take pictures but leave them unpicked; stay on trails and keep dogs on leash in wildflower areas.

Because flowering begins in earnest on the east side of the Gorge each spring, this overview begins there:

*NOTE: this book only lists a few of the flowering plants you may be most likely to encounter in your travels through the Gorge; it does* not list *all plants found in the Gorge. Other books and field guides noted in the Chapter heading or Notes provide additional information.*

Primarily Eastside Native Wildflowers *(typically begin bloom earlier in the spring, so noted first here)*

Lupine (*Lupinus spp*) There are at least 12 different species of Lupine found in the Gorge, growing from river level to the higher elevations. Some are small (4" to 10" high) such as Bi-colored, Prairie or Small-flowered lupine, while others grow up to 4 feet tall (Large-leaf, Broad-leaf and Riverbank). The flowers grow on upright stalks and are mostly blue or blue/white in color (although Velvet Lupine has white flowers), and they bloom variously from April through late summer (the bloom is later as you rise in elevation). Abundant in the lowlands in early summer, they "blue" the hills of the eastern Gorge around The Dalles, often appearing mixed with yellow Balsamroot. Columbia Gorge Broad-leafed Lupine is one of the 15 species of flowering plant endemic to the Gorge (found nowhere else).

Northwest Balsamroot (*Balsamorhiza deltoidea*) is a perennial plant that grows at lower elevations on the eastside up to 3 feet tall. The large flowers are bright yellow, the leaves long and tapered. A similar plant is the Arrowleaf Balsamroot, which grows almost as tall but lives at middle elevations farther east in the Gorge hills (Arrowleaf has more pointed leaves with soft hairs on their underside). The yellow-colored Balsamroot is striking in early Spring on the east side, often seen adjacent to blue Lupines.

Poet's Shooting Star (*Dodecatheon poeticum*) There are 7 Shooting Star species present in the Gorge. Most of the plants live on the eastside, but two species grow on the westside (Few-flowered and Tall Mountain). All are members of the Primrose family. The flowers appear inside out and hang over the end of the stems. The petals are light pink to purple, although one species has white petals (appropriately called the White Shooting Star). Poet's Shooting Star is one of the 15 plants endemic to the Gorge. It grows from 6" to 14" tall with purple flowers, and blooms from late March to early April around the Memaloose and Tom McCall viewpoints, and east of the Lyle tunnel.

Bi-Colored Cluster Lily (also known as Douglas' Brodiaea or Howell's Tritelia) (*Triteleia grandiflora var. howellii formerly classified as Brodiaea howellii*) is an attractive lily that grows up to 2 feet high on slender stalks in the eastern Gorge. Blooms in April and early May. The flowers are white with blue streaks along the petals.

Oregon Sunshine (*Eriophyllum lanatum*) (also called Wooly Sunflower) has distinctive yellow blossoms. One variety (*integrifolium*) grows primarily on the eastside, in low groupings from 6" to 12" high, appearing in May. The other variety (*lanatum*) grows primarily on the westside, from Crown Point through the waterfall areas, and grows a bit taller, from 10" to 12", appearing in June.

Blanket Flower (*Gaillardia aristata*) grows on the eastside, primarily on the Washington shore at low elevations. The yellow flowers appear in mid to late June. The plant typically grows taller than Oregon Sunshine, from 1' to 2'. Blanket Flower also has a dark brown to purple corolla (center), compared to the all yellow flower of Oregon Sunshine.

Poppy (*Eschscholzia californica*) is abundant at low elevations on the east side of the Gorge, especially on the north bank. Despite its name, California Poppy is native to the entire west coast, and flowers most of the summer. The plant grows from a few inches high to over a foot. Flowers are typically orange but can vary from red to pink to white.

Lomatium (Desert Parsley or Biscuit Root) (*Lomatium spp*) At least thirteen species of this perennial herb grow in the eastern end of the Gorge. Whether called Desert-parsley, Biscuit Root or just Lomatium (the latter, Linnaean name is often used, pronounced "*low-MAY-shum*"), it is a fairly common plant on the eastside, with a distinctive aroma. Two Lomatium are endemic to the Gorge (found nowhere else): Columbia Gorge and Suksdorf Desert-parsley. The former, *L. Columbianum,* has dark purple flowers and grows on rocky slopes east of the Lyle tunnel and east of the Memaloose rest area, and grows up to 2.5 feet high. *L. Suksdorfii* has yellow flowers and grows up to 6 feet high on middle elevations between the Little White Salmon river and The Dalles. Lomatium roots were an important foodstuff for First Peoples in the Gorge.

Strict Buckwheat (*Eriogonum strictum*) There are several species of native buckwheat in the Gorge, all on the eastside. Strict Buckwheat is fairly common, growing from 10" to 24" high. It has small whitish-pink flowers in late August, which dry and remain intact through the winter. Douglas' Buckwheat is also common, presenting with round yellow flowers in the Spring.

Fiddleneck (*Amsinckia* genus) can grow from 6" to 36" high in the Gorge. There are several species (Tarweed, Small Flowered and Rigid). Small-flowered and Rigid Fiddleneck have small leaves and small yellow flowers that curve tightly at the top of the plant, like the neck of a fiddle. Small-flowered rarely grows taller than 1 foot, while Rigid grows up to 3 feet. Tarweed has slightly larger yellow flowers that show open petals; they also grow up to 3 feet tall like Rigid Fiddleneck.

Primarily Westside Native Wildflowers *(but some such as Penstemon may also bloom eastside)*

Bleeding Heart (*Dicentra formosa*) is a distinctive flowering plant that blooms from spring to early summer in cool, moist and shady habitats on the west side of the Gorge. The plant grows to 18" high in a spreading form with fern-like leaves. The flowers are purple and hang in drooping abundance.

Indian Paintbrush (*Castelleja spp*) At least four species of Paintbrush grow in the Gorge: Common, Harsh, Cliff and Bog. All are members of the Figwort Family, and all have orange to red petals. The plants grow from river level to higher elevations, and from 6 inches to 2 feet high. Flowers bloom from April through July, with the bloom following elevation.

Forget Me Not (*Myosotis laxa*) grows throughout the Gorge at low elevations, primarily on the westside. The distinctive flowers are small, with five light blue petals surrounding a yellow center. Flowers bloom from May through August, depending on location.

Cliff Larkspur (*Delphinium menziesii*) There are 5 species of Larkspur in the Gorge; 2 found primarily on the eastside. All have deep blue flowers and grow from 1 to 2 feet high. Cliff Larkspur can be found on shaded cliffs and rocks in May, at the base of Rooster Rock and along the Historic Highway's waterfall loop.

Douglas' Aster (*Symphyotrichum subspicatum*) There are at least 14 Asters in the Gorge. Most are light purple, but a few are whitish. Growing up to 4 feet high, Douglas' Aster can be found in moist bottomlands from Dalton Point to Ainsworth on the Oregon side and around Beacon Rock on the Washington side. Blooms in late August to early September.

Barrett's Penstemon (*Penstemon barrettiae*) There are at least 11 species of Penstemon in the Gorge, ranging from the west side to the east side. Most are blue to purple in color, although two are red and one off-white. They grow from 4 inches to 3 feet in height. Barrett's Penstemon is one of the 15 flowering plants endemic to the Gorge (found nowhere else). Light purple in color and growing up to 24", it typically blooms in rocky areas at low elevations east of Hood River and Lyle.

Beargrass (*Xerophyllum tenax*) grows at higher elevations, primarily on the westside and central Gorge. A member of the Lily Family, Beargrass has long grass like leaves with white flowers that grow in a rounded form atop the 2 to 4 foot tall plants. Note that the poisonous plant Death

Camas has some similarity in appearance to Beargrass but grows at lower elevations on the eastside, typically less than 2 feet high.

Columbia Lily (*Lilium columbianum*) Growing from 2 to 5 feet high in woods of the western Gorge, the Columbia Lilly presents in a dramatic orange color with the flower hanging down from the stem. It can be found in June and July from Larch Mountain through the waterfall loop to Ainsworth State Park.

Non-Native (Introduced) Plants and Flowers

Filaree (*Erodium circutarium*) is an introduced ground cover plant that is by now well naturalized to the Gorge. The plant is native to southern Europe and northern Africa. It came to the Americas with the Spanish conquistadores in the 1500s as seed in the hay brought for their horses. The plant spread north as Spanish horses escaped or were captured by American Indians. The plant has found a home along the east side of the Sierras and Cascade Mountains and has been well settled here for centuries. Filaree covers the ground in locations on the East Side with small light purple flowers that last through the season.

Foxglove (*Digitalis purpurea*) is a common and showy west side plant, but it was introduced from Europe. It grows from 2 to 6 feet high in moist areas of the westside. The flowers are usually light purple but can appear as pink or white. The flowers grow on tall upright stems, are large and pendulant. It blooms from June to July (later in higher elevations). The plant provided the basis for the heart medicine digitalis (but the plant itself is poisonous to humans).

## C. GRASSES

Grasses occupy a special niche in the plant world and they are a significant part of the biota in the Gorge, especially on the east side. Grasses propagate by wind (not by pollinating birds or insects), and the Gorge has wind in abundance. Unfortunately, the winds in the Gorge spread invasive grass seed as effectively as native plant seed, and many of the original grasses are now crowded out by non-native species.

Historically, the eastside of the Gorge was dominated by shrub-steppe grass varieties such as Bunchgrass, Needlegrass and native Rye and Barley. The westside also provided habitat for a variety of native grasses. Most native grasses grow in bunches, but after the introduction of livestock (horses and cattle) that used winter hay often containing non-native species, many non-native grasses became introduced to both ends of the Gorge that grow in a spreading form that occupies a site. Additional non-native grass species were introduced intentionally, with the Willamette Valley soon becoming one of the nation's largest lawn grass seed producers.

Today it is a challenge to find large areas of native grass, but they are there to be found. The Native Plant Societies of both Oregon and Washington, as well as local County Extension services, are useful sources of information on where to see native grasses. Most Pacific Northwest bunchgrass prairie ecosystems have been converted to cropland and rangeland. In the Gorge, roadsides and pastures are primarily dominated by a mix of non-native cool season greases introduced for grazing. But native greases can still be observed in areas with minimal disturbance on the east side of the Gorge where shrub-steppe habitats are preserved and intact.

## D. FERNS

Ferns form a bridge between flowering plants on the one hand, and lichens and mosses on the other. Like trees, shrubs and flowers, ferns are vascular plants with stems that draw water up from the soil. Ferns also have leaves and roots like vascular plants. Unlike most vascular plants, however, ferns do not have flowers or seeds; they reproduce instead by spreading spores, like most lichens and mosses.

Ferns are ancient plants, first appearing around 360 million years ago during the Carboniferous Period. Many of the ferns found in the Gorge today display essentially the same form they have presented for millions of years. Others have changed remarkably. Horsetail Ferns, or *Equisetum*, for example, stood from 40 to 100 feet tall and lived as dense forests some 100 million years ago. Today they rarely grow taller than 2 to 3 feet, but they are widespread in both the westside and the eastside of the Gorge, and appropriately sometimes referred to as "living fossils."

Visitors from other parts of the country (or the world) may be surprised at the abundance and variety of ferns that are found here. Ferns occupy niches that other plants cannot use, often favoring poor soils and shaded, moist environments that support their reproduction through spores. Worldwide, there are more than 12,000 species of ferns. In the Gorge, there are more than a dozen species present. The most common Gorge ferns include the following:

> Bracken Fern (*Pteridium aquilinum*) is found throughout the Gorge, tolerating even dry sites on the eastside. It has broad triangular fronds that taper to a point and grow 2 to 4 feet high. The plant has separate forms with the larger form producing spores while the smaller one produces sex cells (both eggs and sperm). People eat the immature fronds known as "fiddleheads," but the mature plant can be poisonous to livestock.
>
> Deer Fern (*Struthiopteris spicant*) is a forest understory plant that lives primarily on the westside and grows in a circular form (typically about 2' x 2'). It has erect central fronds that are fertile, surrounded by outward spreading fronds that are sterile. It is an important winter food for deer and elk, and there are several traditional medicinal uses.
>
> Lady Fern (*Athyrium filix-femina*) is a perennial upright fern found throughout the Gorge, growing from 2 to more

than 3 feet tall. It is light yellow-green in color, and grows from a central clump instead of separate stalks.

Maidenhair Fern (*Adiantum aleuticum*) is a rare beauty in the central to west end Gorge, growing in moist areas, often attaching to rocks around waterfalls where it receives moisture from the waterfall spray. Maidenhair has distinctive, deep blue to black stems that form a nearly complete circle of delicate fronds. You can find Maidenhair around many of the waterfalls along the Historic Highway (but please do not pick or disturb them!)

Sword Fern (*Polystichum unitum*) is common on the west end of the Gorge and appears in the ground layer of the forest. It grows from over 1 foot to nearly 5 feet tall. The fronds are long and blade like, as well as evergreen and sturdy. Sword fern fronds attach to their stalks with small stems, while deer fern fronds (which may appear similar) attach directly to the stalks.

Horsetail (*Equisetum hyemale*) is an unusual plant that looks nothing like other ferns, growing as an upright reed up to 5 feet tall, with segmented stalks. You can find it throughout the Gorge (east and west side) usually near water or available groundwater (like a perched aquifer). *Equisetum* is an ancient genus of ferns (often called a "living fossil") that grew up to 100' tall in the early Jurassic period. There are fifteen species still in existence globally, mostly in the Northern Hemisphere. It is known variously as Horsetail, Scouring Rush or just Equisetum. The plant retains silica in its roots and stems, which makes it useful for scouring purposes. Like all ferns, it reproduces by spores.

## E. LICHENS AND MOSSES

It is late February (in a wet year) as I write this section, and the lichens and mosses all through the Gorge are bursting in their subtle bloom of color. Lichens and mosses are ancient, primitive plants – older than ferns – and they play a key role in creating habitat for other plants. Lichen and moss have a much more immediate relationship to their substrate than do vascular plants (those plants that – unlike lichens or mosses – have hollow stems that can draw water from the soil). Lichens and mosses obtain moisture directly from the air, or from the rock or soil surfaces that they attach to, and when moisture is available (usually in late winter to early spring in the Gorge), they make the most of it.

These primitive plants help break down rock and wood, slowly turning it into bits of soil that can be used by other plants. They can withstand extremes of temperature and precipitation. As it happens, the Gorge presents extremes of temperature and moisture along its course, and lichens and mosses find the Gorge to be a wonderful habitat on both the westside and the eastside.

Lichens and mosses are often discussed together because they often live together, and because their existence differs so substantially from vascular plants. Although they are often discussed together, they belong to wholly separate kingdoms (*Plantae* for mosses but since lichens are comprised of both algae and fungi, they are classified by the fungi present, as part of the *Fungi* biological kingdom).

Lichens and mosses can live for a long period of time, and in part for that reason they are important sentinels for signaling deteriorating environmental quality. In recent years, scientific studies have tracked changes in the range and health of lichens and mosses in the Gorge, using them as monitors in the attempt to understand the impacts of air pollutants that may affect the Gorge. So turn your eyes to the lichens and mosses when you encounter them in your travels, and use them as your own sentinels to the smaller green (or gray or yellow or red) world around you.

### Lichens

Lichens are a most unusual organism: part fungus (or cyano-bacteria) and part algae. You see them on trees, rocks and soil. They are usually seen as simply a part of the patina of the natural world, looking little like a growing plant, and they are sometimes mistaken as moss. If you look closely, however, you will see that their tissue is quite different.

Lichens are a pioneer plant is the best sense of the term. They often grow where no other plant can survive. There are more than 15,000 species of lichens worldwide, with several dozen living in the Gorge. Lichens are classified and named within the binomial taxonomic system based on their fungal association (the algal component is more a descriptor than a classifier). They can be hard to classify individually, but relatively easy to recognize by type.

There are several informal classifications of lichen, with three of the more common types being: *crustose*, *foliose*, and *fruticose*. Crustose are those lichens that appear scaly or crusty, and typically reside on rocks. Crustose lichens are the type most people associate as a lichen. They become almost as hard as the rock in dry periods but become more three dimensional and colorful when moist. Foliose lichens are leafy or stringy and grow on trees or directly on the ground. Fruticose lichens grow on stalks from the ground and can be brightly colored. Lichens appear in diverse colors, from brown to gray to green to yellow to orange or red. Many species are more brown or gray when dry, and more green or colored when moist.

Lichens usually reproduce by spores but can also break off pieces that begin new organisms. Lichens grow slowly (only millimeters per year) and can become incredibly old. Lichens you see on rocks in the Gorge may be hundreds, if not thousands of years old.

Many traditional cultures use lichens as food (more occasional for survival use than routine). Lichens have also long been used for making dyes.

## Mosses

I learned long ago that there are so many species of willow than unless you are a specialist or extremely dedicated, it is usually best to simply identify a willow as "a *Salix* species" and move on. So it is with moss. Moss is in the *Bryophyta* phylum. There are more than 700 genera of mosses worldwide, and at least 10,000 individual species. Thus it is usually best to simply identify a "moss" as a moss and appreciate it for what it is.

Mosses are typically greener and more three dimensional than lichens. They have flat tissue that looks like tiny leaves but lacks veins, which restricts their growth to moist environments. They usually grow on soil or rock or trees that have been altered by lichens, which is why lichens and mosses are so often found together. Although individual mosses may be relatively long lived, they do not persist like lichens.

Mosses have *rhizoids* that help attach the moss structure and look like roots but do not transport water. There are two broad types of moss. *Acrocarpous* mosses grow upright and form a cover over the ground, often mounded, and are usually drought resistant. *Pleurocarpous* mosses lie more flat and form mats on the ground or substrate. Examples of this type are often called "feather" or "fern" mosses.

## F. MUSHROOMS AND FUNGI

Several thousand species of mushrooms can be found in the Pacific Northwest, and there are many in the Gorge. Mushrooms are a type of fungus, a distinct enough life form to have its own biological Kingdom (*Fungi*). Mushrooms are fascinating, beautiful, tasty and... sometimes poisonous. There are many edible mushrooms in the Northwest, but unless you are experienced, you are strongly encouraged to consult an expert mycologist before consuming any mushrooms you may find in your foraging (you can also find wild mushrooms in many local grocery stores in the Gorge during the spring and fall).

> *NOTE: collection of mushrooms in the National Scenic Area is not allowed. Collection may be allowed in adjacent areas of the Mt. Hood and Gifford Pinchot National Forests but depending on the area a permit may be required (check with the Ranger Stations).*

Mushrooms can be found here almost any time of the year, but they are most abundant in the spring and fall and most numerous on the west and central side where conditions are more conducive.

In recent years the importance and complexity of *mycorrhizas* have become better known. Mycorrhizas are a mutualistic, symbiotic association between mushrooms (fungus) and the roots of plants. The Pulitzer Prize winning fiction book *Overstory* by Richard Powers (W.W. Norton 2019) discussed this, and the subsequent book *Finding the Mother Tree: Discovering the Wisdom of the Forest* by Suzanne Simard (Alfred Knopf 2021) (the real-life central character in "The Overstory") explores the intriguing science behind the extensive and complex relationships involving fungi, forests and other life.

# CHAPTER NOTES

## Chapter IV: Plants (Flora)

1. *Linnaeus' Name and Latin.* Nils Ingemarsson was the father of Linnaeus. Nils was an academic and botanist who greatly influenced his son, and who already used Latin in his scientific activities. When Nils applied to the University of Lund in Sweden, he changed his last name from Ingemarsson (a name following the patronymic practice common at the time that used one's father's first name as a surname) to "Linnaeus," intentionally adopting a Latinate surname, after the Swedish word for a Linden tree. Nils' son Carl was therefore born as a Linnaeus (instead of having what would have been the surname of Nilson). The King of Sweden later gave Linnaeus nobility status, and henceforth he went by the name Carl von Linne (at times converting that to the full Latin version of Carolus Linnaeus).
2. *Succession, Climax and Species Diversity.* Thoreau first described the concept that became known as biological succession in a speech/essay given in September of 1860.
3. *Binomial Nomenclature* Linnaeus expanded on Aristotle's attempts to classify organisms (more than 2,000 years prior). Aristotle sought to classify organisms by both "genera" and by individual characteristics ("species"). His approach was much more broad than that of Linnaeus (his initial distinction was whether an organism had red blood or not). Linnaeus focused more on *morphology* or the shape of things, as well as reproductive effects where possible (early naturalists and scientists often only had dead specimens to examine). In recent decades it has become possible to further classify organisms using DNA. Taxonomy includes both identification of a specimen and then classification of that specimen in comparison to others similar. That is how we get from genus to family to order, etc. DNA helps in this, but the Linnaean system remains well established.
4. *Krummholz trees and shrubs.* The word is of German derivation, meaning "bent or crooked wood," and it refers to trees or shrubs that are stunted in growth at timberline or in response to other climate extremes. It usually applies to conifers that are hardy enough to

withstand harsh conditions. A tree or shrub becomes krummholz when wind or ice on the upwind side is strong enough to kill the apical growth buds of the plant. As a result, the tree or shrub only grows on the downwind side, where it is further shaped by the winds and usually sheared off at a stunted height. Because of the strong and persistent winds of the Gorge you can find krummholz trees and shrubs at lower elevation that in surrounding mountains. Gorge winds also create an effect called "*banner*" or "*flag*" trees, where a tree is not stunted vertically but its branches are strongly pruned to the downwind side. This effect is common on both ends of the Gorge, even at river level, with the prevalent wind direction clearly shown for that location by branches reaching downwind.

5. *Plant Lists*. The Washington Native Plant Society maintains a list of plants for the Gorge (counting ten miles either side of the river); their current count is 769 native plants, and another 178 introduced (for a total of 947). www.wnps.org/plant-lists.
6. *Plants endemic to the Gorge* (found nowhere else). There are 15 endemic plants in the Gorge, including: Barrett's Penstemon; Columbia Desert-parsley; Columbia River Gorge Broad-leaf Lupine; Poet's Shooting Star; Suksdorf Desert-parsley; Columbia Gorge Daisy; and Dalles Mountain Buttercup.
7. *Lichens and mosses* uptake water more directly than the higher plants, thus there is no filter to pollutants (like soil) that may be in the air or water that is provided to plants with stems and leaves. The Finnish naturalist William Nylander was the first to recognize this fact in 1866, when he linked the disappearance of certain lichens from downtown Paris to deteriorating air quality.
8. *Latourell Falls lichen*. Latourell Falls is the closest waterfall in the Gorge to Portland, and an easy walk from the parking area. The large yellow powder lichen growing on the walls behind the waterfall are dramatic.

# CHAPTER V: ANIMALS

## *(Fauna)*

### Recommended Reading

*No single book discusses all animals in the Gorge but there are several good handbooks on animals for both the larger region and specific topics. For example, Wildlife of the Pacific Northwest by David Moskowitz (Timber Press 2010); Birds of the Pacific Northwest by Shewy and Blount (Timber Press 2017); Sibley's Field Guide to Birds of Western North America (Knopf 2003); and Butterflies of the Pacific Northwest, by Robert Michael Pyle and Caitlin LaBar (Timber Press 2018). For spiders and other insects there is Merrill Peterson's Pacific Northwest Insects (Seattle Audubon Society 2018). On birds generally, Cornell's Ornithology Department has an excellent website at www.allaboutbirds.com. The Columbia River Intertribal Fish Commission, the National Fish Hatcheries in the Gorge, the Northwest Power Council and the Bonneville Power Administration all have websites with good information on fish in the Gorge and related issues. Professor Michael Blumm of the Lewis & Clark Law School has written extensively about legal issues related to salmon and steelhead, and about natural resource issues affecting the Gorge generally (see the Notes to this Chapter for some references). Finally, Mammal Tracks and Sign: A Guide to North American Species (Stackpole Books, 2d Ed. 2019), by Elbroch and McFarland provides insight on tracking or reading sign.*

# CHAPTER V

## *Animals*

**(<u>Fauna</u>)**

THE COLUMBIA RIVER Gorge is home to a wide range of animals. This Natural History notes some of those species native to the Gorge and currently present, along with some discussion of *extirpated* species (once present but that no longer include the Gorge in their range).

Animals that can be found in the Gorge include the following:

- more than 200 species of birds;
- more than 60 species of mammals (including marine mammals);
- more than 40 species of fish;
- more than 20 species of amphibians and reptiles; and
- a host of butterflies, spiders and other insects.

The narrative in this Chapter provides information on some of those species you are most likely to encounter during a visit to the Gorge. The Chapter Notes provide reference to more information.

| *NOTE: this book only discusses a few of the animals a visitor or resident is most likely to encounter. Field guides and other information sources are listed above, and the reader is encouraged to pursue more information as they gain interest on particular topics.* |
|---|

## A. MAMMALS: MARINE & LAND

The Gorge provides a wide range of habitats and there is accordingly a wide variety of mammals present. There are marine mammals (at least as far upstream as the Bonneville Dam), numerous salmon species and other fish, large and small mammals (from elk to pika) and a surprising variety of birds living in or traveling through the Gorge.

### Marine Mammals

Two marine mammals – seals and sea lions – visit the Gorge frequently, both members of the *Pinnepedia* taxonomic Family (often called pinnipeds). Both species are carnivorous and eat fish. That fact has generated considerable controversy in the Gorge over the past several decades, as pinnipeds (primarily sea lions) prey on salmon and steelhead runs returning to the river. Sea lions are much larger than seals, thus eat more fish and get more attention.

Seals, sea lions and salmon have lived together for millennia, but the construction of dams and changes in the respective populations of the species have led to conflict. There has been a dramatic decline in salmon and steelhead over the past century due to human actions such as overfishing and construction of dams. Those and other changes have affected the natural balance among these animals. Lewis & Clark noted in 1805 that "Phoca" (seals) were "very numerous" around rapids in the Gorge up to Celilo Falls, where they gathered to feed on salmon and steelhead. Of course, there were more salmon then (and likely more seals and sea lions), but over the next two hundred years what had been huge numbers of salmon in the river dropped dramatically while the pinniped populations did not suffer such a significant population change.

As salmon and steelhead populations began to decline and then became threatened, seal and sea lion predation became more of a concern.

In the first half of the 20th century Oregon and Washington paid bounties to hunters who killed seals or sea lions in the lower Columbia River to limit predation on salmon and steelhead, and hired professional hunters when volunteers were low. Seal and sea lion populations were also in some decline, however, largely due to ocean conditions. In 1972, the Marine Mammal Protection Act (MMPA) extended hunting restrictions to seals and sea lions, only allowing removal of marine mammals that proved to be a nuisance to resident fisheries. By the end of the 20th century the number of predatory sea lions consuming salmon and steelhead in the river increased significantly. As a result, in 1994 Congress amended the MMPA to allow the lethal take of sea lions at areas of salmon and steelhead predation (especially at Bonneville Dam, and then later at Willamette Falls). The trade-off between two threatened species (salmon and sea lions) continues to generate controversy.

Sea Lion**s** *(Steller and California)* Two different sea lions visit the Gorge: the Steller Sea Lion (*Eumetopias jubatus*) and the California Sea Lion (*Zalophus californicus*). The California Sea Lion is the one most often found upriver at the Bonneville Dam. Male Sea Lions are typically dark brown while the females are typically a lighter, golden shade of brown. Males can grow from 600 to 850 pounds and up to 7 feet in length, while the females are much smaller.

Harbor Seal *(Phoca vitulina)* Seals are widespread along coasts of both the Pacific and Atlantic oceans. There are 5 subspecies; the one in the Gorge is the Pacific Common Seal (*Phoca vitulina richardsi*). This seal is smaller than male sea lions and feeds off fish and some shellfish. The seal's average length is up to 6 feet and they can weigh up to 300 pounds. Their color ranges from gray to brown, sometimes with spots. Their round heads and V shaped nostrils are distinctive. Harbor seals dive and can stay underwater for several minutes at a time.

## Land Mammals

The most common large mammals a visitor is likely to see in the Gorge are deer and coyote. Less commonly seen but definitely present are elk, bear and bobcat (mountain lion live here, but are not often seen). Beaver, marmot and pika are present if you seek out their habitat. Common smaller mammals you are likely to see include several species of rabbit and squirrel.

Mammals *extirpated* from the Gorge (once present but not currently resident) include mountain goats, bighorn sheep and wolves. These species extirpated from the Gorge currently have populations in the Northwest close to the Gorge. These animals will likely re-inhabit the Gorge in the near future, either by natural migration or by re-introduction (see Section F below for further discussion).

> Elk *(Cervus canadensis)* also known as Wapiti, usually stay at higher elevation forested areas and adjacent open space or edge, but they come down occasionally in the winter to forage in locations like Rooster Rock, Catherine Creek and Seven Mile Hill. Elk are much larger than deer, with large spreading antlers. They weigh from 600 to 1,000 pounds. They are tan to reddish brown in color, darker brown on head and neck. They are distinctive by size, antlers and the light-yellow colored fur on their rear (a "butter butt").
>
> Deer There are two species of deer in the Gorge, one on each end of the Scenic Area: Black-Tailed in the west and Mule in the east. Some overlap and hybrids occur.
>
>> Black-Tailed Deer *(Odocoileus hemionus* var *columbianus)* are most common on the west side of the Gorge. They are smaller than the eastside Mule Deer, usually weighing less than 200 pounds. Black-tailed deer appropriately have a much larger and a more black tail than does a Mule deer.

Mule Deer *(Odocoileus hemionus* var *hemionus)* are most common on the eastside of the Gorge but overlaps and hybrids do occur. Mule Deer are larger and lighter in color than Black-Tailed, growing from 150 to 250 pounds. Distinguishing features between the two are larger ears and a distinctive white rump on the Mule Deer.

Coyote *(Canis latrans)* Coyotes are common throughout the Gorge (indeed, they are increasingly common even in larger cities). They are intelligent and adapt readily to available or changing resources. They are typically light gray to brown in color, with black tips on their hair, especially on the shoulders or tail. They range in size from about 3 to 4 feet in length, with a 16" to 18" long tail. Males weigh between 20 to 45 pounds, while females are usually less than 30 pounds. Coyotes are omnivores, eating whatever they can find, from insects, plants, amphibians, fish, snakes, mice, voles and rabbits (and where available domestic chickens).

Black Bear *(Ursus americanus)* are common across America and present in the Gorge. You are not likely to see one from busy roads but you may encounter one hiking or camping in the backcountry of the Gorge. They are usually all black in color but can have variations, and often have a brown snout. Their weight also varies greatly over the course of a year and can run from 100 pounds for females to 400 pounds for adult males. Although usually shy, as with all animals the females can become protective and aggressive if with cubs in the Spring.

Bobcats *(Lynx rufus)* are present in the Gorge but not often seen, in part because of their *crepuscular* behavior (active most at dawn or dusk). They are usually about 20" to 50" long, standing between 1 and 2 feet at the shoulders and weighing from 15 to 40 pounds. They are grayish brown with spotted or mottled coloration, with tufts on pointed ears.

Beavers *(Castor canadensis)* unintentionally played an important role in the history of the American West and the Gorge, as trappers came in search of furs for fashionable hats in England and the East Coast. Beavers are large: 31" to 46" bodies with another 10" to 20" tail, weighing from 25 to 60 pounds. They are semi-aquatic, building lodges on dams they make on creeks or streams (they enter their lodges underwater). You may see beaver dams and lodges in a wildlife refuge or on tributary streams or rivers in the Gorge, but you may also see distinctive marks and cuttings on branches along the Columbia shores (that may be local or have floated downriver).

Yellow-Bellied Marmot *(Marmota flaviventris)* live in rocky areas of the east Gorge. They are about 18" to 27" in length with a short (~5") tail and weigh from 4 to 12 pounds. They are reddish brown in color with a yellow chest and belly and a white patch between the eyes. They dig dens to live in, sometimes in colonies of up to 20 individuals. Females often group together while males typically occupy single dens. They hibernate in winter and *estivate* (sleep) in the heat of summer. A Marmot will sound a single high pitched CHEEP alert, then if approached further will issue a loud series of chattering sounds. You can still observe them as they run to their dens, since they are not fast runners.

Rabbits There are various species of rabbits in the Gorge. Unfortunately, many species of rabbit have been released to the wild (unwanted pets set free) and hybrids occur, so identification can be difficult.

Brush Rabbits *(Sylvilagus bachmani)* are fairly common on the westside of the Gorge. They are small rabbits with short legs. They are dark gray on the sides and lighter gray on the belly, measuring from 12" to 15" long and weighing about 1 to 2 pounds. They prefer thickets, where you can find runways for their use to and from foraging sites.

Mountain Cottontails *(Sylviagus muttallii)* are fairly common on the eastside. Grayish-brown in color with a white tail and distinctive large ears, they have longer legs than Brush Rabbits and stand more erect. Most active at dawn and dusk. Since they typically live in very dry areas on the east side they often obtain their water from the vegetation in their diet.

Squirrels Several squirrel species are present in the Gorge, occupying different habitats. Among the more common are the following:

The Western Gray Squirrel *(Sciurus griseus)* can be found throughout the Gorge but more commonly on the westside. It is dark gray in color, about 17" to 24" long, including the tail. It lives in trees.

The California Ground Squirrel *(Otospermohilus beecheyi)* is found only on the eastside, and lives in burrows it digs in the ground. Mottled gray color above, with lighter gray on neck and sides, it is slightly larger than the Gray or Douglas squirrels. It is often preyed on by eagles and rattlesnakes. Ground squirrels on the eastside hibernate in the cold months and estivate (sleep) in the heat of summer.

The Douglas Squirrel *(Tamiasciurus douglasii)* has some traits from both its Gray and Ground squirrel cousins; it lives in the coniferous forests (so primarily on the westside and central Gorge) but sometimes uses burrows in the ground. Its color is distinctive: gray on top and reddish-brown underneath. It is similar in size to the Gray Squirrel, and quite noisy.

Pika *(Ochotona princeps)* are a small mammal (6" to 8"), gray or brown colored with large ears and no tail. They live in rocky areas and talus slopes, usually at high elevation, and they have a distinct high pitched single note call. Somewhat surprisingly, a population of pika has been found living in the central Gorge at low elevation (only a few hundred feet above the river). Another population has been identified in mid elevations in the Washington Cascades, but the Gorge pika are living at the lowest level known. Recent research suggests the Gorge pika inhabit a north facing area with low temperatures and near year-round ice under the rocks. The Gorge pika population survived the 2017 Eagle Creek fire.

## B. FISH

Fish have been important to peoples living in or using the Gorge from prehistoric to historic and modern times. More than 40 species of fish are found in the Columbia River and its tributary streams within the Gorge. Because the Gorge is so close to the ocean (Lewis & Clark recognized influence of the Pacific Ocean tides as far upstream as Beacon Rock), there are several unusual species present that make use of both fresh water and saltwater environments. Native salmon, steelhead, sturgeon, smelt and lamprey were abundant in the Gorge in prehistoric and early historic times, and they provided a resource that invited and sustained concentrations of humans over time.

Native Anadromous Fish Species: Salmon & Steelhead

Native fish present in the Gorge include salmon, steelhead, sturgeon, euchalon (smelt), lamprey (look like eels but a distinct species), trout, bass, pikeminnow and others. Many of the native fish are *anadromous*, meaning they are born in fresh water then travel to saltwater to live and grow, returning to their freshwater origins to spawn and die. Anadromous fish currently present in the Gorge include several species of salmon, steelhead, eulachon and lamprey.

Salmon and steelhead are central to the history of the Gorge. Columbia River salmon and steelhead comprise one of the most fascinating and productive fisheries in the world, and they have sustained human populations here for thousands of years. Thirteen species or subspecies of salmonid fish have become threatened or endangered over the past hundred years, due to overfishing from the late 1800s through the 1900s, impact on migratory fish passage by the dams and declining ocean conditions.

All salmon and steelhead are born in freshwater then travel to the ocean where they mature for several years before returning to their home streams to spawn. All salmon species (male and female) die after spawning while steelhead sometimes return to the ocean and go through another cycle of returning and spawning before they die. Salmon change color dramatically from their ocean to spawning phase. When salmon eggs *(roe)* hatch they are referred to as *fry*. When they grow large enough to begin their anadromous voyage to the ocean they are called *smolt* or just juvenile salmon. Since 1955 large numbers of smolt have been barged downstream the Columbia in an attempt to increase survival as they pass through dams.

The following five species of salmon are most common in the Gorge (with several runs of some species occurring at different times of the year, which recently have been shown to be genetically distinct from one another). There is one species of steelhead and one primary species of sturgeon present.

Chinook (or King) Salmon (*Oncorhynchus tshawytscha*) are the largest salmonid in the river. They can grow to over four feet in length and more than 100 pounds in weight, although they more typically weigh between 10 to 40 pounds. There are distinct runs of Chinook occurring in the spring, summer and fall (each run is distinct from the others). Recent studies show that the runs are not just seasonal, but that each run is genetically distinct. Chinook are greenish with black spots on the back, with silver sides.

Chum (or Dog) Salmon *(Oncorhynchus keta)* typically have long migration travels in the ocean. The average about 2 feet in length and weigh about 9 to 20 pounds. They often spawn in small streams and intertidal zones, and usually return to fresh water to spawn later than other salmon species.

Coho (or Silver) Salmon (*Oncorhynchus kisutch*) are significantly smaller than Chinook and are distinct in appearance. They average around 8 pounds in weight and turn dark red as they return to the Columbia to spawn, usually in the fall. They typically spend a year or two in salt water before returning to the river to spawn.

Sockeye Salmon (*Oncorhynchus nerka*) average 6 to 8 pounds in weight. They are unique in that they usually return to and spawn in tributaries just upstream of lakes. They typically spend more time in the ocean than Coho.

Pink Salmon (*Oncorhycus gorbuscha*) are typically less than 5 pounds. They spend relatively little time in fresh water and return to spawn in just a few years, usually in late summer.

Steelhead (*Oncorhynchus mykiss*) are a most amazing fish. Although they are a true salmonid species, they are essentially just an ocean going (anadromous) rainbow trout. They spend more time than salmon growing in freshwater before migrating to the ocean (up to 2 years), and they typically return to freshwater after just a couple of years at sea. Some steelhead return to the ocean after spawning for another cycle (although, like salmon, most die after their initial spawn). They can weigh up to 55 pounds, and usually return to freshwater in the summer but can return any time of year.

All salmon and steelhead in the Gorge are currently listed as "threatened" under the Endangered Species Act, as a result of more than a century of over-fishing, agricultural and stormwater runoff, dams and destruction of spawning grounds. Restoration plans are in place, but recovery is gradual.

## Other Native Anadromous Fish

White Sturgeon (*Acipenser transmontanus*) are an ancient fish that can grow to very large size (more than 12 feet long and over 1,000 pounds) and can live from 80 to 100 years. Like salmon, they are technically anadromous, but sturgeon above Bonneville Dam must now be considered "historically anadromous," because the dams so greatly inhibit their migrations. Populations of sturgeon left sequestered in the pools behind large dams are declining, but the Treaty Tribes, states and BPA are working on sturgeon restoration efforts.

Lamprey (*Entosphenus tridentatus*) are long snake like fish that look like and are sometimes referred to as eels, but they are distinct from the American Eel found on the east coast. Unlike eels, lamprey have teeth and sucker mouths. They attach themselves to other fish (as parasites) or hard surfaces (such as rocks, or the viewing windows at the Bonneville Dam fish ladder). Lamprey are an ancient fish, from 350 to 400 million years old (compared to a

200 million year history for sturgeon and 6 million years for salmon). Lamprey are anadromous fish, born in fresh water then traveling to the ocean to grow, before returning to the river and its tributaries to spawn and die. Adult Lamprey grow up to 2.5 feet long. Lamprey have been an important food source and ceremonial fish for First Peoples in the Gorge, but their population is in decline, primarily because dams limit their migration patterns. There are 3 different species of Lamprey in the Gorge: *Pacific, River and Western Brook* (Western Brook spend their lives in freshwater). Pacific is the most common.

Eulachon (Smelt) *(Thaleichthys pacificua)* Smelt are a small (6" to 8" long) anadromous fish endemic to the Northwest with a high fat and oil content (sometimes called "candlefish" because they can be burned when dried). A food source for humans from prehistoric to recent times, there were no limits on when or how many smelt one could catch in the Gorge until 1997, when the fall runs began to decline significantly. Eulachon were listed as "threatened" under the Endangered Species Act in 2010. Closure of fishing seasons helped the species recover initially, but it continues to decline due to poor ocean conditions.

Other Non-Anadromous Native Fish

Pikeminnow *(Ptychocheilus oregonensus)* are a native fish that prey on salmonid juveniles. They grow up to 25" in length and can weigh up to 7 pounds. Although native to the river, they eat millions of juvenile salmon and steelhead every year (so while they may not be invasive, they have become intrusive). In 1990, as the number of salmonid fish declined, the states established a Pikeminnow Sport Reward program, funded by BPA, where anglers are paid to remove pikeminnow that are 9" or more in length.

The goal is not to exterminate Pikeminnow but only to reduce the population of larger pikeminnow that cause most harm to salmonids.

Trout There are several species of trout in the Columbia River drainage. Rainbow Trout that do not migrate to salt water are resident in the Gorge rivers, streams and lakes. There are also native Bull Trout present in the river and tributaries. The Redband Trout *(Oncorhynchus mykiss gairdneri)* is a native in the Salmonidae family, with three variations. One of those variations is anadromous.

Introduced Fish Species

American Shad *(Alosa sapidissima)* are native to the North Atlantic but were introduced to the Columbia River in the late 1800s. They are anadromous like salmon and steelhead. Shad are a type of herring, growing to about 3" to 8" long. Shad is considered a food fish on the east coast but there has been little interest to date in the Columbia River stock. There is no current limit on the number of Shad caught. In recent years more shad (by orders of magnitude) return to the Columbia River than any other species of salmon or steelhead.

Tiger Muskie *(Esox masquinongy x Esox lucius)* is a sterile cross (meaning they do not reproduce) between a Northern Pike and a Muskellunge. It was introduced to the Columbia River by the State of Oregon in 2013. It can grow to 4 feet long and weigh up to 30 pounds. It is currently a catch and release sport fishery only. Northern Pike are non-native fish that are very aggressive in consuming salmonid species. Some have been illegally introduced in upstream tributaries to the Columbia, but various federal, state and local agencies are working to control any spread.

## C. BIRDS

More than 200 species of birds can be found in the Gorge. The dramatic topography and cliffs provide perfect habitat for raptors like eagles, falcons and osprey, and the river itself provides an abundant food source for waterfowl, including geese, pelicans and numerous species of ducks. The forest to desert environment offers habitat for all sorts of perching birds and songbirds.

Referring back to the *Linnaean* system of taxonomical classification (see Chapter IV), birds are in the class *Aves*, which has 23 Orders. Each Order of birds share similar characteristics. Nearly half of all bird species are in the Order *Passeriformes*. The primary characteristic shared by Passerines, or perching birds, is their feet: all passerines have four toes; three facing forward and one backward. This arrangement allows them to grip a branch or wire tightly ("perch"). When passerines rest or sleep, as they relax their legs their toes reflexively grip the branch or wire tightly even as the bird falls asleep. Passerines include all raptors, songbirds, wrens, hummingbirds, etc.

Within the 23 Orders of *Aves* there are 142 Families at present. Among those Families there are roughly two thousand *genera,* which finally break down to the genus-species taxonomical nomenclature discussed above.

*NOTE: this book only describes a few of those bird species that a visitor or resident is most likely to encounter in average outings. The reader is encouraged to get one or more of the Field Guides to birds noted above or participate in outings with various birding groups in the Gorge to learn more about the rich avian life present here.*

What follows is a short list of the some of the birds you are most likely to see in your travels through the Gorge, generally following the taxonomical order, with an emphasis on larger or more distinctive birds you may be able to identify without binoculars. There are several Wildlife Refuges in or near the Scenic Area that provide excellent opportunity to view birds (but binoculars and a good bird book are recommended there).

*Raptors (Birds of Prey)* are large birds and thus among those birds you are most likely to see in your travels in the Gorge. They typically have large talons and beaks and highly developed eyesight for spotting prey. The raptors you are most likely to see in your travels in the Gorge include Eagles (both Bald and Golden), Osprey, Hawks and Falcons. Vultures and Owls are also classified as raptors.

Eagles and Osprey

Bald Eagles *(Haliaeetus leucocephalus)* are fairly common in the Gorge, especially on the eastside, up the Klickitat River and around The Dalles Dam and Bonneville Dam visitor centers. Eagles stand out as large birds with wingspans of 6 feet or more. They have large yellow beaks and distinctive finger-like feathers at the end of their wings. Juvenile Bald Eagles do not develop the characteristic all white head and tail until their 3d to 5th year, but juvenile Bald Eagles are easy to spot by their overall size (their bodies grow quickly even though adult coloration takes time) and by the size and hook of their beak. They feed mainly on fish, but are opportunistic if small mammals are available.

Golden Eagles *(Aquila chrysaetos)* are less common than Bald but present in the Gorge, especially in the winter on the eastside. Adults are uniformly dark colored (the golden neck feathers only appear gold in the right light), while immature have white tail bands and white wing patches. They often grow larger than Bald Eagles. Like Bald Eagles, Goldens have wide wing spans with finger-like feathers at the ends. Their bill is less heavy than Bald (and not yellow), and they have feathers that extend down to their feet. Feed mainly on rodents.

Osprey *(Pandion haliaetus)* (sometimes called Fish Hawks) are fairly common throughout the Gorge and likely to be seen around bridges, posts or pilings. They are sometimes mistaken for Bald Eagles, but they are smaller (wingspan

5 feet or less), they have a dark line running through their white head feathers and they hold their wings bent back. Osprey often hover while searching for fish.

Hawks, Falcons and Vultures comprise the Order *Falconiformes.*

*Buteos* are the largest subfamily in the Order Falconiformes and the group most commonly thought of as hawks. Four buteos may be found in the Gorge; the two most common are noted below (the two less common are the Ferruginous Hawk, an infrequent summer visitor, and the Rough-Legged Hawk, a winter visitor).

Red Tailed Hawks *(Buteo jamaicensis)* are common throughout the Gorge year-round and familiar to most people. They are a dark colored bird with a distinct reddish tail. They grow up to 18" long with a 4 foot wingspan. Red Tails sometimes hover while hunting over open ground. Their call is a high pitch descending scream (*PSSHHsshh….*).

Swainson's Hawk *(Buteo swainsoni)* is often seen in the summer on the east side of the Gorge. Similar in size to a Red Tail, the Swainson's Hawk is darkly colored. Distinguished from a Red Tail by lack of a red tail and by bands on the tail, ending with a wider dark terminal band.

Harriers are in the Falconiformes Order. There is only one species, but it is fairly common in the Gorge.

Northern Harriers *(Circus cyaneus)* or just Harrier, were previously known as Marsh Hawks. They can be found throughout the Gorge hunting rodents over open ground. Their bodies are thinner than Buteos and are distinguished by a white patch on their rump and upward tilted wings. They typically fly low to the ground but occasionally rise and hover.

Falcons are streamlined birds with pointed wings and narrow tails, known for rapid flight. There are 5 North American falcons, 4 of which can be seen in the Gorge (the largest falcon – the Gyrfalcon – is a secretive bird of northern forests and only visits the Gorge on rare occasions). Two of the more commonly seen falcons in the Gorge are noted below. The other two are present but less commonly seen: the Merlin (sometimes called "Pigeon Hawk") and the Prairie Falcon (occasional visitor to the eastside in late summer or fall).

> American Kestrel *(Falco sparverius)* is the most common and smallest falcon, with length about 8" and a wingspan of about 20" (sometimes called a Sparrow Hawk). It has a reddish-brown back, bluish wings and distinctive dark colored vertical bands on either side of its face. It can be seen hunting (sometimes hovering) over open ground.

> Peregrine Falcons *(Falco peregrinus)* are twice as large as Kestrel, with an average 15" length and 40" wingspan. They have a dark cap and facial stripes like Kestrel, but overall the bird is darker in color. Peregrines are slowly making a comeback across the U.S. after having losses from pesticides in prior decades. They can be seen around cliffs (which abound in the Gorge) where they perch before hunting small birds (often seen above the Cape Horn area, above Doug's Beach and elsewhere). Peregrines are the fastest bird known, capable of reaching speeds over 180 mph in a dive.

Vultures have their own Family. There are two vultures in the U.S., but only one in the Gorge. It is only here in the summer, but it is impossible to miss.

> Turkey Vultures *(Cathartes aura)* are large birds (2 feet long with 5 foot wingspans) that hold their wings in an upward dihedral position, tilting back and forth as they search for carrion. They are darkly colored but with

featherless red heads (juvenile heads are gray). Usually silent, they will gather when one bird finds food.

Ravens and Crows are both common residents in the Gorge. Although they are both all black in color, the similarity ends there.

Ravens (*Corvus corax*) are intelligent birds found throughout the northern hemisphere. They have held spiritual significance in several cultures, from Vikings to the tribes of the Pacific Northwest (raven flags were flown on many Viking ships and ravens have long been featured in stories of First Peoples). They are inquisitive birds and although they often follow people they avoid densely populated areas. Ravens can be seen throughout the Gorge. They are solid black and larger than Crows, with heavy beaks (the best identifying feature is that the beak is as long as the head is wide, while a Crow's beak is shorter and less heavy). The *"g-r-r-a-a-c-ck"* or *"HAW!"* call of a Raven is also deeper and more raspy than the *"caw-caw-caw"* of a Crow. On average, Ravens are about 24" – 27" long, weighing between 1.5 and 3.5 pounds. Ravens are omnivores and eat opportunistically.

Crows (*Corvus brachyrhynchos*) are widespread in North America and common in the Gorge. They are all black like ravens but smaller with a distinctively smaller beak. They often travel in groups, as compared to ravens who are often alone or in pairs. A crow's call is more frequent and repetitive than a raven (*"caw-caw-caw"*). Crows average about 16" to 20" in length and weigh about 2 pounds. They are also omnivores and will eat almost anything (including eggs and hatchlings of other birds).

Jays and Magpies: You can find three Jays in the Gorge, each fairly distinct in their habitat: Steller's Jay on the west side; Scrub Jay on the east side and Gray Jays at higher elevations. All Jays are fairly large (larger than robins) with long tails and relatively short wings. The Magpie is a showy relative of Jays that lives at the east end of the Gorge.

Steller's Jays *(Cyanocitta cristata)* are distinguished by a black feathered crest and back, with blue wings and underbelly. They live in coniferous forests on the west side from river level to mid-elevation (between the river and timberline). They are quite vocal and you are likely to hear them giving a harsh scolding before you see them.

Scrub Jays *(Aphelocoma californica)* live exclusively on the east side of the Gorge in open areas or sparse oak woodlands, as compared to the coniferous forests where you will find Steller's Jay. The Scrub Jay has no crest, but it has a distinctive blue and gray coloring: blue covers its head and wings, while the top of its back is grayish, and there is a whitish underbelly. Scrub Jays have long tails that are held straight downward when they perch. They have a loud, raucous call.

Gray Jay *(Perisoreus canadensis)* In 2018 the American Ornithological Association voted to change the name of Gray Jay to Canada Jay (but Gray is used here because it is so descriptive). Canada/Gray Jays live at higher elevations in forested areas. They are dark gray with white forehead and throat, with a lighter gray colored belly. They are inquisitive and bold, frequently coming right up to hikers or campers. Unlike most birds, they hatch their young in winter (February and March).

Clark's Nutcrackers *(Nucifraga columbiana)* are often found with Gray Jays and look somewhat similar. The Nutcracker is distinguished by its longer spike-like bill, and in showing white in the wings and tail when it flies. Nutcrackers pull seeds from conifers like Whitebark Pine and you can see piles of seed husks around trees they've worked.

Black-Billed Magpies *(Pica hudsonia)* are hard to miss; they are larger than Jays with very long tails, heavy bills and a striking mix of black and white on their body (with blue-green iridescent tinges on the wings and tail). They have two white stripes that run down their back. They are curious birds (Lewis & Clark reported that Magpies often entered their tents to inspect things). Magpies can be found at the eastern end of the Gorge, along Dalles Mountain Ranch Road, Columbia Hills and Deschutes State Parks and along the lower Deschutes River.

Woodpeckers: There are several woodpeckers present in the Gorge. Two of the more colorful are noted below.

Lewis's Woodpecker *(Melanerpes lewis)* Named for Meriwether Lewis who first described the bird on the Expedition's down-stream trip through the Gorge in 1805, Lewis's Woodpecker lives on the eastside in pine and oak forests and openings, usually at mid-elevation between the river and ridge tops. About 10" long with a 20" wingspan, it is a fairly large bird, distinguished by its light pink belly, with a gray collar and dark green back.

Red-Breasted Sapsucker *(Sphyrapicus ruber)* is another colorful woodpecker, with a bright red head and breast. It is a bit smaller than the Lewis's Woodpecker, at 8" in length and 16" wingspan, and usually found among pine or alder on the west side to central Gorge, where it drills rows of small holes on tree trunks, then collects the sap when it runs.

Geese: There are several species of geese resident in the Gorge, and more that winter here or pass through on migration. One of the most common is noted below, along with one easy to recognize.

Canada Geese *(Branta canadensis)* are common and distinctive. They are a large bird (nearly 3 feet long with 4 to 5 foot wingspans) with a black neck and head that is made distinct by a large white chinstrap running from under the bill toward the top of the head. Some Canada Geese are resident in the Gorge; others spend the winter then return north. There are 11 subspecies and considerable variation among populations. They usually gather in gaggles and form Vs in flight. They can be seen throughout the Gorge.

Snow Geese *(Anser caerulescens)* are smaller than Canada (30" long with 50" wingspan) but distinctive as a nearly all white bird (with black trailing edges on their wings in flight). They often gather on fields as well as water. They can be seen throughout the Gorge, usually in winter. They are often seen during migration but some may become resident.

Swans and Pelicans Two nearly all white, large birds easily recognized; one that winters here and the other that is seen in summer.

Tundra Swan *(Cygnus columbianus)* (previously called Whistling Swan) is a large (up to 46" long with a 7 to 8 foot wingspan) all white bird with a black bill. It breeds in the Arctic but both migrates through and over winters in the Northwest. Lewis & Clark were the first non-Indians to describe these birds. Lewis thought their wingbeats sounded like whistles. Tundra are often seen in the Gorge during the winter.

White Pelicans *(Pelacnus erythrorhynchos)* are *very* large birds (second in size among North American land birds only to Condors), with wingspans greater than eagles (body up to 4 feet long with 9 foot wingspans). The body and leading edges of the wings are all white with black on the trailing end of the wings. The large bill with pouch and the legs are orange. There are breeding colonies of White Pelicans in Eastern Oregon and in refuges near the Portland area, but in recent years a large group (up to 100) of non-breeding adult White Pelicans have spent summers just below The Dalles bridge. They often soar and circle high in the air, and at times you can see them cooperating in fishing by forming a circle in shallow water to drive small fish to the center where they take turns feeding.

Ducks Many species of ducks are found in the Gorge, especially in the winter months. They can be seen on ponds and lakes and along the shores of the Columbia itself. Among the many species you are likely to see, two ducks most noticeable for their plumage and chosen habitats are noted below.

Bufflehead *(Bucephala albeola)* Buffleheads are the smallest diving duck, but they are often seen on ponds and lakes and along shorelines in the winter. They have a distinctive black and white coloration, with a large white patch on the back of their otherwise black (and large) head and neck, and an all-white breast and sides under a black back.

Common Merganser *(Mergus merganser)* are large diving ducks, about 2 feet long with wingspans nearly 3 feet wide. They are found on fast moving streams and rivers in the summer, and in winter often join flocks of mixed waterfowl along the Columbia River shores. Unlike many birds, the female is the more colorful, with a rusty-red head topped with a plume-like crest, light gray breast and gray back and sides. Males have bright red bills but dark green heads and black backs with white sides.

Thrush and Meadowlarks are noted together here, although distinct taxonomically, because both provide easily recognizable songs, one on the west and the other on the east side of the Gorge.

> Varied Thrush *(Ixoreus naevius)* are common in the coniferous forests of the westside Gorge. They look like a Robin but with an orange eye band and a black stripe across the orange breast. They have a beautiful and easily recognizable call, as a series of long notes on different pitches. *Swainson's Thrush (Catharus ustulatus)* are also fairly common in the summer on the westside, but more secretive. Their song is even more distinctive, though, as a series of flute like notes rising up the scale.

> Western Meadowlark *(Sturnella neglecta)* are common in open areas of the eastside, especially in the spring and summer when they sing most often. They have a distinctive black band across a bright yellow throat and breast, and their song is a loud melodic medley of notes. They are the State Bird of Oregon.

Hummingbirds are the smallest birds you will find in the Gorge, but they are aggressive and make themselves known, especially if you out looking at wildflowers or wearing colorful clothing. Four hummingbirds may be found in the Gorge in summer (over winter at feeders). The two most common are noted below (the others, Calliope *(Selasphorus calliope)* and Black Chinned *(Archilochus alexandri)* are typically found at higher elevations).

> Anna's Hummingbirds *(Calypte anna)* are the most common in the Gorge, but far from common in appearance. They have iridescent green feathers on their body, and the males have bright rose-colored throats. Like all hummingbirds, they are small (3" in length). As the Cornell website *All About Birds* says, an Anna's hummingbird is "no larger than a ping pong ball and no

heavier than a nickel." But they are distinctive both in appearance and in behavior.

Rufous Hummingbirds *(Selasphorus rufus)* are quite aggressive, frequently attacking flowers, feeders and people. When the light hits directly the males have a vivid orange-red color on their back and underside, with a darker red throat. Females and immature males have greenish backs with rusty colored wings. Rufous breed in the Gorge and northward.

## D. AMPHIBIANS AND REPTILES

A few of the amphibians or reptiles you may encounter on a visit to the Gorge are noted below (plus one you should know about even if you don't see it).

Northern Alligator Lizards *(Elgaria coerulea)* are a fairly large lizard (4" body plus a 6" tail) that can be found primarily on the west side of the Gorge year-round. They are dark brown and do look like tiny alligators. They feed on insects, and sometimes small lizards and baby mice. They are harmless (well, not to small lizards or baby mice).

Western Fence Lizard *(Sceloporus occidentalis)* This medium size lizard is common and often seen on the east end of the Gorge. It is about 8" long with a dark colored back (from gray to tan to brown). They often pose on rocks (or fences, of course) and are easily seen. Their most notable feature is a bright blue belly on adult males (another interesting fact about fence lizards is that a protein in their blood kills the bacterium that causes Lyme disease, so effectively that if a tick bites a fence lizard the bacterium will be killed off in the tick).

Pacific Tree Frog *(Pseudacris regilla)* These small (about 2" long) frogs are common throughout the Gorge. They are typically a bright green color but also have brown morphs (they can also change color over time, but slowly, not quickly like chameleons). They are very vocal, and you are more likely to hear them (often indoors when they slip in) than see them. The frog has been designated a *keystone species* because other animals depend on its existence.

Western Pond Turtle *(Actinemys marmorata)* OK, so you are not likely to see this little turtle because it is considered endangered and there are few to be seen. But of the few remaining known populations of the animal two are in the National Scenic Area. In a show of collaboration among government agencies and public interest groups the Forest Service, Gorge Commission, Washington Department of Fish & Wildlife and the Columbia Gorge Land Trust (associated with Friends of the Columbia Gorge) acquired several parcels of land containing pond turtle habitat, and in 2019 cooperatively released more than a dozen young turtles that were raised in captivity.

There are several species of snakes in the Gorge, including garter snakes, racers, gopher snakes, etc. Rattlesnakes are present, especially on the eastern end of the Gorge, but they are usually as interested in avoiding you as you are them. They are often mistaken for more common snakes like the Gopher Snake (which is about the same size with similar coloration and can coil and hiss like a rattler but is not poisonous).

Western Rattlesnakes *(Croatus viridis)* are not as large (or venomous) as eastern diamondbacks or timber rattlers, but you should be wary of them. They can grow to 4feet long and are usually a mottled gray, brown or olive in color. They have a diamond pattern on their back, but what distinguishes a western rattler from other similar size snakes (like gopher snakes) is that the rattlesnake has a triangular shaped head that is much wider than its body and it usually has rattles.

## E. BUTTERFLIES, SPIDERS AND OTHER INSECTS

There are nearly 100 butterfly species in the Gorge. In general, the further east you go the more species and more individual butterflies you are likely to find. Different species are associated with specific habitats (*e.g.*, open fields with flowers, willows, oaks, pine, etc.). Some of the more common butterflies in the Gorge include Swallowtails, Checkerspots, Blues, Admirals and Painted Ladies. Similarly, there are many spider and insect species in the Gorge, but it is impractical for a book on this general level to do justice in describing them. The reader is encouraged to follow some of the recommended books and sources at the beginning of this chapter to learn more about butterflies, spiders and insects.

## F. ANIMAL POPULATIONS EXTIRPATED FROM THE GORGE (NO LONGER PRESENT)

Several animals that lived in the Gorge in the past are no longer present, either through loss of habitat, over-hunting or decline in population generally. It is possible that some of these species may be reintroduced to the Gorge in the future (such as Mountain Goats), and other species appear to be making their own comeback (such as Wolves). Bighorn Sheep historically included the Gorge in their range, and herds can now be found in the Deschutes River drainage just upstream of the National Scenic Area. It is possible that someday Condors may be re-introduced as well.

California Condor *(Gymnogyps californianus)* Condors are the largest land bird in North America, with a wing-span up to 10 feet and weight up to 26 pounds. Condors can live to 60 years in age. They are related to Vultures (and were sometimes referred to as vultures by Lewis & Clark and other naturalists). They have made a remarkable comeback from near extinction through captive breeding programs, and they are slowly being re-introduced to areas of previous natural habitat.

Mountain Goats *(Oreamnos americanus)* were seen in the Gorge by Lewis & Clark and Hudson Bay trappers, but their population declined by the 20th century. Efforts to re-introduce them have already occurred: in 2010 the Warm Springs tribe and Oregon Fish & Wildlife Department released 45 goats on the eastern slopes of Mt. Jefferson. Similar efforts for Mt. Hood are pending, due to increased human use in prime goat habitat. At least one goat has independently returned to the Gorge (seen between Stevenson and Carson in 2021and another on the Oregon side in previous years). An established population of Mountain Goats are in the Goat Rocks Wilderness and Mt. Adams area just north of the Gorge.

Bighorn Sheep *(Ovis canadensis)* There were two varieties of Bighorn Sheep in the Northwest historically: the Rocky Mountain sheep (*Ovis canadenis canadensis*) and the California subspecies (*Ovis canadensis californica*). The Rocky Mountain variant lived in the Snake River highlands, while the California variant lived in much of eastern Oregon and Washington, including the John Day and Deschutes drainages. Both variants declined due to hunting and loss of habitat to the point few were left by the middle of the 20th century. Efforts to re-introduce Bighorn have been underway for decades, and there is now an established population in the Deschutes River drainage again.

Gray Wolves *(Canis lupus)* were nearly hunted, trapped and poisoned to extinction before being given protection under the Endangered Species Act (ESA) in the 1970s. They have been re-introduced in Eastern Oregon and some individuals have traveled through the Mt. Hood

> area to northern California. In recent years several states were allowed to de-list wolves and resume hunting, but a federal court in 2022 reinstated ESA protection in areas of the Northwest, including areas near the Gorge.

Other animals once present in the Gorge include Whooping Cranes (noted by Lewis & Clark around the Narrows in 1805), and Lynx.

# CHAPTER NOTES

## Chapter V: Animals (Fauna)

1. *Salmon & Sea Lions*. Salmon and sea lions are both native to the Columbia River (the sea lions limited to the lower Columbia by rapids and subsequently by dams) and both are now considered threatened species. In recent decades sea lions have been preying on salmon below Bonneville Dam and Willamette Falls more than in the past, while salmon populations have been in decline. Salmon are protected by the Endangered Species Act and sea lions by the Marine Mammal Protection Act, but one species is clearly harming the other. Both species have their advocates, but to date, Congress, the federal agencies and courts have come down on the side of protecting salmon over sea lions. Human activities have largely contributed to the population declines for both salmon and sea lions, and many observers believe the long-term answer to the issues is removal of more dams from the Columbia system (specifically, four dams on the lower Snake River) which could help salmon recovery without further take of sea lions.
2. *Mountain Lions (Felis concolor)* (also called Cougar) are present in the Gorge, but they are largely nocturnal and seldom allow themselves to be seen – although in recent years Mountain Lions have been seen within the city limits of both Hood River and The Dalles. Tawny brown in color, they are typically about 7 feet long (with the tail a distinctive distinguishing characteristic by being as long or longer than the body) and they can weigh from 75 to 150 pounds. Mountain Lions have large territories and spend much of their time alone. They are noted in the Guinness Book of World Records as the animal with the most names (Mountain Lion, Cougar, Panther, Catamount, Puma, etc.). Linnaeus himself is the person who gave Mountain Lions their taxonomic name of *Felis concolor.*
3. *Plans to re-introduce Mountain Goats to the Gorge* met opposition in earlier proposals by, among others, Russ Jolley, author of the book Wildflowers of the Columbia Gorge. Russ objected to re-introduction plans in 2005 out of concern about goats having an impact on native plants and wildflowers.

4. *Safety When Hiking or Camping* is important to help discourage any unwanted encounters with wildlife. When camping make it a practice to hang your food (at least 10 feet high and 5 feet from a tree trunk). This is prudent not just to avoid attracting large mammals but also the more common pests of squirrels, skunks, porcupines, etc.
5. *Fishing Regulations* on the Columbia are complex and updated frequently because so many fish species are in threatened status, thus seasons must be adjusted often based on returning run size and catch data. Oregon and Washington have cooperative agreements regarding licensing and limits, which are coordinated along the Columbia. The States also coordinate their efforts with the Treaty Tribes through the Columbia River Inter-Tribal Fish Commission.
6. *The Reward Program for Catching Larger Pikeminnow* can be lucrative. The program runs from May through September and anglers are paid $5 per fish (they have to present the fish to state wardens), which increases to $8 for more than a set number of fish. Anglers have made from $20,000 to $48,000 in the 5-month season (they need to catch more than 2,000 fish to make that much, but some do).
7. *Barging of Juvenile (Smolt) Salmon & Steelhead* was first tried in 1955 by the State of Washington then evolved to be done by the Army Corps and other entities. Over 20 million juvenile fish raised at fish hatcheries in the Gorge are barged downstream every year. Without barging, many juveniles historically were lost in passage through the turbines or spillways at the dams. Fish bypass structures have been improved in recent years, however, with more extensive screens that divert juvenile fish around the turbine and spillway streams. Studies have shown that barging greatly improved juvenile survival downstream, but recent data show that barged juveniles have more difficulty returning upstream than their cohorts who passed the dams unaided. That finding led to improved barge configurations to allow smolt to "sense" the native waters while in transit.
8. "*The Columbia River Gorge and the Development of American Natural Resources Law: A Century of Significance*" is a law review article by Prof. Michael Blumm of Lewis & Clark School (NYU Environmental Law Journal 2013). The article provides a thorough overview of legal

issues involving fishing rights, the Northwest Power Act, land use disputes and the ongoing controversy about salmon and sea lions. Prof. Blumm has authored many other articles about the Gorge and salmon in particular.

# CHAPTER VI: PEOPLE

## *(Prehistory, History & Current Life)*

**Recommended Reading**

*Written histories about the Gorge include: Empire of the Columbia, A History of the Pacific Northwest, by Dorothy Johansen (Harper & Row 2d Ed. 1967); Nch'i-Wana: The Big River: Mid-Columbia Indians and Their Land, by Prof. Eugene Hunn (Univ. of Wash. Press 1991); Native River: The Columbia Remembered, by William Layman (Washington State Univ. Press 2002); When the River Ran Wild: Indian Traditions on the Mid-Columbia & the Warm Springs Reservation, George Aguilar, Sr. (Univ. of Wash. Press 2005); Shadow Tribe: The Making of Columbia River Indian Identity, by Emil and Kathleen Sick (Univ. of Wash. Press 2010); and A River Lost: The Life and Death of the Columbia, by Blaine Harden (Rev. Ed. Norton 2012).*

*There are several good biographies about some of the early explorers, such as The Collector (about David Douglas) and Sources of the River (about David Thompson) both by Jack Nisbet (Sasquatch Books 2009, 1994 respectively). The Lewis & Clark Journals are available in several formats, and there are other good books about early explorers such as Astoria by Peter Stark (Harper Collins 2015). There are many other articles and long form news entries about recent issues that can be found through search. See Notes for references to hikes, trails and other current issues.*

*Oral history remains one of the best sources of information about human history in the Gorge. The Yakama, Warm Springs, Umatilla, Cayuse, Nez Perce and other First Peoples retain extensive knowledge about this place and share their knowledge more than is commonly known, at cultural exchanges and various gatherings. Whenever you have a chance to hear traditional speakers you are encouraged to listen and learn.*

# CHAPTER VI

## *People*

**(Prehistory, History & Current Life)**

### A. PREHISTORY: 15,000+ YEARS BEFORE PRESENT TO THE 1500S

The Gorge may be one of a few areas in North and South America that has been continuously occupied by humans for at least as long as 15,000 years. Scientists believe that modern humans (*Homo sapiens*) began a large-scale migration out of Africa around 50,000 - 60,000 years ago (tentative ventures to the Middle East and Southern Europe began even earlier). By at least as early as 10,000 to 15,000 years ago, humans had explored almost the entire planet (it is possible they did so 20,000 years ago or earlier). Recent archaeological sites show that the peopling of the Pacific Northwest occurred at least as early as 14,500 years ago (evidence from Paisley Caves in Oregon, among other locations), but evidence from other sites around the country show that people have been here for at least 15,000 and likely 20,000 years (evidence of earlier life in the Gorge may have been lost to the glacial floods some 15,000 to 18,000 years ago). By any measure, the native peoples living here when the initial Euro-American contacts occurred in the 1500s through the early 1800s were indeed the "First People" in the Gorge, and they remain so today.

Due to its unique habitat and fisheries, the Gorge is believed to be one of the longest continuously inhabited areas in North or South America. Conditions in the Gorge were conducive to long term habitation early on, while other sites may not have had such long term resources available. First People were present when the Gorge was still in the process of being created, at the end of the last Ice Age. The landscape then was already much the same as you find today, although the last of the many Lake Missoula (or Bretz) glacial floods still poured down the course of the river, carving out rapids and landforms through the Gorge. Imagine what it would have been like to witness the glacial floods that formed the Gorge. First Peoples were clearly present for the massive landslide in 1450 that created the Bridge of the Gods, and for the most recent subduction zone earthquake in 1700. Recent generations have also witnessed geologic change in the Gorge, with the eruption of Mount St. Helens in 1980, and less dramatic but continuing earthquakes, landslides and mudflows. The landscape in the Gorge is still a work in progress and First People continue to witness all these changes.

## Tribes and Groups using the Gorge

Several tribal groups lived in or used the Gorge in traditional times, and even more tribes visited the Gorge annually to trade. Groups that have lived in or near the Gorge for millennia include Wasco, Wishram, Yakama, Klickitat, Nez Perce, Umatilla, Cayuse, Walla Walla, Paiute, Chinook, Cascade, Molalla, Tenino, Clackamas, Cowlitz, Multnomah and Kalapuya. The principal groups here when the first Euro-Americans arrived primarily spoke languages grouped as Chinookan or Sahaptin. Chinookan languages were spoken in the middle and west end of the Gorge, with Sahaptin speaking groups from The Dalles eastward.

## Traditional Life

Like traditional peoples around the globe, First People living in the Gorge developed annual life cycles associated with the seasons and foodstuffs available in this location. The river was the central part of annual cycles; it allowed for easier travel than by foot, and provided food and social interaction. Each spring, summer and fall brought its own run of salmon species, steelhead, sturgeon, lamprey, smelt and other fish. Family groups and bands would come together at traditional fishing spots to gather food and socialize.

In the spring, in addition to fishing there were plants and roots to gather, notably camas, biscuitroot and wapato. In summer and fall, expeditions would hunt birds and go higher in the surrounding mountains to hunt deer, elk, bear and gather berries. Over the course of the summer and fall, foods would be smoked or dried and prepared for the winter. Dried salmon was pounded into a fine grind, then often mixed with dried berries or animal fat, and stored. The stored salmon was used as a trade good for other foodstuffs and items coming to Celilo Falls and the Narrows from all over the West.

Housing types in the Gorge varied from the west to the east. On the western end of the Gorge, multi-family cedar longhouses were often used (and became more common further toward the coast, and northward). On the far eastern end of the Gorge buffalo hide tipis were seen in the summer, but most eastside winter dwellings usually consisted of extended family (smaller than on the west side) lodges dug into the earth as much as six feet. These had wooden walls, sturdy branches for rafters and grasses and mud used for a roof. In the area around The Dalles on the east end of the Gorge most lodges were rectangular, but smaller than the larger version found further west toward the coast and northwest coast. East of The Dalles semi-subterranean lodges were often circular. Lewis & Clark noted that many Chinookan peoples in the Gorge used small rectangular lodges that were level with the ground for summer and fall fishing but moved to semi-subterranean locations for the winter.

The social and trade network that existed among American Indian tribes in the Gorge area before European contact was extensive and efficient. Annual gatherings at Celilo Falls and the Narrows brought people from all over the West to trade. A striking example of how effective the trade network was described by Lewis & Clark, who forged an axe while spending the winter at the Mandan-Hidatsa villages in the Dakotas and traded it there, only to encounter the same axe several months later a thousand miles west in a Nez Perce village, providing evidence that traditional trade networks carried that axe ahead of Lewis & Clark in their travel.

Languages and Chinook Jargon

Many different languages were spoken by resident First Peoples in the Gorge in prehistoric times. In the Northwest there were more distinct languages than all of present day Europe. Chinook and Sahaptin language types were most common in the Gorge (the latter including Yakama, Klickitat, Walla Walla and Umatilla, and related but distinct from Nez Perce). During the summers at Celilo Falls more languages were heard, from California, Northwest Coast and Plains groups.

In addition to the numerous native languages, a jargon for trade among different language speakers was developed through the Gorge (and spread up the Northwest coast), using Chinookan as a base. This jargon was expanded upon arrival of Euro-Americans in the 1790s and early 1800s, to encompass words and terms used by the new English, French and American visitors. This lingua franca was known as *Chinook Jargon (or Chinuk Wawa).* Generally speaking, *jargons (or pidgin)* languages result from peoples creating common words out of two or more languages on contact, while *creole* languages are those jargons that become more developed in both grammar and syntax and are passed on over generations. By that definition, Chinook Jargon became more of a creole, if not an independent language (Chinook Jargon is being taught on the Grande Ronde-Siletz reservation in western Oregon today).

Chinook Jargon grew in use as a result of interactions among First Peoples, French, British and American explorers, trappers and traders. It originally had a fairly limited lexicon (or vocabulary) of around 300 to 500 words, but it grew. In Chinook Jargon, existing words in English, French or Chinook became slightly modified, with some interesting derivations. For example, the Chinook Jargon word for people from Great Britain was "*key-chutch*," shortened from "King George." The word for Americans was "*bush-ton*," from "Boston." Some words from Chinook Jargon have found their way into general English, especially in the Northwest (e.g., *tillicum* = friend; *tyee* = leader or boss; *skookum* = strong; *muckamuck* = big deal, person in charge; etc.).

## B. EXPLORATION: 1579 – 1824 (INCLUDING FIRST OCEAN CONTACTS, LEWIS & CLARK, TRAPPERS & NATURALISTS)

Non-Indian exploration of the American West is often thought to have begun with the Lewis & Clark expedition from 1804 to 1806. The Lewis & Clark expedition was remarkable in many ways, providing the American equivalent of Homer's epic story of the *Odyssey*, but Lewis & Clark were not the first non-Indian contacts with the American West, or the Gorge. The Captains were well aware of prior explorations (they relied on maps and earlier reports of coastal and overland voyages by the Spanish and British, and by American Robert Gray – the first non-Indian to enter the Columbia River) – but their journals do not discuss or reflect much on those facts.

Claims to the New World

European nations in the 15th and 16th centuries believed they could lay claim to vast tracts of territory simply by assertion, with the slightest physical presence. This "Doctrine of Discovery" was originally used by the Pope in 1452 to justify Portugal's colonial claims to non-Christian lands in Africa. So it was that in 1493, the year after the (largely lost) voyage of Columbus to the New World on behalf of Spain, another Pope gave Spain the rights to all the Western Hemisphere (the Popes claiming authority from God). Exploration and exploitation of the Americas soon began in earnest, at least on the Atlantic side of the continent, by both the Spanish and the competing French.

In a sailing expedition in 1513 Spanish explorer Vasco Balboa finally reached the western coast of North America in what is now northern Baja and California. As the first European to reach land on the west coast, Balboa promptly named the huge body of water the Pacific Ocean, then claimed all lands touched by that ocean for Spain – including the Pacific Northwest. Of course, neither Balboa nor any other European had yet seen the Pacific Northwest, or any lands on the other side of the vast Pacific Ocean.

## Explorations by Sea and Discovery of the Columbia River

Embarking around the same time as Balboa, fellow Spaniard Ferdinand Magellan's expedition was the first to circumnavigate the globe (1519 - 1522). Unlike Balboa, Magellan never even came close to North America, much less the Pacific coast (he sailed directly from the southern tip of South America to the Far East) but his voyage signaled the beginning of many other expeditions to come. No other Spanish ship explored further north than Balboa for many years, but the Spanish were already well ensconced on the ground in Central America, and they soon influenced what is now the American Southwest and California.

After Balboa's visit to the Pacific in 1513, Great Britain and Russia began funding sailing expeditions to the west coast of North America in search of trade as much as empire. In 1579, British captain Francis Drake (knighted by the Queen and becoming "Sir" Francis Drake upon his return in 1581) led an expedition that had, in part, the purpose of staking British claim to lands not yet fully explored by the Spanish. Drake sailed up the coast of California, Oregon, Washington and Alaska. Although his ship the *Golden Hind* never made land on the Oregon or Washington coast anywhere near the Columbia River (and Drake never recognized the presence of the river), one of his goals was to discover the imagined Northwest Passage between the Atlantic and Pacific oceans.

Nearly two hundred years after Sir Francis Drake unknowingly sailed by the Columbia River a Spanish sea captain became the first European to notice the Columbia River. Sailing in his ship the *Santiago*, on August 17, 1775, Bruno de Hecata observed the mouth of the Columbia and the bay just across the bar. Hecata attempted unsuccessfully to enter the river, but his ship was too large. Considering how dangerous and daunting the Columbia River bar is at its confluence with the Pacific even today, it must have been a harrowing experience for Hecata to attempt a first crossing and then fall back.

The following year, in 1776, as Americans were declaring independence from England on the Atlantic coast, British captain James Cook sailed north on the Pacific coast in his ship the *Resolution*, also looking for signs of a Northwest Passage. Cook was almost solely focused on finding a Northwest Passage and based on prior expeditions and mapmaker predictions he presumed the Passage was far to the north. As a result,

Cook also passed by the mouth of the Columbia River without noticing it and continued north in his travels.

It was not until May 11, 1792 – seventeen years after Hecata tried unsuccessfully to cross the Columbia River bar – that the river was finally entered by non-Indians. This time the exploration was not undertaken by Europeans, but by the new nation of America: it was the American Captain Robert Gray who finally crossed the bar and entered the river. Gray named the river after his ship, the *Columbia Rediviva.* Even though acting as a private citizen, in keeping with the best European tradition Captain Gray claimed the river and all it drained for the United States (some accounts say Gray noted that the local Indians called the river "Ouragon," but that is not certain: see Notes).

Several months later, having managed to get a copy of Captain Gray's chart of the mouth of the Columbia (Gray had left a copy of his chart with traders in Nootka Sound), the British sea captain George Vancouver sailed to the mouth of the river in October of 1792. One of the smaller ships in his fleet was able to enter the river, sailing all the way upstream to the Sandy River, just east of what is now Portland. Vancouver's expedition named both Mt. Hood and Mount St. Helens after British patrons and – of course – also claimed all land within the Columbia basin, meaning that now both America and Great Britain claimed the Gorge as theirs…neither having ever set foot in it. Dr. Archibald Menzies was the naturalist on board Vancouver's ship the *Discovery*, and Menzies identified many plants found in the Gorge (his name is attached to many of the Gorge's trees and plants, including the Doug-fir tree), even though Menzies himself never visited the Gorge (his studies were primarily on Vancouver Island).

## Initial Explorations and Influences by Land

Meanwhile, influence of Spanish forces far to the south had already reached the native peoples of the Gorge and the surrounding areas. The Spaniards introduced the horse to North America in their land explorations to the south. Escaped or stolen horses quickly made their way throughout the American West. Horses reached tribes of the northern plains by the mid-1700s, and other artifacts of trade with the Spanish began to appear as trade items working north from California and the Southwest. Those overland influences from California and the Southwest, combined with continued landings by Spanish, British and Russian ships on the Northwest coast contributed to trade and outside contact with peoples in the Gorge.

The British subject Alexander Mackenzie attempted twice to cross the North American continent from the East Coast to the Pacific Ocean, in search of the Northwest Passage. His first attempt began in 1789, but he ended up on the Arctic Ocean, not the Pacific, at the mouth of what is now the Mackenzie River. He tried again in 1792, and after spending a winter in the mountains short of the coast, he followed the Fraser River to the Coast Range, then crossed to the Bella Coola River and finally reached the Pacific. Mackenzie missed George Vancouver's stop at Bella Coola by only a matter of weeks. Mackenzie's route down the Fraser River did not promise an easy water route across the continent, but he published a book about his travels in 1801 titled *Voyages from Montreal.* President Jefferson was aware of Mackenzie's voyage, and book, and it further encouraged him to sponsor the Lewis & Clark expedition to get an American presence in the Pacific Northwest as quickly as possible.

Sadly, early coastal contacts by Europeans also brought disease. Small-pox epidemics ravaged several Indian tribes in and near the Gorge in the late 1700s. The Kalapuya, for example, living along the Willamette River, were still suffering greatly from small-pox when Lewis & Clark first visited a group of them near current downtown Portland in 1805.

## The Lewis & Clark Expedition

President Thomas Jefferson secured the Louisiana Purchase from Napoleon in 1803 (France having laid claim to the Mississippi and Missouri river watersheds by explorations and settlements in the 1500s and 1600s). The acquisition was conducted for a sum slightly less than $15 million in 1803 dollars. Well aware of the French exploration of large areas of Canada and the Mississippi River, and aware of both the Spanish and British coastal explorations along the Pacific, Jefferson wanted Lewis & Clark to find trade routes overland from the new Louisiana Purchase to the Pacific (recall that by 1792 both Britain and America had laid claim to the Columbia River watershed, without having actually visited or explored it). It was still widely believed in the late 1700s (and at the time of the Louisiana Purchase) that there must be a natural and easy water passage connecting the Mississippi River with the Pacific Ocean, the fabled Northwest Passage. No non-Indian had yet encountered the Rocky Mountains, which (although not yet known to the western world) made any Northwest Passage by water from the Mississippi/Missouri watersheds to the Pacific Ocean impossible.

The Lewis & Clark expedition left St. Louis in May of 1804. The expedition was and remains remarkable in many ways. Over the course of 28 months, the expedition explored and carefully recorded the natural history of the west, identifying numerous watersheds and ecosystems new to the Euro-American world. They met and exchanged goods with tribes who had not previously encountered Europeans or Americans. They kept detailed records of their journey, finding their way to the Pacific Ocean and back.

Despite all the challenges and hazards encountered on the Lewis & Clark expedition, there was only one death (caused by a ruptured appendix in the first weeks out of St. Louis). There was also a birth, a son born to the wife of an interpreter that the expedition picked up in its first winter with the Mandan-Hidatsa Indians. Sacajawea and her baby Pomp accompanied the expedition the entire way, and at a critical juncture Sacajawea helped defuse a tense encounter when she recognized her brother among a war party of the Shoshone. A black man named York also accompanied the expedition, being a slave who grew up with Clark. Remarkably, Lewis and Clark led the group by sharing responsibility as co-captains (even though Lewis was appointed by President Jefferson to be in charge). Even more remarkable, the group made major decisions by vote, and both Sacajawea and York were given votes at those moments.

Although the Lewis & Clark expedition was the first to encounter many native peoples and the first non-Indians to see much of the American West, they also encountered several rather startling events that made obvious the fact that Euro-American influence was already established in the lower Columbia River. On October 21, 1805, near the John Day River, the expedition saw some natives in a canoe, one of whom was wearing a blue British sailor's jacket. Over the next few days, they observed brass tea kettles and other trade goods that had found their way upriver from visiting British ships along the coast. They also recognized those mountains that the English Captain George Vancouver's group had named in late 1792:

Mt. Rainier, Mt. Hood and Mount St. Helens (the first two named after British admirals and the third a British diplomat).

The expedition spent a total of 36 days in what is now the Columbia River Gorge National Scenic Area (13 days downriver in 1805, and 23 days upriver in 1806). They identified many new plants, shrubs and trees previously unknown to Euro-Americans, observed large numbers of white pelicans, whooping cranes and condors, and confirmed that both mountain goats and bighorn sheep lived in the Gorge. They marveled at the number of salmon and steelhead in the river.

## The Astorians and Fort Astoria

Less than four years after Lewis & Clark returned to St. Louis, New York businessman John Jacob Astor presented President Jefferson with a plan to develop a global trading business, hinged on the establishment of a new fur trading post at the mouth of the Columbia River. Astor's idea was to gather beaver pelts at the mouth of the Columbia and take them to China to sell, then bring spices and other goods from the Far East to England and the East Coast of America (making profits at each waypoint), then re-supply and start the route again. Jefferson endorsed the idea, but only as a private enterprise (in large part because the Columbia River basin remained unclaimed fully by either the U.S. or Great Britain, and because Jefferson had already exhausted what funds Congress had appropriated for exploration of the west).

In 1810, Astor sent out two expedition parties, one by sea and one by land. Each party had dozens of members, many of whom were French-Canadian voyageurs and trappers, or from Scotland, and who had been previously employed by the Hudson Bay Company or other Canadian companies (which turned out to be an unfortunate choice by Astor). The Ocean group arrived at the mouth of the Columbia in early 1811 but lost eight men crossing the Columbia River bar through bad decisions by the ship's captain. The ocean party faced many other hardships (including loss of their ship The Tonquin a few months later further up the coast, in a dramatic conflict with local tribes caused by the captain's rude actions). The Ocean expedition had departed from New York and sailed around Cape Horn in South America, then replenished supplies in Hawaii and added several native Hawaiians to the expedition.

The Overland expedition suffered even more greatly, getting lost in the Snake River and Hells Canyon and losing expedition members as well as supplies. Some members of the Overland expedition began to straggle in to Fort Astoria by late 1811 and early 1812. The Overland expedition had departed from St. Louis, electing to travel further south than Lewis & Clark had to avoid confrontation with the Sioux and Blackfeet. So instead of following the Missouri River they went up the Platte River to the Rocky Mountains. They spent the winter in travel up the Platte, then crossed the Rockies the following spring. They began to descend the Snake River (which Lewis & Clark's route had fortunately avoided) but lost boats and men and ended up splitting into two groups, which further fragmented. Those who were left struggled into what is now the Blue Mountains of eastern Oregon, then slowly made their way downstream to the small gathering of travelers at what was then being called Fort Astoria.

Meanwhile, Canada's Northwest Trading Company had sent one of its own explorers to the mouth of the Columbia River, also with the intent of establishing a trading center. Unfortunately for the Canadians, David Thompson arrived a few months after Astor's ocean party had arrived in early 1811, only to find Fort Astoria already under construction (Thompson was the first non-Indian to canoe the entire length of the Columbia River).

The following year, in 1812, word reached Fort Astoria that the U.S. and Great Britain were at war (the War of 1812). Astor's men were already dispirited, and since many of them were either of British/Canadian ancestry or had worked for Canadian trading and trapping companies, they switched their allegiance to Britain. The American members of the Astorian expedition ended up selling Fort Astoria to the British (who renamed it Fort George in 1813) and began their trek home. John Jacob Astor was shocked when he learned his expedition had sold Fort Astoria, at a price well below his investment, but there was nothing he could do. So despite the fact that the first non-Indian to enter the Columbia River from the ocean was American, that the Americans Lewis & Clark made the first exploration down the river through the Gorge and that the American Astor party was the first to establish a settlement in the Columbia Basin with Fort Astoria, by the end of 1812 Americans had abandoned their foothold and sold Fort Astoria to the British. Americans continued to explore the lower Columbia River after sale of Fort Astoria, but the British and Canadian influence grew.

## Naturalists

Naturalists were included on almost all early British ocean explorations, and they later accompanied most of the American and Canadian overland expeditions. By the 1820s naturalists were traveling up and down the Columbia River gathering (and naming) new species of plants and animals. Part of the reason so many naturalists were included in these early expeditions is that England (and later America) had a great appetite for new plants for medicinal, agricultural or horticultural use. The other reason was that scientific enquiry generally was expanding rapidly in the 1700s and 1800s. President Jefferson sent Meriwether Lewis to Philadelphia in advance of the Lewis & Clark expedition for the express purpose of studying botany, biology and geology.

The first naturalist to have relevance to the Gorge did so without setting foot here. Archibald Menzies was on British Captain George Vancouver's ship in the early 1790s, and while he was on what is now Vancouver Island Menzies first identified Doug-fir as an unusual tree new to western science. Doug-fir is the most common tree in the Gorge. Several decades later, David Douglas was the first naturalist to spend considerable time in the Gorge, in two separate visits (from 1824 to 1827 and then again from 1829 to 1832). Douglas provided more detailed description of what became known as the Doug-fir tree, and many other plants. Other naturalists on early expeditions through the Gorge included Thomas Nuttall and John Townsend. Nuttall started out on the overland party of the Astor expedition in 1810 but left early. Nuttall later joined the second (1834) expedition of Nathaniel Wyeth (see below), along with Townsend. Later naturalists included Wilhelm Suksdorf, whose brother founded Bingen in the 1870s. Suksdorf became an accomplished botanist who provided specimens and assistance to various academic institutions.

## The Wyeth Expeditions

In 1832, twenty years after Astor's interests were sold to the Hudson Bay Company, a Boston inventor attempted again to launch a new American trading empire in the lower Columbia. Nathaniel Wyeth became wealthy by holding several patents for preserving ice in ships (the secret was wrapping it in sawdust) and he became devoted to the idea of a trading empire in the Gorge and lower Columbia River. He left Boston in 1832 with a group of 20 expedition members but arrived at Fort Vancouver in 1833 with only 8 remaining members of the group (some left, some died). His scheduled ship of supplies also failed to arrive, so Wyeth returned to Boston.

Undaunted, Wyeth embarked on another attempt in 1834, this time leading a group of 70 members. His plans to acquire trade goods again fell through, and he ended up establishing a small trading post near what is today Pocatello, Idaho (Fort Hall), and then a smaller post (Fort Williams) on Sauvies Island across from Fort Vancouver. Neither of these ventures were successful, and like Astor's representatives before him, by 1837 Wyeth had sold all his interests to the Hudson Bay Company. A rail station and post office were established near the small unincorporated community of Wyeth in the eastern Gorge, on the Oregon side of the river, and that namesake is all that remains of the Wyeth expeditions.

## C. SETTLEMENT: 1825 – 1889 (ESTABLISHMENT OF FORT VANCOUVER, THE OREGON TRAIL, ESTABLISHMENT OF CITIES AND THE CREATION OF TERRITORIES AND STATES)

### The Establishment of Fort Vancouver

Although Americans were still present after Fort Astoria was sold to the British in 1812, most of the non-Indians in the lower Columbia basin were French-Canadian trappers who maintained allegiance to Canada and Great Britain. They developed enough of a fur trade that in 1825 the Canadian Hudson Bay Company established a new fort upstream from Fort Astoria, across from the Willamette River's confluence with the Columbia River. The new Fort Vancouver was named after British captain George Vancouver (whose fleet entered the Columbia after American Robert Gray in 1792). The Fort was located at the site of modern Vancouver, Washington (the National Park Service maintains a historical restoration of the original Fort Vancouver on the original site). Over the next few decades, Fort Vancouver was the organizing center of early non-Indian life along the Columbia.

The establishment of a permanent fort by the British at the western end of the Gorge in 1825 marked the fact that Euro-Americans had become a permanent fixture in the Gorge. There was still considerable exploration going on (trappers and naturalists were going up and down the Gorge both before and after 1825), but the establishment of Fort Vancouver was a signal change. Americans made the first explorations of the Gorge (Captain Gray in 1792; Lewis & Clark in 1805-06) and made the first attempt at settlement along the Columbia (Fort Astoria in 1811-12), but the British were the first to put down roots with Fort Vancouver. The tension between British and American influence in the Gorge was much in play after 1825, and it was not resolved until the international boundary was finally settled with the Treaty of Oregon in 1846 (see below).

Missionaries and the Whitman Mission

In the 1830s several missionaries also arrived in the Gorge, intent on converting First Peoples to their version of Christianity. In 1836 Marcus Whitman and his family established a Presbyterian Mission near Walla Walla. Two years later, Daniel and Jason Lee established a Methodist Mission in The Dalles (Jason Lee had been a member of Wyeth's second expedition). Neither mission was very successful, as indicated by diary entries and letters from trappers, naturalists or soldiers passing by each mission. Reportedly the attendance of potential converts was greatly influenced by whether and when food was provided. The Dalles had long been a place of Indian community, called WinQuatt (French-Canadian fur trappers had called the place "*the dalles*" since at least 1814, referring to the layered rock lining the rapids).

Both the Whitman Mission near Walla Walla and the Wascopam Mission in The Dalles provided comfort and what assistance they could to early emigrants coming west on the Oregon Trail (which was used from about 1841 to 1869). After some Euro-American visitor to the Whitman Mission brought measles to the local Indian community in 1847, however, anger led to violence and as a result Marcus Whitman and twelve members of his group were killed. The Mission closed soon after, and The Dalles mission also closed by 1849.

The U.S. Army used the Whitman incident as reason to establish a military presence in the Gorge. Fort Dalles was constructed in 1849 as The Dalles mission was closing. The fort was initially called Camp Drum, then Fort Drum and finally Fort Dalles (The Dalles was incorporated as a city in 1857). Fort Dalles housed soldiers who patrolled the territory. Officers stationed at Fort Dalles over the years included names that later became familiar landmarks in eastern Oregon, such as Alvord, Harney and Jordan.

## Migration and The Oregon Trail

What became known as the Oregon Trail started as the route taken by some of the Astorian expedition's travels in 1811 and 1812. It was on a return trip to bring messages to Astor that members all but accidentally found South Pass in southwestern Wyoming as a more favorable place for crossing through the Rockies. South Pass is really two mountain passes around 7,500 feet in elevation about 35 miles apart. In contrast to the struggles of the Lewis & Clark expedition crossing the Rockies up Lolo Pass west of Missoula, or some of the overland group of Astorians who became lost in the Snake River and Hells Canyon on their initial trip west, South Pass was gentle enough to allow relatively easy horse and wagon traffic.

Thirty years after the Astorians first used South Pass, it was used again by settlers emigrating from the East to the Northwest. The Bartleson-Bidwell party in 1841 was the first wagon train credited to use the route that became known as the Oregon Trail (although that group later split in Idaho from a larger group headed to California). A much larger group followed the same route in 1843 (referred to as "the Great Migration"). That and subsequent wagon trains, many trailing cattle and other animals with them, found their way to The Dalles. From there some went down river to Portland on boats or rafts, while others went south and west over Mt. Hood on the Barlow Road, which was really just a cleared and well-used track similar to the Oregon Trail. The Barlow Road was laid out in 1846 by Sam Barlow, Joel Palmer and Phillip Foster. The road was privately funded and intended to be a toll operation, but its popularity triggered the Oregon Territorial government to provide some funding. Wagon wheel ruts and rope marks on trees (for lowering wagons down steep slopes) can still be found in some areas and are memorialized at Timberline Lodge on Mt. Hood.

As many as 400,000 people started their journey on the Oregon Trail, with some splitting off to go places other than what would take them to or through the Gorge. The primary destination for those following the Oregon Trail the entire way was the Willamette Valley, based on glowing descriptions of the broad and fertile valley carried East by Lewis & Clark, the Astorians and others. The pioneers that traveled the Oregon Trail had a significant impact on subsequent development and life in the Gorge. The last organized wagon train to use the Oregon Trail is believed to have been in 1869. Use of the Oregon Trail all but ceased as railroad connection to the west coast became possible by the late 1860s.

## Portages, Ferries and Steamboats

Native Americans used canoes to travel along and across the Columbia River for thousands of years. Many of those canoes were large, sufficient to transport a number of people as well as cargo. Early explorers and pioneers also used large canoes for transport. The major rapids in the Gorge (Celilo, the Narrows and the Cascades) required portage for larger canoes, especially during summer low water.

As the influx of pioneers came to The Dalles on the Oregon Trail in the mid 1800s, some travelers built rafts to carry their wagons and belongings downriver to what is now the Portland area, or to Oregon City. Some of the rafts were ultimately used again for river crossings once a party landed. Many pioneers were headed for what is now the Oregon side of the Columbia River to settle in the Portland area or up the Willamette Valley, but for several decades the center of trade for everyone (including the new arrivals) was still the Hudson Bay Company trading post at Fort Vancouver. That required frequent crossings of the Columbia River for goods and supplies.

The first commercial ferry across the lower Columbia River is thought to have been started by John Switzler in 1846, running from Hayden Island on the south bank of the Columbia River to the Hudson Bay Company fort and supplies at present day Vancouver, Washington (the Fort Vancouver National Historical Site maintains many replicas of the original buildings). Over the next several decades, ferries began operation throughout the

Gorge, including runs between the Sandy River and Washougal, Cascade Locks and Stevenson, Hood River and White Salmon, Rowena and Lyle and between The Dalles and Dallesport. The early ferries were situational in use, but as time went on there was enough demand for some crossings to have regular schedules and fees. Steamboats also began making runs all along the Gorge during the mid-to late 1800s, either using landings for loading and offloading, or docks that were constructed at several growing cities.

## A New Boundary with Canada: the 1846 Treaty of Oregon

As Americans began using the Oregon Trail in increasing numbers the number of Americans in the Northwest quickly exceeded the number of British or Canadian citizens. As a result, pressure grew to solidify America's claim to the Pacific Northwest. On June 15, 1846 the Treaty of Oregon finally established the present day boundary between U.S. and Canada at the 49th parallel, ending joint occupancy of the Northwest by Britain and the U.S. (Canada did not gain independence from Great Britain until 1867, thus the British led the negotiation of the Treaty of Oregon). Britain and Canada had argued for the Columbia River itself to be the international boundary, while the U.S. Congress had wanted to claim northward to 54' 40" latitude, to include Vancouver Island. This was the source of the "54-40 or fight" political cry of the day. The nations settled on the 49th parallel in order to avoid another military conflict like the War of 1812, giving Vancouver Island to Canada, but keeping most of the Columbia River basin in the United States.

## Government: Territories, States and Communities

In 1848, two years after location of the boundary with Canada was resolved by the Treaty of Oregon, the U.S. Congress created the Oregon Territory, which included an area encompassing the modern states of Oregon, Washington and Idaho. Five years later, in 1853, Congress created the Washington Territory (originally proposed to be called the Columbia Territory). The new Washington Territory sub-divided the existing Oregon Territory, so that the current state of Washington, plus northern Idaho and northwestern Montana became the new Washington Territory. Congress gave concurrent jurisdiction over the Columbia River to the Oregon and Washington Territorial governments.

County governments along the Gorge were established shortly after the Territories were created. Clarke County was established first, in 1849, under the provisional government of the Oregon Territory (the spelling was changed to just "Clark" in 1925). In 1854, Skamania, Wasco and Multnomah counties were each incorporated (in March, July and December, respectively). Klickitat County was established in 1859. Hood River County was not established until 1908, carved out of the large existing Wasco County (the largest county ever in the U.S.). Of the six counties in the National Scenic Area four are named using Indian words, one is named after the Lewis & Clark expedition, and one is a local place name.

In 1843 the City of Portland was founded (incorporated in 1851), and by the mid-1800s Portland was the largest population center in the Pacific Northwest, eclipsing the prior center of activity at the Hudson Bay outpost in Fort Vancouver (present day Vancouver, Washington). As Portland grew it became a center of commerce for inhabitants of the Gorge. Portland's name, incidentally, was determined by a coin toss between two of its founders, Asa Lovejoy and Francis Pettygrove (now recognizable street names in downtown Portland). The founders agreed that the City would be named after the hometown of one of them, as determined by the coin toss. Lovejoy came from Boston, while Pettygrove came from Portland, Maine. Obviously, Pettygrove won the coin toss.

Oregon became the 33d state of the Union in 1859. Thirty years later, in 1889, Washington became the 42d state. From the start of the Oregon Trail through creation of state governments, the various cities in the Gorge developed and grew. The Dalles was first incorporated as a city in 1857, having served as a military fort and population center for years. The Hood River Post Office was created the following year, in 1858, but the city was not platted until 1881 and not incorporated until 1895.

The City of Lyle was named in 1878, followed by the City of Stevenson in 1893 (Lyle was named after James Lyle, its first Postmaster, and Stevenson was named after George Stevenson, who owned and developed the land that became the City). White Salmon was incorporated as a city in 1907 (named after diary entries from Lewis & Clark who first observed bleached out salmon after spawning in what is now the White Salmon River). The Jewett family founded White Salmon. Bingen was incorporated in 1924. The Suksdorf family originally settled at that location in 1892 and named the community after their home along the Rhine River valley in Germany, which they thought bore striking resemblance to the Gorge.

## The Stevens Treaties of 1855 and the Donation Land Act

A law called the Oregon Donation Land Act (passed by the U.S. Congress) became effective in 1850. The stated purpose of the Act was to dispossess native peoples from their land by allowing "whites and half-breed Indians" to claim 320 acres of land (another 320 if married) if they occupied and improved the land. The law expired in 1855 – when the Treaties (discussed below) more fully disposed tribes of land – but in the few years the Donation Land Act was in effect more than 7,000 claims were filed on more than 2.5 million acres.

Congress was intent on settling the Northwest, and to that end it decided native peoples needed to be removed to reservations. Four separate treaties were signed during 1855 affecting Indian tribes living in or around the Gorge: (1) Treaty with the Yakamas (June 9, 1855); (2) Treaty with the Walla Walla, Cayuse and Umatilla (June 9, 1855); (3) Treaty with the Nez Perce (June 11, 1855); and (4) Treaty with the Tribes of Middle Oregon (Wasco, Wishram and Paiute) (June 25, 1855). Each of these treaties created a reservation and resulted in people being relocated away from traditional homelands and placed with different groups than they had associated with historically. In the case of the Warm Springs reservation, for example, three entirely different language groups were brought together (Sahaptin, Chinookan and Shoshonean), and some groups were traditional enemies (Wishram and Paiute).

Two non-Indians were appointed by Congress to negotiate the treaties: Isaac Stevens represented the Washington Territory and Joel Palmer represented the Oregon Territory. Isaac Stevens was initially tasked by Congress to survey a northern route for a railroad to the Northwest but was then appointed Governor of the new Washington Territory when it was established. Once Governor, Congress asked Stevens to negotiate treaties with various tribes to open the Northwest for settlement and development. Joel Palmer was appointed by the Oregon Territory when it was created in

1853 to be its Commissioner of Indian Affairs and joined Stevens in the negotiations.

Stevens was criticized by his own Territorial Legislature for being too harsh in negotiations with tribes, especially the Yakama and Nisqually, although he survived calls for removal from office. Palmer, on the other hand, was criticized by many settlers for giving "too much" to Indians – being any reservation land at all – while the tribes criticized him for moving them off traditional homelands. Palmer's perceived pro-Indian policies caused him to be removed from office by Oregon's Territorial Legislature in 1857, after the treaties had been signed.

The Treaties of 1855 all contained a clause that would prove significant in preserving American Indian rights to fish in the Columbia and the Northwest generally. That clause reads as follows:

> *The right of taking fish, at all usual and accustomed grounds and stations, is further secured to said Indians in common with the citizens of the territory...together with the privilege of hunting, gathering roots and berries, and pasturing their horses on open and unclaimed lands.*

See "Realization of Treaty Indian Fishing Rights" in Section D, below, for further discussion of how this important provision of the 1855 Treaties has been given effect.

## Rise of Fish Wheels and Canneries; Decline of Native Fish Runs

The Native American fisheries on the Columbia River had existed for many thousands of years in balance with the natural abundance of fish. Not long after Euro-Americans entered the Gorge, fishing became more aggressive, and overfishing occurred quickly. It is estimated that pre-contact First Peoples caught roughly 10 to 18 million pounds of fish (of all species) annually from the Columbia River. Those fish were used for subsistence and ceremonial purposes, and for trading. When Lewis & Clark and the Hudson Bay trappers came to the river in the early 1800s, they marveled at the number of fish in the river. But marvel soon turned to commercial harvest, then over harvest.

In 1866 the first commercial salmon cannery was established on the Columbia River near Cathlamet (downstream of the Gorge). That first cannery was started by two individuals from the East Coast with some prior canning experience, John Hume and Andrew Haygood. It would be the first of many canneries operating through the end of the 1800s, which contributed to the significant decline of the historic salmon runs in the Gorge. Hume and Haygood came to the Columbia after having already overfished the Sacramento River in northern California (even as early as the mid-1800s). By 1883 there were 39 canneries on the Columbia River, taking on average an estimated 42 million pounds of fish per year out of the river (some years exceeded 50 million pounds), using fishwheels, seine nets and set nets to serve the growing demand. Some fishwheels were extremely large, literally mining salmon, steelhead and other species in astounding quantities. Oregon eventually banned their use in 1926, followed by Washington in 1934.

More than 50 canneries operated in the lower Columbia from 1866 to the end of the 1800s. Gorge salmon was exported to the east coast, to Europe and China. The fisheries began to decline almost immediately, and by the early 1900s canneries were closing for lack of fish, although the last salmon cannery on the lower Columbia was not closed until 1980.

## D. GROWTH & DEVELOPMENT: 1890 - 1985 (ESTABLISHMENT OF AGRICULTURE AND INDUSTRY; CONSTRUCTION OF ROADS, RAILROADS AND DAMS)

By 1890 the boundary between the U.S. and Canada was long settled, with the Columbia Gorge being fully within American territory as agreed to in the 1846 Treaty of Oregon. The U.S. had also recorded treaties with many of the tribes of the Gorge in 1855, and established reservations intended to remove First Peoples from the Gorge. By 1890 Oregon and Washington had also both become states (statehood occurring in 1859 and 1889, respectively). So by 1890, the dominant presence of First Peoples was gone, the influence of the British was gone, and the relative lack of government that was associated with the Territorial system was also gone. In 1890, the way in which people lived in the Gorge was about to change again.

## Communities and Population Change

For most of the next hundred years following 1890 the story of the Gorge was about population growth and the rise of various agricultural and industrial commercial enterprises, and then construction of dams which changed the Columbia River and life in the Gorge even further.

When the National Scenic Area was created in 1986 thirteen urban areas were recognized in the statute as were the established off-reservation rights of those Indian tribes subject to the 1855 Treaties. These communities were already in existence in 1890 (in fact, most had been places of traditional life for thousands of years). The identified urban areas on the Oregon side (south bank) included: Cascade Locks, Hood River, Mosier and The Dalles. Urban areas on the Washington side (north bank) included: North Bonneville, Stevenson, Carson, Home Valley, White Salmon, Bingen, Lyle, Dallesport and Wishram.

There are no reliable records on the population of the Gorge communities in 1890, but what data exists suggests there were less than 5,000 people total living in these urban areas. The rural population was likely much greater (in the U.S. more people lived in rural areas than urban until after 1910, when a majority of the population moved to cities). The Indian population in the Gorge was likely at least as large as the non-Indian in 1890. So although no reliable data exists, the total population of the Gorge in 1890, urban and rural, was almost certainly greater than 10,000. By the time the Scenic Area was established in 1986 – nearly 100 years later – some additional Indian residents had relocated to reservations, but other population growth (Indian and non-Indian) also occurred. An estimate of the Gorge population within the National Scenic Area boundaries was about 44,000 in 1986. At the turn of the century, in 2000, the resident population in the National Scenic Area was about 50,000. Twenty years later the 2020 Census showed the population of the Gorge had grown to around 75,000, with most of those people living in one of the thirteen designated Urban Areas (which combined only comprise about 10% of the land area within the National Scenic Area boundaries).

The population of the Gorge has clearly grown over the past one hundred years, but not as much as larger urban areas nearby, such as Portland or Seattle (see Notes for more data).

## Dams and Further Impact on Declining Fish Runs

Chapter II describes the construction of dams on the mainstem of the Columbia River, which began with the Rock Island dam in 1933 and concluded with the Revelstoke dam (in Canada) in 1984. Looking back, it is unfortunate that all the planning that went into construction of 14 major dams on the Columbia over the span of decades did not consider more fully or attempt to better mitigate the impact the dams would have on fish migration and survival.

Dams affect fish in several ways. They are an obvious obstacle for migrating fish. Not all dams on the Columbia had effective fish ladders when constructed, and since the average height between impounds on Columbia River dams is roughly 70 to 100 feet, upstream passage often remained an unsurmountable challenge. The impounds behind dams also flooded spawning grounds and changed the ecology of the river, increasing water temperature which can lead to disease. When the juvenile fish begin downstream migration, the dams present another obstacle that lead to mortality for some fish that do not survive passage through the turbines or spillways.

Considerable research and efforts to mitigate losses to the fishery have been undertaken, but many runs of salmon in the Columbia remain in threat. Chapter V discusses the impacts on specific species and efforts to restore certain runs.

## Railroads and Roads

Canoes carried traffic and cargo up and down the Gorge for millennia. By the mid-1800s rafts and then steamboats began plying the river. In the late 1800s and early 1900s railroads were constructed on both sides of the river, and in the early 20th century roads lined both sides of the river through the Gorge. The railroads largely displaced the role of steamboats for hauling people and cargo, and the new highways opened new uses for the Gorge, including sightseeing and tourism.

The first railroad in the Gorge was built in 1851, as a short mule powered wooden rail portage around the Cascades rapids (another 12-mile rail was constructed around Celilo Falls in 1862, replacing a wagon road portage). The first complete railroad through the Gorge was constructed on the south bank of the river by the Oregon Railway & Navigation Company. That line became operational in 1882 and eventually became owned and operated by the Union Pacific railroad company. The first railroad on the north bank of the river began operation in 1908, constructed by the Spokane, Portland & Seattle Railway. That line eventually became owned and operated by the Burlington Northern Santa Fe company. Both companies currently run numerous trains through the Gorge every day. In recent years concern has grown about coal and oil carried on many of these trains, on both sides of the river, because the tracks of both lines are close to the river. A Union Pacific oil train derailed in 2016 near Mosier, causing an oil spill and fire.

The Oregon Trail stopped at The Dalles because there was no road through the Gorge. Pioneers either rode rafts from The Dalles down river to Portland or took the Barlow Road over Mt. Hood. The Barlow Road was little more than a path similar to the Oregon Trail, but it provided a way to get wagons to Portland and the Willamette Valley (even though the wagons needed to be belayed by ropes down the steeper sections). The Barlow Road was marked in 1846 by Sam Barlow, Joel Palmer and Phillip Foster (Palmer was appointed Commission of Indian Affairs in 1853 and with Isaac Stevens negotiated the Treaties of 1855 with tribes living in the Gorge). A primitive road was built on the south side of the Gorge in the 1870s called The Dalles and Sandy Wagon Road, but it was too rough and steep to be of much use.

The first serviceable road to be completed through the Gorge was the Columbia River Historic Highway, stretching 74 miles from Troutdale to The Dalles. Sam Hill, who constructed MaryHill at the east end of the Gorge, promoted the idea of a Gorge highway as an attraction comparable to the great scenic routes in Europe. He recruited landscape architect Samuel Lancaster to help design the road, intentionally focusing more on views than direct routes. The road was constructed in sections from 1913 to 1922 (the western section was dedicated in 1916). It was the first road in the U.S. to be designated as a Scenic Highway. It became State Highway 30 in 1926. Sections of the original Historic Highway are currently being restored and will be incorporated into the biking and hiking trail that will become part of the Towns to Trails trekking destination.

On the north bank, a survey was made in 1905 to construct a wagon road from Washougal to Lyle. The road was to be known as State Road 8. A second road began in 1913 aligned more closely to the river, and that was called the North Bank Highway (which made use of existing State Road 8 where possible). As with the Historic Columbia River Highway on the Oregon side of the river, the North Bank road was built in sections, and the work was difficult (numerous tunnels had to be blasted). The road was open for use by the mid-1920s but work continued into the early 1930s. It was renumbered as U.S. Route 830 and then in 1967 became State Route 14 (also known and marked as the Lewis & Clark Trail).

In 1957 work began on a new interstate highway at river level on the south bank of the Columbia (Oregon side). The new road was largely complete by 1963 but it was not until 1968 that it met federal interstate highway standards. The new interstate was planned to be numbered as I-82, but that plan was changed in 1958 with the new designation of I-80N. In 1980 the interstate designation changed again, to I-84. Parts of the Historic Columbia River Highway (Route 30) were damaged or destroyed during construction of I-84, but the State of Oregon began reconstructing Route 30 from Troutdale to The Dalles in the early 2000s. Much of the revised Route 30 will be open to vehicles but some of it will be limited to foot or bike traffic. The restored Route 30 will be called the Historic Highway State Trail, which in turn will become part of the Towns to Trails trekking loop around the Gorge.

Bridges

Three vehicle bridges cross the Columbia River within the Gorge National Scenic Area, one each at Cascade Locks, Hood River and The Dalles. A stand-alone railroad bridge crosses the river further upstream at Celilo, at the east end of the Scenic Area. The first bridge built across the Columbia within the Gorge was the Hood River bridge. It was completed and opened in 1924, but then rebuilt in 1938 to raise it above the higher water levels created by completion of the Bonneville Dam. In 1950, the Hood River bridge was purchased by the Hood River Port Authority (for $800,000) and began to collect tolls for crossing. The bridge is now approaching 100 years in service as a narrow steel grid over the river with 2 nine-foot wide lanes and no shoulder. The Hood River bridge carried horse drawn carriages and Model T autos when it opened. It now carries log trucks, semis, commercial trucks and passenger cars. Plans are underway to replace the bridge in the coming years.

The "Bridge of the Gods" was the second bridge built in the Gorge, at Cascade Locks. The name of the bridge was appropriate because of the traditional First Peoples story of a bridge of the gods at that location, which reflected the fact that a landslide completely blocked the river for a few years, beginning in 1450, which subsequently created the Cascades Rapids (see Chapter II). The Bridge of the Gods was completed and opened in 1926, then rebuilt in 1940 to raise it above the higher water levels created by the Bonneville Dam, which is about 4 miles downstream from the bridge. The Bridge of the Gods is part of the Pacific Crest Trail. After construction, the bridge was purchased by the Port of Cascade Locks, and like the Hood River bridge it continues to charge a toll for passage.

The final bridge to be built across the Columbia within the Gorge was The Dalles bridge, completed and opened for use in 1953. Unlike the Hood River bridge and the Bridge of the Gods, The Dalles bridge only charged a toll from time of construction until 1974, when the construction bonds were paid off. The bridge underwent a re-surfacing and guardrail upgrade in 2021-2022.

## Barge Traffic

Although the Columbia River through the Gorge has been used to haul cargo for thousands of years, modern barges carry huge volumes of material on a weekly basis. Barges typically haul various natural resources downstream, such as timber, wheat and gravel. These commodities are increasingly loaded onto ocean vessels at the ports of Portland or Longview and shipped to Asian markets. Upstream barges typically haul empty containers, wastes (such as scrap metal), etc. Two companies manage the bulk of barge traffic on the lower Columbia River at present: Shaver and Tidewater.

## Realization of Treaty Indian Fishing Rights

Salmon, steelhead, sturgeon, lamprey and eulachon (smelt) have been a part of the Columbia River ecosystem since the Gorge was formed. The lives of the First Peoples who lived in the Gorge centered around these fisheries for millennia. In the early 1800s, when non-Indians first began to settle in the Gorge, salmon and other fish were abundant to an extent that amazed the Euro-American explorers. Everyone assumed that these fish runs were so remarkably abundant that they would never decline. But decline they have, due to overfishing, dams, pollution and loss of habitat.

The tribes that were signatories to the Stevens treaties of 1855 were guaranteed the right to continue to fish in the Columbia "*at usual and accustomed places in common with others*." The impact of those treaty words became evident in 1905 when the U.S. Supreme Court declared in *U.S. v. Winans* (198 U.S. 371) that treaty tribes had reserved rights to fish in the Columbia River and the Gorge. The case precluded the non-Indian owners of a fishwheel below Celilo Falls from fencing out tribal fishing. The U.S. Supreme Court further upheld tribal fishing rights in the case of *Tulee v. State of Washington*, 315 U.S. 681 (1942). In that case the Court held that the State could not charge license fees for fishing to Yakama tribal members.

One of the most significant cases upholding Treaty tribal rights to fishing was specific to the Gorge, arising in the 1960s. *Sohappy v. Smith*, 302 F. Supp. 899 (D. Or. 1969) began when fourteen members of the Yakama Nation filed suit against the State of Oregon for abrogating tribal fishing rights. Judge Belloni sided with the tribes in that case, declaring that the Treaties of 1855 required that tribes be allowed a "fair share" of the fishery harvest in the Columbia River. That decision was upheld by the Ninth Circuit Court of Appeals, 529 F.2d 570 (9th Cir. 1977) but remanded back to the District Court for the parties to develop management plans that fairly shared the fishery resource.

The Belloni "fair share doctrine" laid the groundwork for the next significant decision affecting Treaty tribe fishing rights in the Gorge, this time regarding the State of Washington's fishery regulations and management. The case of *United States v. State of Washington*, 384 F. Supp. 312 (W.D. Wash. 1974) is known as "the Boldt decision" for the name of the judge who signed the original Order and maintained jurisdiction over the case for years. The U.S. Attorney's office in Washington filed suit in 1970 against the State on behalf of various tribes (the Yakama joined the case as an intervenor), seeking to stop the State from arresting tribal members for fishing in alleged violation of state fishing regulations. The case took several years to reach an initial decision, but in 1974 Judge Boldt ruled in favor of the tribes, interpreting the phrase "in common with" found in the 1855 treaties to mean that there should be an equal sharing of the fisheries resource between Treaty tribes and non-Indians.

The Boldt decision created considerable controversy and further litigation that went on for years, but it was upheld by the Ninth Circuit federal appeals court, and the U.S. Supreme Court denied review of it. As remanded to Judge Boldt, the District Court was told to work out details of the rights to harvest with the State and other parties.

The *Winans* and *Tulee* cases, combined with the *Sohappy* and *Boldt* decisions, not only upheld Treaty rights to fish at usual and accustomed places, but they ultimately required various parties to work together in developing fish management plans in accord with Treaty rights. These cases contributed to the creation of the Columbia River Inter-Tribal Fish Commission in 1977, and they continue to influence fishery issues in the Gorge today.

At present, the Columbia River from Bonneville Dam upstream through the Gorge is designated as part of "Zone 6" for fishery regulation purposes (Zones 1-5 apply from the mouth of the Columbia upriver to the Bonneville Dam). Zone 6 is designated as an exclusive Treaty Indian commercial fishing area. Non-commercial sports fishers may still fish in this area, but are limited by season and run size that apply per species (there are separate rules and exclusions for salmon, steelhead, sturgeon, etc., and non-Indian fishing times and catch are closely regulated and often brief). Treaty tribe members may fish for subsistence and ceremonial purposes at any time.

## Agriculture and Industry

Euro-Americans came to the Gorge in the early 1800s in search of trapping (coastal expeditions sought sea otter while inland explorers trapped for beaver). As the Hudson Bay Company put down roots at Fort Vancouver in 1825 early settlers began logging, then commercial fishing and then construction of canneries. In the early 20$^{th}$ century apple, pear and cherry orchards were planted in the Hood River Valley and elsewhere.

Industry bracketed both ends of the Gorge for many years. The editor of the Portland Oregonian newspaper constructed a pulp and paper mill in

Camas, Washington in 1883 to provide newsprint for his papers. The mill grew over the decades, and the sulfur smell associated with pulp mills was noticeable for years in the west end of the Gorge and eastern Portland (the pulp lines were closed and the mill downsized by the early 2000s). In the 1940s and 1950s aluminum smelters were constructed at both Troutdale and The Dalles, and they also contributed noticeable air pollution to the Gorge. The smelters closed by the turn of the century. Both sites were then placed on EPA's National Priorities List (NPL) under Superfund. EPA certified cleanup for both sites and removed them from the NPL list by the late 1990s.

The most significant long-term impacts from commercial development in the Gorge are associated with construction of the dams from the 1930s to the 1950s. Hydroelectric power has been generated in the Gorge for nearly a century, at both the Bonneville and Dalles dams. The dams provide renewable energy for the Pacific Northwest and they are non-polluting, but their impact on fisheries has been long lasting.

Finally, following establishment of the National Scenic Area, tourism and recreation has become a leading industry in the Gorge. More than 90 vineyards and more than 40 wineries now exist in the Gorge, and in 2004 the eastern Gorge was designated an American Viticultural Area (the Columbia Gorge AVA), including portions of four counties (Hood River, Wasco, Skamania and Klickitat). In 2005 Google built a Data Center in The Dalles that has been expanded several times (representing an investment of more than $1.8 billion). Unlike the prior large business ventures Google is non-polluting (although like the paper mill and aluminum smelters they located in the Gorge to take advantage of available electricity generated by the dams). Logging and gravel production also continued as active commercial undertakings in the Gorge (gravel deposits courtesy of the Missoula floods).

## Recreation

Even before the Gorge received protected status it had long been a destination for hiking, biking, camping, kayaking, rafting, fishing, windsurfing and other outdoor pursuits. Today there are some 57 designated trails on Forest Service land (totaling over 200 miles of trail), 13 state parks, 7 day-use sites and 4 developed campgrounds (Eagle Creek, Wyeth, Hermann

Creek and Eagle Creek Overlook). There are also several State Parks that provide picnicking and camping opportunities. White water services and guides are available for both the White Salmon and Klickitat rivers. The Pacific Crest Trail crosses through the National Scenic Area (and across the Bridge of the Gods). There are numerous hiking trails in the National Scenic Area.

Windsurfing was introduced to Hood River and the Gorge by the late 1970s, and today the Gorge is an international windsurfing destination. Kite boarding and standup paddleboard activities have also developed. Visitors can see world class water sports in action at several points in the Gorge, such as the waterfront in Hood River, the "Fish Hatchery" just west of the Hood River bridge on the Washington side of the river, and Doug's Beach off Washington Highway 14 near milepost 79.

The three primary roads through the Gorge (I-84, Historic Highway 30 in Oregon and State Highway 14 in Washington) offer visitors picturesque views along their entire length. The Historic Columbia River Highway Trail is nearing the end of reconstruction (work visible from I-84 in several places), and the 200-mile loop Towns to Trails trekking project is more than half complete. There are shuttle bus tours, and several boat tour cruise options available.

Multnomah Falls is the most frequently visited spot in the Gorge, receiving more than 2 million visitors per year. Other sites frequently visited include The Columbia Gorge Discovery Center & Museum just west of The Dalles, MaryHill Museum at the east end of the Gorge off Highway 14, and the Bonneville Dam visitor center off Exit 40 of I-84 (which includes a remarkable viewing room to the fish ladder at the dam).

Increased recreational visits to the Gorge have helped build the local economy, from vineyards and wineries to breweries and brew pubs, restaurants and food provisions, guides and shopping. But with increased visits comes increased responsibilities to help preserve and protect the natural resources that make up the Gorge.

### Early Efforts Toward Preservation of the Gorge

There was interest in protecting the Gorge as a public resource as early as the beginning of the 20$^{th}$ century, when the first National Forests were established that bordered the river in both Oregon and Washington.

National Forest lands constitute a considerable percentage of the National Scenic Area as enacted in 1986 (roughly 40%). The Pacific Northwest Regional Planning Commission noted in 1937 that the Gorge was an asset of national significance and was deserving of protection (but then that Commission went on to plan for the development of dams in the Gorge and the upper Columbia River).

Other efforts to consider the Gorge for protected status surfaced on several occasions after WWII. In the 1950s the states of Oregon and Washington both created Gorge Commissions to study the issue, but both disbanded with no concrete results. Efforts re-surfaced in the 1970s, where interstate commissions worked with counties to consider zoning provisions that could help protect Gorge acreage.

In 1979, the National Park Service conducted a study of the Gorge, issuing a report that recommended protection of the Gorge to avoid further loss of undisturbed acreage and habitat. The presence of established communities and population made National Park status unrealistic, and for the same reasons the Gorge did not meet the criteria for wilderness designation. After Mount St. Helens erupted in 1980, the call for protection of the Gorge became more focused as Congressional efforts to preserve the St. Helens blast area were fast tracked (in part because there was pressure to conduct salvage logging at the perimeter of the blast zone).

There was also a major change in political will for creating new federal lands after the 1980 Presidential election, as the new Reagan Administration appeared to have less interest in creating new areas of federal protection. The fast-track negotiations on the preservation of Mount St. Helens were effective in achieving creation of the Mount St. Helens National Volcanic Monument in 1982 (encompassing 110,000 acres), only two years after the volcano erupted. As it became obvious that the Gorge would not meet the criteria for a National Park, other types of protection were considered. In 1984 Mono Lake became the nation's first National Scenic Area, and the Columbia River Gorge ended up following that track, finding Legislative (and Executive) branch approval in late 1986. Several groups had been either proposing or objecting to federal land management in the Gorge. Those groups in favor of protecting the resource, including the Friends of the Gorge, managed to effectively help marshal Congressional support that was able to finalize passage of the Columbia River Gorge National Scenic Area Act in late 1986.

## E. CURRENT LIFE & PROTECTION OF THE GORGE: 1986 TO PRESENT

There were significant changes in human use of the Gorge and numerous environmental impacts to the Gorge in the century after Oregon and Washington became states in the late 1800s. Largely in response to those impacts, a new chapter in Gorge history began in 1986 with enactment of the Columbia River Gorge National Scenic Area Act.

### The Columbia River Gorge National Scenic Area Act

Decades of interest in preserving the natural beauty of the Gorge culminated in 1986 with Congressional creation and Presidential approval of the Columbia River Gorge National Scenic Area Act (16 U.S.C. 544 *et seq*) (the Gorge was the second National Scenic Area created in the U.S., after establishment of the Mono Lake National Scenic Area in 1984). Senators Mark Hatfield of Oregon and Dan Evans of Washington were instrumental in getting the Scenic Area legislation passed, as were various House Representatives and citizen groups, most notably the Friends of the Columbia Gorge.

The Scenic Area as created by Congress in 1986 established a boundary that contained approximately 292,500 acres. The area was a mix of federal, state and private land. The statute designated 13 existing towns or municipalities within that boundary as Urban Areas, including in Oregon: Cascade Locks, Hood River, Mosier and The Dalles; and in Washington: Bingen, Carson, Dallesport, Home Valley, Lyle, North Bonneville, Stevenson, White Salmon and Wishram (16 U.S.C. 544b(e)). Those Urban Areas, along with rural residents, combined to include a population within the Scenic Area of about 44,000 people at the time of enactment (increased to about 50,000 by 2000 and 75,000 by 2020). Roughly half of all residents in the Gorge live in one of the designated Urban Areas.

The statute also created Special Management Areas (SMA) to include existing federal lands, primarily U.S. Forest Service, and General

Management Areas (GMA), which include private property within the Scenic Area boundaries, as well as the Columbia River. The Forest Service oversees federal lands (SMA) in the Scenic Area, while the Columbia River Gorge Commission oversees lands in the GMA, including private property. Private property in the GMA designation is subject to National Scenic Area Act land use and construction permit requirements, as are roads and bridges in the Gorge. Private property within the 13 Urban Areas is not subject to the building permit requirements applicable in the GMA. At the time of enactment, the 292,500 acre Scenic Area was comprised of approximately 40% SMA, 50% GMA and 10% Urban areas.

As enacted, the Columbia River Gorge National Scenic Area Act has two express purposes:

> "*(1) to establish a national scenic area to protect and provide for the enhancement of the scenic, cultural, recreational, and natural resources of the Columbia River Gorge;* *and*
>
> *(2) to protect and support the economy of the Columbia River Gorge area by encouraging growth to occur in existing urban areas and by allowing future economic development in a manner that is consistent with paragraph (1).*"
>
> 16 U.S.C. 544(a), Section 3.

These goals (*protect scenic, cultural and natural resources* but also *protect the economy by encouraging growth...in existing urban areas*) reflect an unusual balance struck by Congress. There was little appetite in Congress for acquiring ("taking") private property, but there was also strong pressure to protect the Gorge from further development. The statutory goals were not intended to be in opposition to one another, but there is clearly some tension in attempting to "protect and enhance" natural resources while "encouraging growth... and economic development" within the same area. Time has shown, however, that these goals can be given effect, and that not without difficulty the goals can in fact be complementary.

The framework established by Congress to manage these potentially conflicting purposes was the Columbia River Gorge Commission (or

CRGC). The CRGC is comprised of 12 Commissioners and 1 non-voting member. Three Commissioners from each state are appointed by the Governors of Oregon and Washington, and one Commissioner is appointed from each of the 6 counties in the National Scenic Area (3 each in Oregon and Washington). By law, one of the three commissioners appointed by each governor must live in the Gorge. In addition, although not required by the statute, in recent years the states have included as one or more of their representatives a member from the four Treaty Indian tribes who have rights to the Columbia River area. The CRGC appoints an Executive Director, who is an employee of the Forest Service and the non-voting member of the CRGC.

The National Scenic Area Act directed the CRGC to prepare a Management Plan and then review and revise it every 10 years. The Commission produced the first Management Plan in 1991. The first revision was issued in 2004. The Commission began working on the second revision of the Management Plan in 2016, and in late 2020 proposed a new amended version. The most recent version of the Plan discusses climate change, increases stream buffers and perhaps most significantly limits future expansion of Gorge Urban Area boundaries to no more than 50 acres (in maximum 20-acre increments). The Gorge Commission issues permits for all new or modified construction on private land (in the GMA) and for new or revised roads and bridges. Five of the six counties write permits under the supervision of the Gorge Commission, while Klickitat County elected not to participate, resulting in the Gorge Commission issuing permits directly in that county.

There were several legal challenges to the Columbia Gorge National Scenic Area Act and the Gorge Commission in early years, but none were successful and both the National Scenic Area Act and Gorge Commission structure remain intact. Challenges to the initial Management Plan and permit decisions on Constitutional "takings" grounds were also rejected. Other legal challenges arose in following years to permits issued or other actions taken by the Gorge Commission. Those decisions, either by the Gorge Commission itself or reviewing courts, have helped refine the permit and management efforts by the Gorge Commission.

Interpretive/Visitor Center and Conference Center

The Scenic Area Act allocated a one-time amount of $10 million in funds to help construct an interpretive/visitor center on the Oregon side of the river and a conference center on the Washington side. 16 U.S.C. Section 544f(d). The Columbia Gorge Discovery Center & Museum just west of The Dalles is the visitor center envisioned by the Act. The visitor center was combined with a new Wasco County Museum, as inclusion of that venue allowed for more funding and a larger facility. Skamania Lodge near Stevenson is the conference center envisioned by the Act. The Lodge has more than 250 guest rooms, 22,000 square feet of conference space, an 18-hole golf course and various activities and programs. It also has interpretative exhibits.

Other than the initial construction funds allocated in the Act, no additional federal funds support either the interpretive/visitor center or the conference center. Skamania Lodge has become a popular destination resort and is self-supporting. The Discovery Center relies on membership and contributions, and various funding assistance from State or local sources.

## F. LOOKING AHEAD

The Gorge finally received protected status as a National Scenic Area more than 35 years ago. The National Scenic Area designation recognized that this place of natural beauty and history was deserving of protection, even though it also contained transportation corridors, urban areas and commercial activities. Time has shown it is possible to both *protect natural resources* while also *encouraging economic growth* consistent with protection of natural resources. That balance is constantly in challenge, though, and new issues often arise. Among future issues to watch are the following:

Traffic and Trail Access

Like many popular national parks the Gorge is at risk of being loved to death. Traffic on the Historic Highway 30 waterfall route has become gridlocked in the summer, and parking areas for major trailheads are overwhelmed with cars parking unsafely along the highways, on both sides of the river. Some effort to manage this overuse has begun at both Multnomah Falls and the Dog Mountain trailhead, but more action will inevitably be required. Beginning in May of 2022, the waterfall route along Historic Highway 30 now requires an online permit to drive through. That system is planned to be in place from May to September of each year. It seems likely that the waterfall corridor of Historic Highway 30 will ultimately need to be closed to private traffic other than shuttle buses, service and emergency vehicles (while still open to hikers and bikes) with visitors using shuttle buses or time permitted parking in the Exit 31 parking area along the Interstate. Similarly, parking areas at several trailheads will likely need to be expanded and/or relocated. And it seems inevitable than a permit system will be required for many of the more popular trails in the summer. None of these restrictions are welcomed by visitors or users, but without them both the visitor experience and – more importantly – the resource itself may be at risk.

### Fisheries Management and Restoration

Salmon, steelhead and other fish native to the Gorge are inextricably bound with the history and current life of this place. The Columbia River was overfished for a century, followed by loss of spawning habitat from construction of dams and limitations on the ability of anadromous fish to navigate the dams. Pressure from the tribes and decisions by the courts have required significant action by state and federal agencies to help restore the fisheries, and some progress has been made. The fate of too many fishery resources is still in jeopardy, however, and more action will be required.

### Hydro and Energy Development

More dams from Columbia River tributaries will likely be removed in coming years (these are aging dams no longer being used for hydropower), and there is continuing effort to remove some of the Snake River dams to help preservation and restoration of salmon and steelhead runs.

There will also be continued efforts to establish wind energy resources in or near the National Scenic Area, even though lands just east of the Columbia Gorge are already thick with wind turbines. The Gorge Commission and the Friends of the Gorge have to date resisted construction of any wind farms in the National Scenic Area, including those beyond the National Scenic Area boundaries but visible from within the National Scenic Area (the National Scenic Area Act expressly seeks to preserve scenic view values). The Gorge Commission does allow individual landowners within the National Scenic Area to construct small private solar or wind installations for residential use, provided they are in compliance with all requirements (especially regarding visibility from *Key Viewing Areas.*)

## Urban Boundaries, the Management Plan and Climate Change

Several of the larger urban areas within the Gorge have expressed interest in expanding their boundaries. The National Scenic Area statute is quite clear on the burden a city needs to carry to show such a need (16 U.S.C. 544b(f)), but the requests continue. Many urban areas, like The Dalles and Dallesport, have considerable vacant land already within their boundaries, and other cities could easily encourage vertical expansion instead of urban growth.

The urban boundary issue was addressed in the 2020-22 update to the Gorge Commission's Management Plan. Climate change was also preliminarily addressed, and stream buffer zones were expanded. These issues will continue to present challenges in the coming years, and visitors and residents of the Gorge can become involved in those decision-making processes through public comment.

## Fire Prevention and Management

A century of overly aggressive fire suppression combined with the effects of climate change have made the risk of forest fire an almost year-round concern in the American West, including the Gorge. Fires in recent years have been driven by extreme heat, prolonged drought and wind. The results have been catastrophic. Fires are influenced by fuel, weather and topography, and the Gorge has heavy fuel, strong winds and steep slopes in abundance.

The Gorge has burned before, and it will burn again. Government officials (at all levels), National Scenic Area and Forest Service managers can help reduce risk of catastrophic fire in the Gorge through prevention and management efforts such as mandating or encouraging more strict building codes that emphasize the establishment and maintenance of defensible fire perimeters around buildings. Continued stationing of rapid response fire suppression resources throughout the ever lengthening fire season can also help prevent catastrophic wildfire in the Gorge (this is already being done with positioning of small water scooping aircraft at The Dalles airport and interagency agreements among state and county fire agencies to respond aggressively to all fire starts without regard to jurisdictional boundaries). Residents and visitors can help reduce risk of fire by exercising care in all activities in and travel through the Gorge, as most wildfires in current times are human caused.

Towns to Trails

This initiative promises to create a world class trekking destination in the form of a 200-mile loop trail around the Gorge, connecting towns, vineyards, wineries, breweries and lodging with scenic trails and viewpoints. These efforts are being done with minimal environmental impacts and will help bring new economic development to the Gorge in a manner fully consistent with the intent of the National Scenic Area Act. About half of the trail is already complete (including reconstruction of the Historic Columbia River Highway/Route 30 which will include walking and biking sections) and more than 80% of the land has been acquired to bring the project to completion. Many governmental entities and other groups are supporting this effort, and public support is encouraged. When complete, the Towns to Trails system is likely to become one of the more popular and well-known features of the Gorge.

The Columbia River Gorge is a place of natural beauty, with a unique geologic history. It provides habitat for a wide variety of plants and animals in various ecosystems that range from temperate rain forest to high desert, in the span of less than 85 miles. It has long been a place of human habitation (primarily by First Peoples), and despite significant development over the past 150 years the natural beauty and ecological diversity of the Gorge perseveres.

The Columbia River Gorge National Scenic Area Act of 1986 and the oversight efforts of both government and public interest groups help preserve and protect the Gorge for future generations. But the Gorge needs your help, too. The more we learn about the natural history of the Gorge, as residents and visitors alike, the better inclined we may be to help preserve it.

# CHAPTER NOTES

## Chapter VI: People (Prehistory, History and Current Life)

1. *Peopling of the Americas*. Since the 1950s the prevailing scientific opinion was that humans came to North America at the end of the last ice age across a land bridge at the Bering Strait between Siberia and what is now Alaska. That theory was based on certain stone tools called "Clovis points" that were found in the U.S. and dated to sites around 13,000 years old, roughly in line with the end of the last glaciation. New analytical methods – including the study of ancient DNA and reconstruction of ancient genomes – now show that the Bering Strait land bridge theory was simply wrong. Humans have been in North and South America for at least 15,000 years, and likely longer than 20,000 years. A recent book summarizing these new developments is *Origin: A Genetic History of the Americas,* by Jennifer Rafferty *(Twelve Books 2022).*
2. *Archaeological evidence in the Gorge*. As Prof. Scott Burns has pointed out, the glacial (Bretz) floods some 15,000 to 18,000 years ago likely scoured out almost all evidence of human occupation in the Gorge preceding those dates. Archaeological evidence of past human presence in the Gorge has to date been limited to activities after the time of the glacial floods.
3. *Some 300 indigenous languages* were spoken in North America at the time of European contact. Some were related enough to be understandable by non-speakers (e.g., Upper Chinookan, Lower Chinookan and Kathlamet were understandable among each other, as were the Sahaptin-Penutian languages spoken by Yakama and related groups, in comparison to the Nez Perce-Penutian language), but most were distinct languages not understood by others. The Gorge had an unusual concentration of languages, both because of the natural resources that allowed population density, and because of the trade that occurred annually at Celilo Falls that brought various groups and languages in contact.

4. *The Doctrine of Discovery* as it affected native peoples is analyzed in a superb summary by law Professor Robert Miller of Arizona State University (formerly with the Lewis & Clark Law School) (also a Kiowa Indian). *See Discovering Indigenous Lands: The Doctrine of Discovery in the English Colonies (Oxford Univ. Press 2012).*
5. *Derivation of the Word "Ouragon."* American Robert Gray is said to have noted that the Indians referred to the river he had just named the Columbia when he first crossed the bar in 1792 as Ouragon, but the source of the word Oregon is not clear. It appeared in writing at least as early as 1765 in an English army report referring to potential travel from the Mississippi River to a western river said to be called "Ouragon" by the Indians (the army report referring to the long sought Northwest Passage). Others theorize the term came from the French word for Hurricane (referring to the strong winds in the Gorge), or from a blend of Algonquin and Cree words meaning big river. Of course, the Indians already had names for the Columbia River, but the source of the word that came to denote first the Territory and then the State of Oregon remains uncertain.
6. *Exploration and Influence of the Gorge by Land before Lewis & Clark*. One of the more interesting entries in the journals of Lewis & Clark is a note Clark recorded on their return trip from the Pacific. On April 11, 1806, Lewis & Clark visited a group of the "Clah-clel-lah" Indians near present day Stevenson, Washington, and were presented with "*a large fine pipe tomahawk*" that was said by the locals to have come from a non-Indian man called Swippeton, who had come from the north and also traded some "*well baked Saylors biscuits*" to the Indians. From this encounter, Clark concluded that there was "*no doubt but the traders who winter in the inlets to the N. of us visit this part of the Columbia by land at certain seasons...*" Swippeton was presumably a sailor associated with some British coastal expedition, but no record of his name has yet been found on ship logs or other documents. Similarly, while spending the winter at Fort Clatsop on the Oregon coast, Lewis & Clark heard many stories of Europeans or Americans who had visited the lower Columbia since Robert Gray and George Vancouver first entered the river in 1792. These encounters illustrate that Euro-American contacts with the Gorge occurred before Lewis & Clark arrived.

7. *The Journals of Lewis & Clark*. The Univ. of Nebraska Press has published the original Journals of the Lewis & Clark Expedition in 15 hard cover volumes, including full reproductions of all maps and drawings. Bernard DeVoto's *Journals of Lewis & Clark* is one of the best single volume abridged versions of the journals. Stephen Ambrose's *Undaunted Courage* adds background and presents more perspectives on the Expedition. One of the more interesting books (of the multitude) on Lewis & Clark is a history of what happened to the various members of the Expedition after their return: *The Fate of the Corps*, by Larry Morris (Yale Univ. Press 2004).
8. *The Astorians Expedition*. Astor had a global plan to trap furs from the Pacific Northwest, transport and trade them to China, then bring goods from China to Europe and finally transport items from Europe back to the U.S. to use as trade goods for procurement of more furs from the Northwest. President Jefferson supported the idea in order to get an American foothold and claim of right in the Northwest. The Astorian expeditions were every bit as adventurous as the Lewis & Clark journey, but unfortunately much more tragic in loss of life and then ultimate failure. An excellent book about the journey is *Astoria* by Peter Stark (Harper Collins 2015).
9. *"The End of the Oregon Trail."* The Oregon Trail effectively ended at The Dalles, where immigrants either went further downstream by rapids, or – after 1846 – took the Barlow Road over Mt. Hood. Many immigrants were headed for the Willamette Valley, but they often had to go to Oregon City to file land claims (all land claims for the entire Northwest were filed there in the early years). Oregon City thus claims to be the official "End of the Oregon Trail."
10. *A Northwest Passage* by water from the Atlantic to the Pacific Oceans was sought from the very first by European explorers. Of course, it did not exist, at least not in convenient form. The Rocky Mountains present a rather significant challenge to water travel from the Missouri River to the Columbia River. A Northwest Passage finally did appear in recent years, although far to the north: climate change has thawed the Arctic enough that in most years since 2007 an ice-free passage from Canada to the north slope of Alaska appears for some perioed of time in the summer, populated with thousands of icebergs.

11. <u>*Current Population of the Gorge*</u>. Angie Brewer, a former planner with the Gorge Commission and currently Director of the Wasco County Planning Department, prepared a paper for the Gorge Commission in 2020 on "*Population Demographics of the Columbia River Gorge National Scenic Area*." That paper showed the increase in population within Scenic Area boundaries from the year 2000 (about 50,000 residents at that time) to about 75,000 residents in 2020. More than half of the residents of the National Scenic Area live within the boundaries of one of the 13 designated Urban Areas, which comprise only about 10% of the land area of the National Scenic Area (and most of that group – some 24,000 people – live in either The Dalles or Hood River, showing that resident/urban area population is concentrated in those two cities on the east end of the National Scenic Area). Further growth is expected in the coming decades, but it will likely continue to be concentrated within the designated Urban Areas.

**Population of Columbia River Gorge Communities 1890-2020**

| City | Early Estimates | 2020 Population |
|---|---|---|
| Bingen | 365 (1930) | 778 |
| Carson | -- | 2,830 |
| Cascade Locks | 703 (1940) | 1,379 |
| Dallesport | -- | 1,328 |
| Home Valley | -- | -- |
| Hood River | 201 (1890) | 8,313 |
| Lyle | -- | 518 |
| Mosier | 259 (1920) | 468 |
| North Bonneville | -- | 1,397 |
| Stevenson | 387 (1910) | 1,491 |
| The Dalles | 3,239 (1890) | 16,010 |
| White Salmon | 682 (1910) | 920 |
| Wishram | -- | 366 |

compare

| Portland | 46,385 (1890) | 652,503 |
|---|---|---|
| Seattle | 42,837 (1890) | 737,015 |

Source: U.S. Census Data; biggestuscities.com (city data only, not metropolitan or county data) Most 1890 U.S. Census records were destroyed in a fire; only some records and estimates remain

Note that by 2020 the greater metropolitan area of Portland had increased to about 2.5 million people, and Seattle's greater metropolitan area increased to about 4 million.

12. *Restoration of Historic Highway 30*. When Congress enacted the Columbia River Gorge National Scenic Area Act in 1986 it included a directive to the Oregon Department of Transportation to "*restore the continuity and historic integrity of the remaining segments of the Old Columbia River Highway for public use as a Historic Road*." 16 U.S.C. 544j.
13. *Early Efforts to Preserve the Gorge*. In the late 1970s and early 1980s several groups formed with varying ideas on how to protect the Gorge. Chuck Williams, a descendant of the Cascades Indians, organized the Columbia Gorge Coalition. Chuck had worked with Friends of the Earth on National Park issues, so he was inclined to pursue National Park status. Gertrude Jensen (who with the Women's Forum purchased then donated Chanticleer Point to the State of Oregon in the 1950s to preserve it) was part of another group called Save the Gorge. Somewhat surprisingly, for all her prior efforts Gertrude ended up opposing the National Scenic Area Act, believing it did not adequately address private property interests.
14. *Biography of Nancy Russell*. Nancy Russell was one of the founders of the Friends of the Gorge citizen group, and she worked tirelessly toward establishing federal protection of the Gorge. Bowen Blair has written a thorough biography of Nancy, titled *A Force for Nature: Nancy Russell's Fight to Save the Gorge* (Oregon State Univ. Press 2022). Bowen Blair is an environmental lawyer who was also involved in the initial organizing of the Friends of the Gorge. Bowen subsequently served on and was a Chair of the Gorge Commission.

15. *Types of Federally Protected Land*. There are more than 25,000 federally protected areas in the U.S. at present, encompassing roughly 14% of America's land mass. The U.S. has always been a leader in land conservation, and at present has approximately 10% of all protected areas in the world. *UNEP World Database on Protected Areas (2015).* The types of protected areas range from National Forests and National Parks to National Preserves, Seashores or Lakeshores, as well as National Wildlife Refuges and National Recreation Areas, National Grasslands, National Conservation Lands, Wilderness, Roadless Areas, National Historic Sites, Wild & Scenic Rivers, Scenic Trails, etc. In addition, there are Marine Sanctuaries, Estuarine Research Reserves, etc. These areas have varying levels of protection.
16. *Vineyards and Wineries*. Early pioneers planted some grape vines for personal use, but it was not until the 1970s and 1980s that vineyards were planted for commercial viticulture purposes in the Gorge. Several wineries followed. In 2004 some 1300 acres in the eastern Gorge were officially designated as the *Columbia Gorge American Viticultural Area (AVA)* (including parts of Hood River, Wasco, Klickitat and Skamania counties). Although a relatively small area, the *terroir* of this eastside area produces some outstanding wines and is referred to as "a world of wine in 40 miles."
17. *Trails and Destinations*. Good trail information is available on several websites, including: the Friends of the Columbia Gorge (www.gorgefriends.org/hike-the-gorge/find-a-hike); Trailkeepers of Oregon (www.oregonhikers.org/field guide/Columbia River Gorge Hikes) and AllTrails (www.alltrails.com/parks/us/oregon/columbia-river-gorge-national-scenic-area). In addition, there is fascinating and informative book titled *Curious Gorge*, by Scott Cook (Maverick Publications 4th Ed. 2017), that is full of little-known facts, locations and interesting hikes and side trips in the Gorge.
18. *Museums and Local Attractions*. Most of the urban areas inside the National Scenic Area boundaries have museums or local attractions well worth a visit, including Troutdale, Cascade Locks, Hood River, The Dalles, Lyle, Bingen, Stevenson and others. Check their websites for details.

# NATURAL HISTORY of the COLUMBIA RIVER GORGE

*--- TIMELINE ---*

©

***Robert Hogfoss***

**(to accompany the book *Natural History of the Columbia River Gorge*)**

*The earth is about 4.5 billion years old, but we can fast forward to set the backdrop for the story of the Gorge as we find it today. The Columbia River has flowed through this area for about 40 million years. Then some 17 million years ago, in the Miocene geologic epoch, huge basalt lava floods began to create the layer cake landscape that we find in the Gorge and eastern plateau today. From there we fast forward again to about 2 million years ago, in the Pleistocene geologic epoch. During that relatively recent geologic time, volcanic eruptions and other events created many of the major features found today in and around the Gorge. Then as the last Ice Age glaciers began to melt and retreat, from 15,000 to 18,000 years ago, a series of massive glacial floods scoured the Gorge to leave the fjord-like river course we find today. And then human and more recent natural events begin to fill the record. But let's start 17 million years ago...*

**17 to 5 million years before present (in the Miocene geologic epoch): Basalt Lava Floods** spread across eastern Washington and Oregon, including the Gorge (some 270 basalt floods occurred across what is now eastern Oregon and Washington, but only an estimated 21 covered the Gorge). These were horizontal floods of lava that accumulated to become as thick as 2,000 feet in the Gorge area. They did not erupt, but simply oozed out and spread. Many of these individual lava floods are visible today as you drive through the Gorge (looking like layer cakes). As flows cooled, many formed columnar basalt (usually as six sided columns of rock), and the tops of such columns often cracked from cooling more rapidly than the bottom, creating stacked columns ("columnar basalt"). When lava encountered water it created more diffuse "entablature" or "pillow" basalt instead of columns. Most of the lava flows occurred during the first two million years of these outpourings but continued for another ten million years.

**5 to 2 million years before present: Columbia River continues to erode its way through the basalt plateau (Pliocene geologic epoch).** The Columbia River has flowed through this area for about 40 million years, so the river valley was present before the lava floods began. Basalt lava followed the flow of the riverbed toward the coast, sometimes changing the course of the river (slowly moving it northward). Then as the lava flows cooled and weather events continued (for millions of years) the course of the river deepened.

**2 million to 500,000 years before present (Pleistocene geologic epoch): hundreds of volcanoes erupt** from south to north across current Oregon and Washington, creating the Cascade Mountain range that forms the base of the stratovolcanoes we recognize today as Mt. Hood, Mt. Adams and other high Cascade peaks. The Cascade Mountains began roughly 37 million years ago, but this relatively more recent period of activity gave us the shape of the mountains we see today. Near the end of this period **the Cascade Range begins uplift, creating synclines and anticlines** in the basalt flood lava flows laid down previously – this is visible in many places in the eastside Gorge, such as at Mosier in Oregon and Coyote Wall in Washington.

**500,000 years before present: Volcanic Eruptions further shape Mt. Hood and Mt. Adams** to the forms we see today, followed by other significant eruptions about 15,000 years ago up to the past two hundred years. Both volcanoes have the potential to erupt again.

**18,000 to 15,000 years before present (we are now in the Holocene geologic epoch):** The **Missoula (or Bretz) Glacial Floods** scour the Gorge at least 40 times as lobes of continental ice sheets form and dam a huge Glacial Lake Missoula as they melt, then break through the dams and flood their way to the coast. Melt water backed up over a very large area and then broke though the ice dams, creating the largest floods in the history of the planet, and in the process carving out the sharp relief we see today in the Gorge. Each time the glacial lobe collapsed and advanced again these ice dams and subsequent floods occurred again and again. A Seattle geologist named J Harlan Bretz was the first to recognize in the 1920s that the Central Washington and Northern Oregon landscapes were carved by some massive flood event, even though he did not yet know the source of the flood or that it occurred repeatedly. His observation was not fully endorsed until decades later, after satellite photos and more ground investigations proved his theory.

**~15,000+ years before present**: **American Indian habitation and use of the Gorge**. There is considerable controversy about when people first came to North America, but it is generally accepted that native peoples have been in the Pacific Northwest for at least the past 14,500 years, and probably much longer. Regardless of the time of first arrival, American Indians truly were – and are – the first people of the Gorge. Because of its unique habitat and fisheries, the Gorge is believed to be one of the longest continuously inhabited areas in North America. Groups that have lived in or near the Gorge for millennia include Wasco, Wishram, Yakama, Klickitat, Nez Perce, Umatilla, Cayuse, Walla Walla, Paiute, Chinook, Cascade, Molalla, Clackamas, Cowlitz, Multnomah and Kalapuya.

**7,700 years before present: Mount Mazama erupts (creating Crater Lake in its caldera).** Mt. Lassen erupts in 1915; and Mount St. Helens erupts in 1980.

**1,500 years before present: Mt. Hood eruptions** contribute lahar mud flows that clog the Sandy River delta.

**1450 CE (common era, or A.D.):** a series of four large **landslides from Table Mountain and Greenleaf Mountain** (covering an area of five square miles) **completely block the Columbia River** between what is now Cascade Locks and the Bonneville Dam. The slides create a 200-foot-high rock and earth dam and land bridge across the River (giving credence to the native stories about a **Bridge of the Gods**). This natural dam backed up the river for nearly 100 miles (roughly to the current location of Pasco), creating a pool that covered rapids upstream to Celilo Falls. As the water backed up, the building pressure eventually cut a new channel near the south bank of the landslide dam, **creating the Cascades Rapids** from landslide debris. The date of this landslide event was estimated by Donald Lawrence in the 1930s to be between 1250 and 1560 (using dendrochronology to compare tree rings). That estimate was later revised (in the 1970s) to 1450 using radiocarbon dating on some of the same tree core samples initially obtained by Lawrence. It is likely that the landslides were triggered by a large earthquake.

**1480-82: eruptions of Mount St. Helens** contribute more lahar mud flows to the Columbia River.

**1559-62: the Strait of Anian** rumored to be a narrow ocean passage between Asia and North America. Likely linked to Marco Polo's reference to the Anian Province in China (in his book published in 1559), this rumor evolved to become part of the **imagined Northwest Passage** of a waterway that would link eastern North America to the west coast. The first map showing Anian was made in 1562.

**1579-1776**: **coastal explorations** sponsored by Britain, Spain and Russia, beginning with British captain **Sir Francis Drake** in 1579 pass the Oregon coast and the mouth of the Columbia River. Many of these expeditions left place names along the West Coast that continue today (**Juan de Fuca** in 1592; **Vitus Bering** in the 1740s; **Bruno de Hecata** in 1775; and **James Cook** in 1776). The only one of these early expeditions that spotted the mouth of the Columbia River was Hecata, who on August 17, 1775 attempted to cross the bar, but found it too dangerous.

**1700 (January 26; 9:00 p.m.): Cascadia Earthquake**, registering between an estimated magnitude 8.7 and 9.2 strikes a 600 mile stretch of the Pacific NW, from Seattle to northern California. The quake moved the ground in and near the Gorge as much as 60 feet and triggered massive landslides. The exact date and estimated time of the earthquake was identified by tsunami records in Japan.

**1709**: **maps of North America** drawn after the written accounts of the Frenchman Louis Armand (the self-described Baron of Lahontan) **show a River of the West** (Louis called it the Longue River) flowing from the center of the continent to the Pacific Ocean. Lahonton was in the French military around the Great Lakes and upper Mississippi in the late 1680s (until he deserted), and he was an avid explorer who learned several Indian languages. He wrote a book that was popular in Europe and was used as a source for maps for nearly 100 years, and it encouraged further exploration of the American West. Even in Lahontan's day, however, it was widely believed that he exaggerated greatly (*e.g.*, he claimed that crocodiles would be found in the Longue River), thus his accounts were viewed with some skepticism. It is likely that his reports of a large river system reaching across the West were based on stories he heard from Indians about the Missouri and Columbia rivers.

**1722**: Pierre Francois Xavier de Charlevoix, **a Jesuit priest and explorer** in the area west of Quebec and the Great Lakes, **writes** to his benefactor (the Duke of Orleans) **about a rumored great western river**: "I have good reason to think that . . . after sailing up the Missouri as far as it is navigable you come to a great river which runs westward and discharges into the sea." His comments were undoubtedly based on accounts by Indians, since tribes from far away had traveled to and traded at Celilo Falls for millennia.

**1730s-60s**: **introduction of the horse** to tribes of the American West (captured or escaped from Spanish explorers in Mexico). A small ancient horse (*Eohippus*) was present in the Northwest some 50 million years ago (but was not a progenitor of the modern horse).

**1780-1781**: **widespread smallpox epidemics** observed by French Canadian trappers in the upper Northwest, accounts of which were later reported to Lewis & Clark by Indians living in and around the Gorge. Various diseases were introduced to the native peoples both from coastal contacts and direct or indirect contacts with inland Europeans (Spanish, French or British).

**1781**: **eruption of Mt. Hood** deposits lahar mudflow to Columbia via the Sandy River (shifting the Columbia River northward as found during both Broughton's visit in 1792 and Lewis & Clark in 1805-06).

**1792 (May 11-20): Columbia River named by American sea captain Robert Gray, who is the first non-Indian to cross the bar into the River.** He names the river after his privately-owned ship (the *Columbia Rediviva*), which was the first American ship to circumnavigate the globe and which Gray was using to pursue the sea otter fur trade when he discovered the Columbia River entrance. Gray noticed muddy water coming from the coast near latitude 46.16 degrees north, and correctly guessed that it might be from "the great river of the west." Even though a private citizen, Gray claimed the Columbia River for the U.S. He made a chart of the mouth of the River and traded with natives, then left after nine days.

**1792: botanist Archibald Menzies first observes what is now called the Douglas fir tree** on the coast of British Columbia, while serving on George Vancouver's British exploration ship. Doug fir (*Psuedotsuga menziesii*) is one of the most common trees found in the Gorge, especially on the west side (although it is neither a fir nor a false hemlock, as the common and scientific names suggest).

**1792 (Oct. 20 – 30):** Several months after American Robert Gray entered (and named) the Columbia River, **British explorer Captain George Vancouver's expedition sails up the Columbia River**, having obtained a copy of Gray's chart of the mouth of the river (Gray left a copy of his chart with traders in Nootka Sound before sailing for China, and Vancouver made a copy while stopped there). Vancouver attempted unsuccessfully to get his large ship Discovery across the bar, but managed to get another, smaller ship from that expedition into the river (the HMS Chatham, under the command of Lt. W.R. Broughton). Broughton sailed **as far up the Columbia as the Sandy River, and** on behalf of Vancouver **named Mt. Hood and Mount St. Helens** (the first after British Admiral Samuel Hood, and the latter after the British diplomat Alleyne Fitzherbert, the "First Baron of St. Helens"). Of course, the River and the mountains were already named by first peoples long before these new visitors presumed to add their gloss (the native name for Mt. Hood was Wy'East; LooWit for St. Helens). **Vancouver's expedition had named Mt. Rainier earlier that year** while in the Puget Sound (named for British Admiral Peter Rainier); the native name for that mountain was and is Tahoma.

**1792: Significantly, American and British explorers both laid claim to the entire Columbia Basin under "the Doctrine of Discovery,"** without either country actually entering or exploring the area. The American Robert Gray made his claim on behalf of the U.S. in May of 1792, and the British Captain George Vancouver did likewise in October of that year. The dispute over which nation held claim over the Columbia River and its basin was not resolved until the Treaty of Oregon in 1846 (agreement between Great Britain and the U.S.).

**1793 (July 22): British explorer Alexander Mackenzie reaches the Pacific Ocean on an overland trek across Canada**, looking for the Northwest Passage. Mackenzie tried to reach the Pacific in 1789 but ended up on the Arctic Ocean in northern Canada, along what it is now known as the Mackenzie River. In 1792 he tried again, and after spending a winter in waiting he followed what is now the Fraser River to the Coast Range, then crossed to the Bella Coola River to the Pacific in B.C. Mackenzie published a book about his travels in 1801, titled *Voyages from Montreal.* Thomas Jefferson read the book and became determined to get an American presence in the Pacific Northwest.

**1801**: **another epidemic of smallpox** occurs among Indians living in and around the Gorge and the Willamette valley, presumably triggered by European contacts from the coast (evidence of a recent outbreak was visible and testimony about it was offered to Lewis & Clark on their return trip upriver in 1806).

**1803**: **President Jefferson acquires the Louisiana Purchase** from France (roughly 828,000 square miles) for an amount equal to about $15M in 1803 dollars (50 million francs cash and cancellation of 18 million francs in debt owed to the U.S.). This gave the U.S. a claim to all land from New Orleans up the Mississippi and Missouri Rivers, and west to the Continental Divide along the Rocky Mountains. The claim did not include the Pacific Northwest, which was not yet fully explored enough to map and not subject to France's claim of ownership, but it was Jefferson's goal to use the Louisiana Purchase as a launching ground to explore and claim the Northwest.

**1804-1806**: sent by President Jefferson, **the Lewis & Clark expedition passes through the Gorge**, spending a total of 36 days in what is now the Scenic Area: 13 days downriver (Oct 22 - Nov 3, 1805), and 23 days on their return upstream (Mar 31 - April 22, 1806). Lewis & Clark provided the first written record and observations of the Gorge, its inhabitants and characteristics (even though the British in late 1792 were first to sail up the Columbia as far as the Sandy River, they never entered the Gorge). Lewis & Clark identified many plants and animals of the Gorge that were new to science, and their names remain associated with many (*e.g.*, Lewis' Woodpecker, Clark's Nutcracker, etc).

> **In the Corps of Discovery's late 1805 downstream trip** through the Gorge, they began to encounter trade goods from the coast

(including a blue sailor's jacket worn by an Indian greeting them near the John Day River on Oct. 21). They made various camps near Wishram, the Deschutes River, Fort Rock (The Dalles), Crates Point, Hood River, above the Cascades Rapids, Beacon Rock and below Crown Point. They passed through Celilo Falls, the Narrows and the Cascades rapids, and through large populations of both Sahaptin and Chinookan speaking peoples. They noted large numbers of White Pelicans, Whooping Cranes and Condors, and marveled at the abundance of salmon and steelhead.

**On their return trip upstream through the Gorge in early 1806** the Corps made a long camp upstream of Washougal, then camped near Sheppards Dell, the Cascades Rapids (near today's Bonneville Dam), near Dog Mountain, near Major Creek (by the Catherine Creek preserve), to Fort Rock (The Dalles), near Horsethief Lake, Wishram, Miller Island, Deschutes River and the John Day River. They made detailed maps of the Columbia River that remain remarkably accurate today. While the larger group camped at Fort Rock, Clark, Sacajawea and 9 men went across the river for several days (ranging between the area of current Murdock to Doug's Beach) to trade unsuccessfully for horses.

**1805 (Oct. 31): Beacon Rock named by Lewis & Clark**, who also noted for the first time (using sticks stuck at the edge of the water) that the ocean tide affected the River this far upstream. **In the 1880s Henry Biddle bought the Rock** to prevent the Northern Pacific Railroad from using it as a quarry, and it was Biddle who built the trail to the top (in 1915-18). In 1935 Biddle's heirs offered the Rock to the State of Washington as a State Park in an attempt to prevent the Army Corps of Engineers from using the rock for the south jetty of the Columbia River. Washington at first declined the offer, but then accepted after Oregon proposed to make it a park. **Coincidentally**, an older relative of Henry Biddle – **Nicholas Biddle – was the first editor of the Lewis & Clark Journals**.

**1806 (March 30): Mount Jefferson named by Lewis & Clark**, noted by them from the vicinity of present Vancouver, Washington on their return trip east (Clark's journal entry for this day noted they "*discovered a high mountain SE...which we call Mt. Jefferson*"). **Lewis' entry for the same day noted** that he found the snow-covered cone of **Mount St. Helens** to be "*the most noble looking object of its kind in nature*". **Lewis also noted that he found the current area of Portland-Vancouver to be the**

**most "*desirable situation for a settlement which I have seen on the West side of the Rocky mountains,*"** suggesting that it "*would be copetent [sic] for the maintenance of 40 to 50 thousand souls*" (a nice thought, but two hundred plus years later the Portland-Vancouver Metropolitan Area has more than 2 million residents, placing it as the 26th largest metro area in the U.S.).

**1810-1812:** encouraged by President Jefferson, and **only 4 years after Lewis & Clark return from the Northwest,** New York entrepreneur **John Jacob Astor finances two expeditions (one by land and one by ocean) to the mouth of the Columbia River to establish a trading post.** Both the Overland party and the Ocean party left in 1810 (the first from St. Louis and the latter from New York), planning to meet at the mouth of the Columbia in 1811. Both parties suffered significant hardship and loss getting to the mouth of the Columbia, with the Ocean party arriving in March of 1811 while members of the Overland party struggled in over a period of months from late 1811 to 1812. As noted below, the venture failed and Fort Astoria was sold to the British by 1813.

> **The Ocean party** sailed around Cape Horn at the tip of South America and stopped in Hawaii for supplies, adding more expedition members. The Ocean party arrived in March of 1811 but lost 8 men trying to cross the Columbia River bar. They ultimately did establish a fur trading post at what is now Astoria, Oregon, as the Pacific Fur Company. Sea otters and beaver were to be the focus of the trade, intended to be traded to China, then carry goods from China to Europe and return to New York.
>
> **The Overland party** followed a route south of the Lewis & Clark expedition to avoid the Blackfeet (going up the Platte River instead of the Missouri). In doing so, they pioneered parts of what would later become the Oregon Trail, but they also blundered into impassable rapids in the upper Snake River and Hells Canyon, suffering incredible hardship. The survivors straggled in to Fort Astoria in several small groups in late 1811 and early 1812. On a return trip to bring news of the expeditions back to Astor, some members discovered South Pass in southwestern Wyoming, which became an important cutoff for pioneers because it was broad and gentle enough to allow wagons to cross the Rockies. **John Day**, a hunter from Virginia (who the river and town in Oregon were later named for), was a member of the Overland party but suffered greatly in the journey and ultimately returned East. Botanist **Thomas Nuttall**, who identified many of the plants and animals

found in the Gorge, was a member of the Overland party for part of the expedition.

**1811: British explorer and naturalist David Thompson is the first non-Indian to travel the entire length of the Columbia River.** Thompson worked with the (British) Northwest Fur Company and was sent to establish a trading center at the mouth of the Columbia in advance of Astor's expeditions, only to find the Astorians had arrived a few months earlier. Thompson continued to work with the Hudson Bay Company for years.

**1812-1813: Fort Astoria is sold to the British** (and renamed Fort George), the result of hardships suffered by both the Overland and Ocean expeditions sent west by John Jacob Astor (loss of personnel and trading supplies), and the fact that many members of the Astor expedition were British or Canadian subjects who upon learning of the U.S. declaration of war against Britain in the War of 1812 decided to switch allegiance (a British warship was also falsely rumored to arrive at the mouth of Columbia shortly, which influenced the decision to sell). British and French-Canadian trappers were far more numerous in the Columbia Basin than Americans at this point. Astor was shocked when he learned that his partners and settlers had sold out (and at a price much reduced from his investment), but Americans and British continued to live in peace throughout the Columbia region.

**1813: the British Northwest Fur Company assumes operation of John Jacob Astor's American Pacific Fur Company** fort and outpost at the mouth of the Columbia River. The Hudson Bay Company subsequently acquired it in 1821. The presence of the large Hudson Bay Company strengthened Britain's claims to the Northwest and Gorge area and brought more French-Canadian voyageurs and trappers to the Gorge.

**1824-25: Fort Vancouver established by the Hudson Bay Company** near present day Vancouver as its Northwest headquarters. John McLoughlin oversaw the Fort and its trading activities throughout the Northwest. Fort Vancouver was the center of commerce for the Northwest and the Gorge for many years, until sometime after the Treaty of Oregon was finalized in 1846. Trappers (and naturalists) canoed or walked the length of the Columbia River several times a year, based out of the Fort.

**1824-27; 1829-32: Scottish explorer and naturalist David Douglas** visits the Gorge on two separate occasions, walking or riding canoes up and down the Columbia River several times over the course of several years, cataloging numerous plants new to science. Douglas was the first fully trained naturalist to spend considerable time in the Gorge (earlier visits were short in duration).

**1827: Hudson Bay Company begins first commercial logging** in the Northwest and begins operation of a water powered sawmill near Fort Vancouver.

**1832-1837:** following the earlier efforts of John Jacob Astor, **American Nathaniel Wyeth attempts to establish trading posts on the Columbia, to compete with the Hudson Bay Company.** Wyeth was a Boston inventor who was friends with Hall Kelly (see below) and became consumed with the idea of settling the Oregon country. He led a group of 20 men to the Gorge in 1832, but only 8 made it to Fort Vancouver, and his trading effort failed. He returned to Boston in 1833 and tried again in 1834 with 70 men. He ran out of trading supplies en route but established a trading post (Fort Hall) near what is today Pocatello, Idaho. He also established a small post on Sauvies Island (Fort Williams) across from the Hudson Bay Company's Fort Vancouver. Those efforts soon fell through as well, and by 1837 Wyeth had sold all his interests to Hudson Bay, at a loss. Members of Wyeth's second expedition included naturalists **Thomas Nuttall** and **John Townsend** (both names associated with plants and birds found in the Gorge), and **Jason Lee**, who later started the Methodist Mission in The Dalles (see 1838 below). A railroad station and post office was later established near the unincorporated hamlet of Wyeth off I-84 at the east end of the Gorge.

**1834**: **Mt. Adams named by American promoter Hall Kelley** (who was trying to rename all of the Cascade volcanoes for U.S. Presidents as part of his unusual efforts to encourage migration to the Oregon country to help sustain an American presence over that of Great Britain). But for a mapmaking error Kelley would have renamed Mt. Hood for President Adams – the current Mt. Adams was not his intended place for the name. The Yakama/Klickitat (Sahaptin language) name for Mt. Adams was and is Pahto.

**1836**: **Hudson Bay Company brings first steam powered boat (a sternwheeler) into the lower Columbia** (named the Beaver). The Oregon Steam Navigation Company managed most boats in the river in later years, up to 1883.

**1838**: **first missionary settlement established in the Gorge**, near The Dalles (Jason and Daniel Lee's Wascopam Methodist Mission). Marcus Whitman had established a Presbyterian Mission near Walla Walla in 1836, and both missions eventually provided assistance to pioneers coming west on the Oregon Trail.

**1841-1869:** the **Oregon Trail** began as a foot and horse path that followed the path of the Astorians return trip in 1812. The trail started in Independence, Missouri, and followed the Platte River west, then crossed the Rockies over the South Pass, which was passable for wagons. The Bartleson-Bidwell party was the first wagon train credited to use the route that became known as the Oregon Trail (splitting from a larger group heading to California). A much larger group (called "the Great Migration") followed the same route in 1843. That and subsequent wagon trains (some bringing herds of cattle) found their way to The Dalles, where some went downriver to Portland on boats or rafts, while others went south and west over Mt. Hood on the Barlow Road and Pass (see entry below). Willamette Valley was the destination of many using the Trail, based on glowing descriptions from Lewis & Clark, the Astorians and others. As many as 400,000 people started their journey on the Oregon Trail (with some splitting off to go places other than what would take them to or through the Gorge and a few turning back). Use of the Trail largely died out when the first transcontinental railroad was completed in 1869. The Oregon Trail pioneers had a significant impact on subsequent development and life in the Gorge.

**1843: City of Portland founded**, when William Overton and Asa Lovejoy filed a claim on land on the west bank of the Willamette River. Overton subsequently sold his interest to Francis Pettygrove, and in 1845 Lovejoy and Pettygrove flipped a coin to decide whether to name the new city after Lovejoy's hometown (Boston, Mass.), or Pettygrove's hometown (Portland, Maine). Pettygrove obviously won the coin toss. The city was incorporated on February 8, 1851 and was the largest population center in the NW for many decades. The Portland metro area was the 26th largest in the U.S. in the 2020 census.

**1846: Barlow Road constructed as the final overland stretch of the Oregon Trail**; Sam Barlow, Joel Palmer and Phillip Foster supervised marking of the road, with subsequent funding from the Oregon Territorial government.

**1846 (June 15): Treaty of Oregon establishes the present-day boundary between U.S. and Canada** at the 49th parallel, ending joint occupancy of the Northwest by Britain and the U.S. (Canada did not become independent of Great Britain until 1867). Great Britain had argued for the Columbia River to be the boundary between the countries, while the U.S. Congress had wanted to claim northward to 54' 40" latitude, to include Vancouver Island (this was the source of the "54-40 or fight" political cry of the day). The nations settled on the 49th parallel in order to avoid another military conflict like the War of 1812, giving Vancouver Island to Canada but keeping most of the Columbia River in the United States. The fact that the Oregon Trail brought so many Americans into the Northwest and Gorge area influenced the negotiations for the boundary between the U.S. and Canada.

**1846: first scheduled ferry across the Columbia River between Hudson Bay's Fort Vancouver and Hayden Island (now the north end of Portland).** Native residents of the Gorge used large canoes to transport people and cargo across the Columbia River for thousands of years. As Euro-American pioneers arriving on the Oregon Trail built rafts to carry their belongings from The Dalles to Portland, some rafts were re-purposed as temporary, personal or limited use ferries, especially since the Hudson Bay Company trading post at Vancouver, Washington remained the main source of supplies. Commercial ferries that operated with some schedule sprouted up throughout the Gorge in the following decades, and the states of Washington and Oregon began regulation of them in the early 20th century.

**1847:** conflict between tribal peoples and missionaries results in the murder of Marcus Whitman, his wife and 12 other non-Indians near Walla Walla, Washington, known as the **Whitman Massacre.** The action resulted in increased military patrols **and construction of outpost forts in the Gorge**, eventually including Fort Dalles. It also led the Mission in The Dalles to close two years later out of concern for more conflict.

**1848 (August 14): Oregon Territory established** by Congress. The new Territory included the current states of Oregon, Washington and Idaho.

**1849: Fort Dalles constructed** as a military outpost (initially called Camp Drum and then Fort Drum). Officers stationed at Fort Dalles over the years included such familiar Oregon place names as Harney, Alvord and Jordan. The Dalles had long been a place of Indian habitation, called WinQuatt.

**1849 (September 3): Clarke County established** by the provisional government of the Oregon Territory. The County initially included all of current Washington State, but was gradually subdivided, until reaching its current boundaries in 1880. The County was named after Lewis & Clark; the spelling was corrected by the State legislature to "Clark" in 1925.

**1850: Oregon Donation Land Act (September 27)** became effective. It was passed by the U.S. Congress and allowed "white and Indian half breeds" to claim 320 acres (another 320 if married), if the filers occupied and improved the land. The open purpose of the Act was to dispossess Indian claims to land. The law expired in 1855 – when the Treaties more fully dispossessed tribes of their land – but in those few years more than 7,000 claims were made to some 2.5 million acres.

**1850**: **Crates Point named** for Edward Crate, a French-Canadian trapper who came to the Vancouver area in 1838 to work with the Hudson Bay Company. He settled near The Dalles in 1850 with a native wife and filed a claim on roughly 640 acres in 1851, encompassing Crates Point. Lewis & Clark camped near here on their downriver journey, on October 28, 1805. Many early French- Canadian voyageurs and trappers intermarried with first peoples and settled in and near the Gorge.

**1851**: **first (mule powered) wooden rail portage in the Gorge around the Cascades rapids** (built by Hardin Chenoweth, who charged $0.75 per 100 pounds carried).

**1851: a steamboat is hauled upstream through the Cascades Rapids**, to ply the middle River in the Gorge (the "James P. Flint").

**1853 (February 8): Washington Territory established by Congress** (initially proposed to be called Columbia Territory), dividing part of the Oregon Territory created in 1848 into a new Territory consisting of present day Washington and the northern parts of Idaho and northwestern Montana. Congress gave concurrent jurisdiction over the Columbia River to the Oregon and Washington Territorial governments.

**1853: first steamship to establish a scheduled route between the Cascades rapids and The Dalles** (the "Eagle").

**1853**: **Isaac Stevens** appointed Governor of Washington Territory and Superintendent of Indian Affairs. He was initially tasked by Congress to survey a northern route for a railroad to the Northwest, but once he became Governor he was asked to negotiate treaties with Northwest tribes to open the country for settlement and development. In contrast to Joel Palmer (see below), Stevens was criticized by his Territorial Legislature for being too harsh on Indians (especially the Yakama and Nisqually), although he survived calls for removal from office. Stevens returned East in 1857, where he was killed in the Civil War (in 1862). His son Hazard was later credited with being one of the first non-Indians to climb Mt. Rainier, in 1870.

**1853: Joel Palmer appointed Commissioner of Indian Affairs for the Oregon Territory.** Palmer worked with Isaac Stevens in negotiating treaties with Indians living in or using the Gorge. Ironically, Palmer was criticized by many settlers for giving "too much" to Indians – being any reservation land at all – while he was criticized by the tribes for moving them off traditional lands. His perceived pro-Indian policies caused him to be recalled from office by the Territorial Legislature in 1857.

**1854 (March): Skamania County established** (the name is from a Chinookan word meaning swift water); population in the year 2020 was roughly 12,000 people.

**1854 (July): Wasco County established** (named after the local Wasco'pam Indians), originally extending from the Cascade Mountains to the Rocky Mountains, bounded by the Columbia River and the California border (encompassing more than 130,000 square miles). Until subsequently reduced in size, Wasco was the largest county ever created in the U.S. Population in 2020 roughly 27,000.

**1854 (December): Multnomah County established** (named after the Multnomah group of Chinookan Indians who lived around Sauvies Island). The smallest, but also the most populous, county in Oregon. Population in 2020 roughly 815,000.

**1854: first Commercial Ferry established at The Dalles** to carry passengers and wagons to and from the Dallesport area (then referred to as the "Grand Dalles"). Although unincorporated, **the City of Dallesport** dates back to establishment of the ferry crossing. Originally called Rockland or Rockland Flats, at roughly 1,300 people the population of Dallesport today is larger than many of the incorporated towns in the Scenic Area.

**1854: Jonah Mosier settles at the mouth of Mosier Creek** and establishes several sawmills. The railroad built a station there in 1882, and the Columbia River Highway came through in 1921. **Mosier** was incorporated in 1914 (2020 population about 500).

**1855: Stevens Treaties** (negotiated by Isaac Stevens and Joel Palmer) were signed by Congress, creating the Yakama, Warm Springs, Umatilla and Nez Perce reservations. The Stevens treaty negotiations continue to be the subject of controversy; they were conducted in relative haste, not all critical tribal representatives were included and groups were lumped together on reservations without reference to natural affiliations. On the other hand, Stevens and Palmer did include language in the treaties that allowed fishing at "usual and accustomed places…in common with," which ultimately helped to preserve native fishing rights in the Northwest and the Gorge.

**1857: The Dalles incorporated as a city**. Long a place of Indian community (called WinQuatt), the area upstream was referred to by Lewis & Clark as the "Narrows," being the rapids between Celilo Falls and the future site of the city. French fur trappers called the area *dalles* (intended to refer to the layered rock lining the shutes and rapids) at least as early as 1814. The U.S. Army sent troops to The Dalles in 1849 (right after the Oregon Territory was established). A U.S. Post Office was first established in 1851. Population in 2020 roughly 16,000.

**1858 (September 30): Hood River** U.S. Post Office **established.** The City was platted in 1881, but not incorporated as a city until 1895. Lewis & Clark named the river Labeasche (incorrect spelling of one of their French-Canadian expedition members: Francis Labiche); the river was also called Dog River in early days, reportedly due to non-Indian eating of dogs in the area. Local residents/pioneers Mary and Nathaniel Coe managed to change the name to Hood River by the mid-1850s. Population of the City in 2020 was roughly 8,000 (population of Hood River County in 2020 was roughly 24,000). Hood River was part of Wasco County until 1908.

**1858: a 19-mile-long wagon road built to bypass Celilo Falls and the Narrows.** This was replaced in 1862 with a 12-mile railway.

**1859 (February 14): Oregon becomes the 33d state.**

**1859 (December): Klickitat County established** (named after the local Klickitat group of Sahaptin speaking Indians, which speakers include the Yakama). Population in 2020 roughly 23,000.

**1859**: **first steamship launched above The Dalles** ("The Colonel"), which carried freight between The Dalles and Walla Walla and the inland empire.

**1862: a 12-mile portage railroad is built to carry freight around Celilo Falls and the Narrows**, constructed by the Oregon Steam Navigation Company

**1866: first salmon cannery established on the Columbia River** by John Hume and Andrew Haygood, near Cathlamet, Washington, downstream of the Gorge. This would be the first of many canneries operating through the end of the 1800s, which contributed to the significant decline of the historic salmon runs in the Gorge. Hume and Haygood came to the Columbia after having already overfished the Sacramento River in northern California.

**1870s: The Dalles and Sandy Wagon Road constructed along the south side of the Gorge** The road had local use but was too rough and steep to be used for extensive travel.

**1870s–1890s: establishment of more fish canneries along the lower Columbia River.** Once canning was developed as a means to preserve salmon and sturgeon, more non-Indians began to harvest the fisheries, using fishwheels, seine nets, set nets and drift nets. More than 50 canneries operated in the lower Columbia by the end of the 1800s. Gorge salmon was exported to the East Coast, Europe and China.

The fisheries began to decline almost immediately, and by the early 1900s canneries were closing for lack of fish. The last salmon cannery on the lower Columbia closed in 1980.

**1870s: use of fishwheels** on the River, to serve the growing canneries. Some fishwheels were extremely large in size, literally mining salmon, steelhead and other species in astounding quantities. Oregon banned their use in 1926, followed by Washington in 1934.

**1876: first orchards planted in Hood River Valley.** Pioneers Nathaniel and Mary Coe were among the first to establish orchards.

**1876: Lyle Post Office established at a steamboat landing** near the mouth of the Klickitat River; from there mail was distributed to all points east in Washington. James Lyle was the first Postmaster.

**1877: the Oregon and Washington Fish Propagation Company began the first fish hatchery to address declining Chinook Salmon runs in the Columbia River.** The hatchery was funded in part by Columbia River canneries (who were concerned about the rapid decline of Chinook for catch) but operated by the U.S. Fish Commission (which became the U.S. Fish & Wildlife Service). Over the next 140 years, the role of fish hatcheries in the Gorge was in frequent controversy. In 2007 Congress ordered a Hatchery Scientific Review Group specific to the Columbia River, which issued a report with various recommendations that remain in discussion today.

**1878: construction begins on Cascade Locks to allow passage around the Cascades Rapids.** The locks became fully operational in 1896 and then eventually submerged in 1938 when the Bonneville Dam was completed. Even before then, by the turn of the 19$^{th}$ century early railroads were reducing the need for sternwheelers so the locks were used less frequently.

**1878 (August 8):** James Lyle recorded title to 107 acres of land at the mouth of the Klickitat River and gave name to **the Town of Lyle.** The location had been used for years as a steamboat landing (largely to transport sheep/wool to market in Portland) and before that was the site of an Indian village visited by Lewis & Clark.

**1882: first railroad on the south shore of the river (Oregon side) becomes operational** from Portland to Walla Walla, operated by the Oregon Railway & Navigation Company (which eventually became the Union Pacific).

**1883: Henry Pittock, editor of the Portland Oregonian, constructs a paper mill at Camas, Washington to provide newsprint for his paper.** Pulp operations at the mill generated the distinctive sulfur smell noticeable throughout the east Gorge and Portland area for decades. In 2018 the Camas Mill closed its pulp line and downsized, now primarily making paper towels.

**1889 (November 11): Washington becomes the 42d state.**

**1893: City of Stevenson established** on land owned and developed by George Stevenson. A ferry connected the town to Cascade Locks on the south bank. The town initially grew as a service and supply source for sternwheelers, then became a center for forestry and logging. Since creation of the National Scenic Area and construction of Skamania Lodge, the workforce has changed again, but unemployment has dropped and the population of the City has grown (to roughly 1,500 by 2020).

**1894 (June): Highest Flow in the Columbia River recorded** at The Dalles, at 1.24 million cubic feet per second (cfs). The average flow of the river through the Gorge is around 250,000 cfs, ranging seasonally from below 100,000 cfs to over 400,000 cfs.

**1896: Little White Salmon Fish Hatchery constructed.** One of the oldest national fish hatcheries on the river, it today produces more than 17 million Chinook annually, primarily Tule fall Chinook (also known as the "white salmon" for the color it becomes after spawning). As with other national fish hatcheries in the Gorge, they coordinate with the Treaty tribes in propagation and restoration of the fisheries.

**1896 (November 5): Cascade Locks completed allowing reliable navigation around the Cascade Rapids**. Railroads limited the need for the locks in the coming years, and in 1938 the locks were largely inundated by commencement of operation of the Bonneville Dam (some remnants remain visible).

**1901: Spring Creek National Fish Hatchery constructed.** Flooded after the Bonneville Dam was built the hatchery was rebuilt in 1972 with a new design that relies exclusively on spring water. The hatchery currently raises more than 10 million fall Chinook annually.

**1902 (September 8): the Yacolt Burn** ignites, which goes on to consume more than a quarter million acres of timber (390 square miles) on both sides of the Columbia west of the Cascade crest (largely in Washington State). The fire was fanned by strong east winds and logging slash and caused the loss of 65 lives. The fire was started by young boys burning a nest of Yellow Jackets near Eagle Creek, Oregon. Ironically, 115 years later the next largest catastrophic fire in the Gorge (the Eagle Creek Fire of 2017) had similar causation: it was also ignited in the first week of September, in Eagle Creek, started by young boys throwing fireworks and fanned by east winds. That fire (see 2017 below) also burned both sides of the River, but while the Yacolt Burn was primarily in Washington, the Eagle Creek fire burned primarily in Oregon.

**1905: construction started on The Dalles-Celilo Canal**, to allow steamships to bypass Celilo Falls and the Narrows rapids. The canal opened for operation in 1915, and once complete allowed steam navigation from the mouth of the Columbia River up to Idaho and the Snake River. By the time the canal was completed in 1915, however, most cargo traffic was already being carried by rail on the south bank of the river. The canal was flooded when The Dalles dam opened in 1957.

**1905: U.S. Supreme Court in _U.S. v. Winans_** (198 U.S. 371) **upholds the 1855 Treaty rights reserved by Gorge tribes to fish at *"usual and accustomed places...*"** The case precluded the non-Indian owners of a fishwheel below Celilo Falls from fencing out tribal fishing.

**1907 (June 3): White Salmon incorporated as a city in the Gorge** (population in 2020 roughly 2,800). The town is named after the White Salmon River, which was in turn named by Lewis & Clark in 1805, upon seeing bleached out salmon after spawning. The Jewett and Suksdorf families were initial settlers of White Salmon and Bingen, respectively. The Suksdorfs first bought property in White Salmon in 1874. **Wilhem Suksdorf became a well-known botanist** in the Gorge and Mt. Adams area, having studied some at both Harvard and U.C. Berkeley.

**1907-1940: MaryHill Mansion and Art Museum.** Sam Hill purchased 5,700 acres at the east of the Gorge in 1907 for creation of a Quaker community (he was raised Quaker). Hill was a lawyer for the Great Northern Railway who married the company president's daughter (and married into her wealth). The remote location and lack of available irrigation caused him to abandon plans for a community, but in 1914 he began construction on a hilltop mansion to be called MaryHill after his daughter. Hill's wife did not want to live in the west, however, and Sam stopped construction in 1917. A friend of Hill persuaded him to complete the mansion as an art museum, and she helped him acquire a collection including 80 works by the sculptor Rodin. The museum was dedicated by Sam's friend Queen Marie of Romania in 1926, although it was not completed and opened to the public until 1940.

**1908: first railway operated on the north shore (Washington side of the river)**, by the Spokane, Portland & Seattle Railway (which eventually became the Burlington Northern).

**1908 (June 23): Hood River County created** out of existing Wasco County. The County boundaries have remained unchanged since it was created. Hood River is the second smallest county in Oregon (Multnomah is the smallest). 2020 population roughly 20,000.

**1908: City of Carson founded,** largely to accommodate growing forestry and reforestation efforts. Population in 2020 roughly 2,800.

**1909: salmon hatchery constructed near what is now Bonneville Dam**, known as the Central Hatchery.

**1909: Wind River Nursery established in Carson, WA.** The first of many attempts to begin to re-forest the thousands of acres of land in and around the Gorge that had been logged, burned or lost to erosion related to human activities. The original goal of the nursery was to grow 1 million tree seedlings per year. That goal was met and exceeded through the 1930s.

**1911: Oregon Trunk Railroad Bridge constructed at Celilo** on the east end of the Gorge (operational in 1912). The single track bridge connects Burlington Northern tracks on the north bank of the Columbia and Union Pacific tracks on the south bank, to a rail line going up the Deschutes River to Bend. The bridge initially had a swing span on the south side, over the Dalles-Celilo Canal. In 1956, during construction of The Dalles dam, the bridge was raised 5 feet and a center lift span replaced the swing span, as The Dalles Dam flooded the Canal as well as Celilo Falls (the rail bridge is just upstream of the Falls).

**1913-1922: Columbia River Historic Highway** constructed on south shore (from west to east), in several sections. Stretching from Troutdale to The Dalles, the road was about 74 miles as it winds along the river. It was the first Scenic Highway constructed in the U.S., officially dedicated (although not yet complete) in a ceremony at Crown Point on June 7, 1916. Re-numbered as Oregon Highway 30 when that was constructed in 1926.

**1915: Columbia River Compact entered by Oregon and Washington to manage fisheries in the Columbia River.** Congress adopted the Compact three years later, making the two states co-managers of all fisheries in the river. The Compact continues in place today, with jurisdiction over all fisheries shared among states, the Treaty tribes and Columbia River Intertribal Fish Commission, and various federal agencies (NOAA, F&WS, etc).

**1915**: **construction on Highway 14 begins** on the north shore (more piecemeal than the south bank U.S. 30 road). Initially called the North Bank Road or Evergreen Highway, it was officially named Primary State Highway 8 (there were five primary state highways in Washington at the time), then designated as U.S. Route 830 until 1968, when the name was changed again to U.S. State Route 14.

**1918: Crown Point Vista House opened** after construction from 1916-18. Intended to be a viewpoint on the new Historic Highway, it was constructed for a cost of about $70,000.

**1918 (July 4): Stonehenge Memorial dedicated in the eastern Gorge**, 3 miles east of the MaryHill museum. Sam Hill initiated the monument in 1918 but it was not fully complete until 1929. Hill intended the replica of Stonehenge to honor the dead from WWI (it was the first monument in the U.S. to so honor the dead of WWI).

**1920: Pear and Cherry orchards planted in the Hood River valley**, introduced after a hard freeze in 1919 killed many of the existing apple trees.

**1920s:** commercial **ferries continue to expand and operate in several locations in the Gorge**, including runs between: the Sandy River to Washougal; Cascade Locks to Stevenson; Hood River to White Salmon; Rowena to Lyle and The Dalles to Dallesport.

**1922: the Broughton log flume**, near Stevenson, began transporting logs from Skamania County to the River. The 11-mile flume remained in operation through 1986. Other log flumes, on both sides of the River, were also used.

**1924 (April 18): Bingen incorporated as a city in the Gorge:** the Suksdorf family from Germany originally settled the site in the late 1800s and named the town after their home in Germany (they thought the Gorge bore a striking resemblance to the Rhine Valley). Population in 2020 about 750.

**1924 (December 9): Hood River lift bridge opened to traffic.** Built by the private Oregon-Washington Bridge Company and originally named the Waucoma Interstate Bridge, the bridge was rebuilt in 1938 upon completion of the Bonneville Dam, to accommodate heightened water levels. In 1950 the bridge was purchased by the Hood River Port Authority (for $800,000), which started (and continues) to collect tolls as a source of revenue for the Port ($2 toll for cars as of 2022). The bridge opened to horse drawn carriages and Model Ts in 1924. Almost 100 years later traffic has increased significantly and plans for construction of a new bridge are being developed.

**1926**: **Bridge of the Gods (Cascade Locks) bridge** opens, replacing a ferry. The bridge was raised in 1940 due to higher water flows resulting from construction of the Bonneville Dam, about 4 miles downstream. The Bridge is part of the Pacific Crest Trail, connecting the Trail sections in Oregon and Washington. The Bridge was constructed by the Wauna Toll Bridge Company, then sold to the Columbia River Bridge Company in 1953 (for $735,000). The Bridge was subsequently purchased by the Port of Cascade Locks, which maintains a $2 toll as of 2022.

**1930s: Civilian Conservation Corps crews work on various projects in the Gorge**, including construction of **Viento State Park** (which, although appropriately meaning "windy" in Spanish, was the name of a nearby railroad station, created from the first two letters of three men named Villard, Endicott and Tolman). The Union Pacific railroad donated much of the land for the state park as in-lieu compensation for trees it had to cut down to construct the railroad. The CCC also constructed **the Eagle Creek Campground** and other facilities that remain in use today. The **CCC camp in the 1930s was at Wyeth.**

**1933: work on Washington Highway 14 continues,** as road and railroad tunnels are blasted out of the rock east of the Klickitat River, and a bridge is built over the river.

**1935: City of Cascade Locks incorporated** (the name obviously associated with the navigational locks completed in 1896). Population in 2020 about 1,400.

**1937: Pacific Northwest Regional Planning Commission recommends creation of a National Interstate Park to protect the Gorge** and recognize its "qualities of national significance."

**1938 (June 6): Bonneville Dam commences operation.** The dam includes a navigation lock and a fish ladder, which counted nearly a half million adult salmon and steelhead passing in the first year (469,027). A second powerhouse was completed in 1981, replacing the lock with a larger structure and increasing electric generation rated capacity to 1.2 gigawatts. The dam was named after Captain Benjamin Bonneville, who mapped much of the Oregon Trail.

**1940: Alcoa builds an aluminum smelter along the Columbia River near Troutdale.** The plant was operated under various ownership and levels of activity until finally closed in 2000. Air pollution from the plant gave rise to lawsuits from neighboring property owners. EPA placed the site on the Superfund National Priorities List (NPL) in 1990, but after cleanup it was removed from the list in 1996.

In 1991 some of the plant land was sold to the State and became the Sandy River Delta Park.

**1941 (May): Woody Guthrie writes songs of the Columbia River** while working (for only 1 month) to narrate and perform in a documentary about the BPA and public works projects in the Columbia Basin. He was let go out of concern that he was too political, but in that 1 month he wrote 26 songs, including *Roll On, Columbia, Roll On* and *Pastures of Plenty.* Seventeen of the 26 songs recorded in 1941 were eventually released as an album in 1988.

**1942**: in the second **Supreme Court decision specific to Indian fishing rights in the Gorge**, *Tulee v. State of Washington* holds that the State cannot charge license fees to Yakama Tribe members, because of the Stevens Treaty of 1855.

**1945: Congress sets aside land for in-lieu fishing sites as mitigation for native fishing sites inundated by completion of the Bonneville Dam.** By the 1960s five sites had been established: Cooks, Wind River, Underwood, Lone Pine and Cascade Locks. A separate Congressional action recognized 26 additional "treaty fishing access sites."

**1948 (May 31): the second highest flow ever recorded on the Columbia** floods the city of Vanport in north Portland, at 1.01 million cfs (caused by record snowpack and a cool Spring, followed by sudden warming and heavy rains in late May).

**1950s: Oregon and Washington both create Gorge Commissions** to explore ways to preserve and protect the resource.

**1950:** the Holocene geologic epoch by this date considered by some to be merging into what is now being called **the Anthropocene epoch**, named because of the significant impact humans have had on the earth in recent geologic time.

**1951: Portland Women's Forum forms a "Save the Gorge" committee, with Gertrude Jensen as chair.** Jensen persuaded the Women's Forum to press the Oregon legislature for action to preserve the Gorge, and the Forum purchased land at Chanticleer Point and then donated it to the State – which became the iconic photo point in the Gorge just west of Crown Point. Jensen pursued other land exchanges with timber companies to preserve more Gorge acreage. She remained active in Gorge issues but ultimately opposed the Scenic Area Act in the 1980s, thinking it would not give proper consideration to private landowners.

**1952: Willard National Fish Hatchery completed.** Managed by the Fish & Wildlife Service in coordination with Treaty tribes and NOAA, the hatchery raises 2 million Chinook and over 1 million Coho salmon annually.

**1953 (December 18): The Dalles bridge completed.** The bridge was initially operated as a toll bridge, but unlike the Hood River and Cascade Locks bridges, the Dalles bridge tolls were withdrawn in 1974, when the bonds were paid off.

**1955: the first use of barges to move juvenile Salmon and Steelhead downstream past dams in the Gorge is undertaken by the Washington State Department of Fisheries**, loading 200,000 juvenile Chinook Salmon onto a barge at the mouth of the Klickitat River and transporting them 165 miles downriver, in the process avoiding mortality at Bonneville Dam and predation in passage. The Corps of Engineers now barges more than 20 million juvenile salmon and steelhead each year around Gorge dams, pursuant to federal, state and tribal agreements, and court orders (see below).

**1956-1969: Interstate 84 constructed on south shore** (originally called I-82 then I-80 North before finally being named I-84); the interstate was initiated in 1956 as part of President Eisenhower's Federal Interstate and Defense Highways Act. The interstate was largely completed by 1963, but the final portion near The Dalles was not finished until 1969.

**1957 (March 10): The Dalles Dam completed.** Although as constructed the dam allowed fish passage along the south bank, it inundated Celilo Falls and the Narrows rapids, which had been one of the longest continuously occupied gathering points for First Peoples on the continent for thousands of years.

**1958: The Dalles Aluminum smelter begins operation.** Located near The Dalles dam for the large amount of electricity needed, the smelter contributed significant pollution to the city and the Gorge until it was closed in 1987 (at which time it became an EPA Superfund site).

**1964: Columbia River Treaty implemented, with the U.S. and Canada agreeing to increase upstream storage on the Columbia for flood control.** Discussions about an agreement for upstream water storage on the Columbia began after the damaging flood in Vanport/Portland in 1948. The Treaty was signed in 1961, but not implemented until 1964. It required Canada to construct 3 new dams for storage/flood control. In exchange the U.S. made payments and promised a significant allotment of hydroelectric power to Canada. One additional dam was constructed in the U.S. (Libby, Montana).

**1969: A significant legal victory for Treaty Indian fishing rights in the Gorge** was decided by a federal court in Oregon. **The Sohappy case** arose from claims brought by 14 members of the Yakama Nation against the State of Oregon alleging violation of treaty fishing rights in the Gorge. The court agreed with the tribes, concluding that the language of the 1855 treaties entitled the Treaty tribes to a "fair share" of the fishery. The case, *Sohappy v. Smith*, 302 F. Supp. 899 (D. Or. 1969) became known both for the judge who decided it as well as his holding, and the "Belloni fair share doctrine" had influence on subsequent legal victories for the tribes. Judge Belloni's decision was upheld on appeal (529 F.2d 570, 9th Cir. 1976). The parties ultimately agreed to a settlement of the case and **established a fisheries management plan for the Gorge**, where non-Indian commercial fishing is maintained below the Bonneville Dam, but commercial fishing for native anadromous species above Bonneville to the McNary Dam is reserved to the tribes, giving priority to treaty Indian fishing rights (non-Indian recreational fishing allowed only when fish runs exceed minimum agreed upon limits).

**1970s: Windsurfing established as a major new recreation activity in the Gorge**. Although the sailboard was invented in the 1950s, it did not become popular until the 1970s, and the strong and frequent winds of the Gorge quickly made it a windsurfing destination. The first world championship for windsurfing was held in 1973, and it became an Olympic sport in 1984 (for men) and 1992 (for women). **Kite Boarding** followed the popularity of windsurfing in the 1990s, and by the 2000s **Stand Up Paddleboards** became popular in the Gorge.

**1974 (February 12)**: following Judge Belloni's 1969 decision in the Sohappy case, **the landmark Boldt decision, concerning treaty Indian fishing rights**, ruled that the promise made in the treaties of 1855 guaranteeing Treaty tribes the rights to fish at all "usual and accustomed places…in common with" should be interpreted to allocate 50% of the annual catch to the tribes. The District Court decision was upheld by the 9th Circuit Court of Appeals in 1975 and the U.S. Supreme Court denied further review. The decision was then applied to other areas, including the Gorge (see below).

**1977: Columbia River Inter-Tribal Fish Commission founded**, including representatives from the four treaty tribes: Yakama, Warm Springs, Umatilla and Nez Perce. Initially organized to help develop fisheries management plans following the Sohappy legal decisions, the Inter-Tribal Fish Commission has become an important part of fisheries management generally, especially for Zone 6 of the river (between Bonneville and McNary dams, including the Gorge).

**1979: National Park Service conducts study of the Gorge, recommending protection.** The study was published in 1980, and (along with the eruption of Mount St. Helens) prompted serious further discussion about the various options for federal protection of the Gorge.

**1980 (May 18): Mount St. Helens volcano erupts** on the west end, north bank of the Gorge: 57 people are lost, and 156 square miles of forest land is devastated. More than 45 million cubic yards of lahar mudflow and debris stops all shipping traffic in the Columbia River.

**1980 (Nov. 18): Friends of the Columbia Gorge formed** with an announcement by Multnomah County Executive Don Clark that Nancy Russell (encouraged by John Yeon, architect and son of the builder of the Columbia River Historic Highway) would lead the group. As a non-profit, the Friends has actively supported various activities related to education about and preservation of the Gorge. Through donations and its Land Trust, the Friends has secured added acreage for protection within the National Scenic Area boundaries. The Friends were also instrumental in securing legislative approval for nearly 26,000 acres of additional wilderness area adjacent to the Gorge in 2009. Most recently, they have protected the Cape Horn area and led the "Towns to Trails" initiatives.

**1980 (Dec. 5): Northwest Power Act enacted by Congress** (as the Pacific Northwest Electric Power Planning & Conservation Act, 16 U.S.C. 39-839h), requiring that salmon be treated "on par" with economic demand for electricity in planning. The Act created the Northwest Power and Conservation Council, which is required to prepare (and update every 5 years) both energy and fish conservation plans.

**1981:** heavy rains create **mudflow off north face of Mt. Hood**, causing expansion of the delta of Hood River into the Columbia.

**1982 (Aug. 27): Mount St. Helens National Volcanic Monument signed into law by President Reagan**, setting aside 110,000 acres of the blast area for research and education. It was the first "volcanic" national monument. In the early 2000s a committee was formed (including Washington Senators Cantwell and Murray) to look into whether Mount St. Helens management should be shifted to the National Park Service to increase public use and economic benefit. The effort did not go far but was instrumental in creating the non-profit Mount St. Helens Institute, which took over responsibility for one of the Forest Service's visitor centers, and provides education and outreach.

**1982 (November): Pursuant to the Northwest Power Act, the Northwest Power Planning Council prepares a plan to mitigate the impacts of dams on salmon and steelhead in the river**, calling for increased restoration of spawning habitat, increased hatchery production to supplement native stock, improved bypass systems at the dams and barge or truck transport of juvenile salmon and steelhead downstream past the dams. Numerous lawsuits in the following years challenged the sufficiency of plans by the Corps of Engineers and other agencies, resulting in ongoing oversight by a federal court in Portland on recovery efforts for salmon and steelhead in the Columbia River.

**1982 (Dec. 22): Glen Jackson Bridge (I-205) opened as a new crossing of the Columbia River**, between the Portland International Airport and the Sandy River. Completion of this bridge triggered real estate speculation along the Washington State side of the River, and into the Gorge. That, in turn, gave further purpose to the Friends of the Gorge and other groups to find permanent protection for the Gorge.

**1984: Congress creates the first National Scenic Area at Mono Lake**, which became a reference for the Columbia River Gorge National Scenic Area two years later.

**1986 (Nov. 17): Columbia River Gorge National Scenic Area Act signed into law** (P.L. 99-663) by President Reagan, becoming the second National Scenic Area in the country (after Mono Lake in 1984). The Scenic Area is divided into federal lands (Special Management Areas or SMA), private and state lands (General Management Area or GMA) and Urban Areas. At present, the National Scenic Area is comprised of roughly 51% GMA, 39% SMA and 10% Urban Areas. The U.S. Forest Service is given responsibility for the SMA, while the Interstate Compact represented by the Gorge Commission is responsible for the GMA and Urban Areas. Population within the boundaries of the Scenic Area was about 50,000 in 2000 but grew to around 75,000 by 2020 (half of which live in one of the 13 designated Urban Areas, which comprise only about 10% of the Scenic Area).

> **The Scenic Area encompassed 292,500 acres as created in 1986**. More acres within these boundaries have been conserved by The Friends of the Columbia Gorge, the Columbia Land Trust and some private landowners to limit further development.
>
> **As part of the National Scenic Area Act the lower sections of both the Klickitat River and Little White Salmon River are designated as part of the Wild & Scenic River system.** Wild and Scenic status was designated for the 10.8-mile section of the

Klickitat River running from the Columbia River upstream, and the Little White Salmon for about 28 miles from the Columbia upstream, with more upstream miles added in 2005.

**1987**: **creation of the Columbia River Gorge Commission.** Created by bi-state compact between Oregon and Washington, the Gorge Commission includes 13 members: 3 each from the states of Oregon and Washington, appointed by their governors (1 of which, from each state, must live in the Gorge) and 1 from each of the 6 counties in the National Scenic Area (appointed by the counties). In addition, the 13$^{th}$ member of the Gorge Commission is appointed by the Forest Service in a non-voting role. Although not required, at least one representative has been a member of one of the four Treaty Tribes in recent years.

**1987: Steigerwald Wildlife Refuge established near Washougal**, as part of mitigation for construction of the second powerhouse at Bonneville Dam, which inundated lowlands and wetlands. At 1,049 acres, much of Steigerwald is within the boundaries of the National Scenic Area. Managed by the U.S. Fish & Wildlife Service, it was first opened to the public (hiking trails) in 2009. **Franz Lake NWR and Pierce NWR** were established about the same time, upstream of Steigerwald. Both are smaller in size.

**1987: the last wild Condors are captured in California** in an effort to save the species through captive breeding programs. Condors were historically common in the Gorge, noted by Lewis & Clark and other explorers. The last confirmed sighting of Condor in or near the Gorge was at the turn of the 20$^{th}$ century. More than half the captive birds have now been released to the wild and the population is recovering (possibly someday to be re-introduced to the Gorge).

**1987-1996:** In the first decade after creation of the National Scenic Area, there were **various legal challenges brought against the Scenic Area Act, the Gorge Commission and decisions by the Gorge Commission.** All substantive challenges ultimately failed, in large part due to efforts by the Gorge Commission, the Friends of the Gorge and others to defend the Scenic Area.

**1991: first Management Plan for the Gorge completed by the Forest Service and Gorge Commission**. The Scenic Area Act called for Plan reviews and revisions at least every 10 years. The initial Plan was not revised until 2004. A second revision began in 2016 but is not complete as of this writing.

**1993 (March): Skamania Lodge opens** in Stevenson (the Scenic Area Act provided funding for both an Interpretive (Visitor) Center and a Conference Center, with

$5 million construction funds allocated for each. The statute specified that one should be in Oregon and the other in Washington. By agreement among the Gorge Commission, state and local officials, the facilities were located on each end of the Scenic Area (the Conference Center becoming Skamania Lodge near Stevenson and the Visitor Center becoming the Columbia River Gorge Discovery Center and Museum near The Dalles).

**1996:** heavy rains create **landslides near Warrendale**, damaging several homes (and illustrating the continuing process of landslides in the Gorge).

**1997: Columbia River Gorge Discovery Center & Museum opens** west of The Dalles, implementing the intent of the Scenic Area Act to have both an Interpretative Center and a Conference Center (the Discovery Center meets the first goal, and serves as the official visitor center for the Scenic Area, and Skamania Lodge west of Stevenson, Washington is the conference center envisioned by the Act).

**1999 (Mar 24): Lower Columbia River Salmon and Steelhead declared "threatened" under the Endangered Species Act**, by the National Marine Fisheries Service. The threats to these fish began with overfishing from the mid-1800s to the early 1900s but decline of the fisheries was made worse by loss of habitat associated with dam building through the mid-1900s, and more recent depletion of ocean food sources. As of 2011, there were 13 runs of salmon and steelhead in the Columbia River system that were listed as either threatened or endangered.

**2002: designation of the Historic Columbia River Highway State Trail** as a 73-mile-long project to convert and restore the 1920s era Columbia River Highway (Route 30), extending from the Sandy River in the west to milepost 88 at The Dalles in the east end of the Gorge. Some of the restored Highway will be open to vehicles and other sections only to hikers and bikes. Work on the trail continues as of 2022, and includes water and rest stops, and bike repair stations. When complete, much of the trail will become part of the Towns to Trails initiative.

**2004**: **creation of the Columbia River Gorge American Viticultural Area**, recognizing the eastern Gorge as an important vinifera grape producing area. Four counties are within this AVA (Hood River; Wasco; Skamania and Klickitat), with some 40 wineries producing wine from more than 30 grape varieties, including award winning Syrah, Pinot Gris, Cabernet and Zinfandel (among others).

**2005**: **Upper White Salmon River designated as a Wild and Scenic River.**

**2005: Friends of the Columbia Gorge Land Trust** formed with initial donations from John Yeon and Nancy Russell. The Land Trust has conserved 26 sites within the Scenic Area, totaling more than 1,500 acres. The Trust manages acquired properties to restore native plants and provide educational opportunities. They continue to pay property taxes to the local communities.

**2006: Google builds a Data Center in The Dalles.** Google has expanded the facility several times, investing $1.8 billion. Located near The Dalles dam to secure the large amount of electricity required to operate, the Data Center generates little pollution, but has high demands for groundwater as well as electricity.

**2007 (October): Marmot Dam Removed from the Sandy River.** Constructed in 1908 as part of the Bull Run Reserve project to provide hydroelectricity for Portland, the 47-foot high dam was decommissioned due to rising maintenance costs and the availability of other energy sources. At the time it was the largest concrete dam removed in the U.S. Within a year native salmon and steelhead returned to waters above the former site of the dam.

**2007: A Northwest Passage finally reveals itself**, as a (seasonal only) path opens through ice floes from Hudson Bay to north Alaska. Not what or where the early explorers imagined, and created largely by climate change.

**2008 (August 23): Confluence Project dedicates Sandy River Bird Blind.** Architect Maya Lin's Confluence Project is constructing several installations along the river to highlight history of the land and people. The elliptical bird blind is at the end of a 1.2-mile trail off Exit 18 at the west end of the Scenic Area. Other installations are at Cape Disappointment and Vancouver. A new project is planned for Celilo Park.

**2008: Celilo Village restoration finished**, more than 50 years after it was promised by the federal government. A number of Indian people did not enroll in or go to reservations when The Dalles dam was completed in 1957, which inundated Celilo Falls; instead, many Wy'am people remained at Celilo Village. In 2003 Congress authorized funds to rebuild Celilo Village, which is one of the oldest continuously occupied sites in North America.

**2009 (Mar. 30): Congress authorizes the Ice Age Glacial Floods Geologic Trail**, with the National Park Service to administer creation and use. Little funding has been allocated to date, but the concept and planning is in place.

**2010 (May): Columbia River eulachon (smelt) designated as threatened under the Endangered Species Act**, with smelt fishing completely closed for the first time ever in the fall; this following a sharp decline from the millions of smelt that would return each fall (as recently as the early 1990s people lined the Sandy River to collect them in baskets). The catch from mainstem Columbia in 2009 was only 5,609 pounds.

**2010**: even as the smelt are declining, the **largest Spring salmon runs pass Bonneville Dam since 1938**, when Bonneville was the first dam on the Columbia (it remains uncertain whether high salmon returns in 2010 were due to habitat and species enhancement or favorable ocean conditions that year).

**2011**: **200th anniversary of David Thompson's first voyage down the entire 2,142 miles of the Columbia River** (the David Thompson Brigade of up to 150 canoeists recreates the voyage in its entirety, but this time encountering 14 main stem dams).

**2011 (Oct. 26): Condit Dam breached to allow the White Salmon River to run free** for the first time since 1913. At the time, this was the largest dam to be removed in the U.S. Only a year later, salmon and steelhead began returning to the river in large numbers.

**2011: Gorge Towns to Trails is launched** by the Friends of the Gorge, working with the Washington Trail Association, Oregon Department of Transportation and other groups. The effort is intended to create a roughly 200 mile loop trail from the west end of the Scenic Area at both the Washougal waterfront park and the Sandy River Oxbow park, going east along a trail network that loops across the Columbia River at The Dalles, then returns down the Gorge on the other side of the river. The project will make it possible for residents and visitors to travel with light packs throughout the Gorge, staying at establishments along the trail, enjoying local restaurants and touring wineries and breweries. It will be the first such major trekking location in the U.S., similar to those found in Europe and Asia. As of 2022, more than half of the trail was complete with roughly 80% of the land to complete the trail secured.

**2014 (Feb): Rockslides close I-84 for days.**

**2017 (Sept. 2): catastrophic Eagle Creek Fire** ignited by two teenage boys playing with fireworks part way up the Eagle Creek trail. The fire was eerily similar to the 1902 Yacolt Burn, in that both began in the first week of September, in Eagle Creek (Oregon) and both were caused by young boys playing with fireworks. Both fires were initially fanned by East Winds and both jumped the river to burn in Oregon and Washington. The Eagle Creek fire burned nearly 50,000 acres (48,861), with another 260 acres burned on Archer Mountain in Washington State. Interstate 84 was closed for 11 days westbound and 19 days eastbound, and both railroad and river traffic was halted for days. Unlike the Yacolt Burn, there were no fatalities associated with the 2017 Eagle Creek Fire, but more than 150 hikers were trapped six miles up the Eagle Creek trail the first night (led to safety the following day).

**2019: National Marine Fisheries issues new Biological Opinion for preservation and restoration of native salmon and steelhead, including areas in the Gorge.**

**2020 (March):** the **Covid pandemic causes road and trail closures** throughout the Gorge; tentative re-openings begin late summer.

**2020 (August 14): National Marine Fisheries Service issues a permit to allow removal of Sea Lions from the river.** Sea Lions have long preyed on salmon and steelhead in the Columbia River, but declining fish runs and the fact that the fish gather below the Bonneville Dam fish ladder has increased the adverse impact of Sea Lion predation on the fishery. Both Oregon and Washington fish and game agencies, along with several Indian tribes, petitioned to allow removal of sea lions.

**2020 (October): Gorge Commission updates Management Plan**, addressing for the first time climate change and urban growth boundaries.

**2020: 40th Anniversary of the Friends of the Columbia Gorge.**

**2020 (December): Whitebark Pine proposed to be listed as endangered**, due to impacts from bark beetles and blister rust fungus, both linked to warming caused by climate change (the proposal did not include critical habitat, however, to the concern of various environmental groups).

**2021: Mountains Goats seen in Gorge**, one between Stevenson and Carson, another on the Oregon side of the river further east. Likely roamed from the Goat Rocks Wilderness near Mt. Adams. Mountain Goats have been re-introduced to the Mt. Jefferson area, but plans for the Mt. Hood area are pending.

**2021: 35th Anniversary of creation of the National Scenic Area.**

**2021 (June-July):** A long lasting **heat wave sets new records** for the Gorge (temperatures up to 116 in Oregon and 118 in Washington). The heat kills or damages thousands of trees in the Gorge. The event is attributed to long term climate change. In addition, **traffic limits, revised parking areas and/or access permits or timed permits are considered or required for summer visits in the Scenic Area.**

**2022 (January): snow and ice storms**, followed by a mudflow near Warrenton, **close Interstate 84 through the Gorge**. Highway 14 is also closed for some time.

**2022: permits required for travel through the waterfall corridor on Oregon Highway 30** during the summer months (May to September). New proposals for improved parking and trail access to Dog Mountain and other areas along Washington State Highway 14 within the National Scenic Area boundary.

**2022 (May): funds authorized** by the U.S. Department of the Interior **to upgrade some the treaty tribe in-lieu and fishing access sites.**

**2022 (September)** Steigerwald National Wildlife Refuge near Washougal, Washington on the west end of the Gorge reopens to the public after several years of restoration efforts to enhance wetlands and stream flows. The more than $30 million dollar restoration was undertaken as a cooperative effort by various federal, State and non-profit entities. The restored Refuge provides enhanced wetlands, additional habitat for wildlife and greater natural flood control.

# TRAVEL IN THE GORGE: BE PREPARED, BE SAFE

*Although there is easy road and trail access to the Gorge, it remains a wild place and can be dangerous for the unprepared. Every year visitors get lost, injured or killed here. Almost all such incidents are preventable. So be smart, be prepared and be safe. Watch your footing even at roadside stops (there are steep slopes and sharp drop offs, loose rocks and slippery moss all around), and watch traffic as it slows, stops or parks haphazardly. If you venture out on even a short trail from a parking area, always have some basics with you.*

*The Crag Rats out of Hood River County were the first mountain rescue organization in the U.S., formed in the 1920s. They are an all-volunteer organization, working in coordination with the Hood River County Sheriff's Department, the National Guard and other emergency services. Every month of the year the Crag Rats help find and rescue hikers, climbers and tourists who are lost or in distress. Set a goal for yourself not to need their services. Better yet, make a donation: www.cragrats.org.*

*Another longstanding Northwest outdoor group is the Mountaineers, founded in 1906. Based in Seattle, they sponsor a variety of outdoor education activities aimed to improve general knowledge about wilderness. In the 1930s the Mountaineers were the first to develop a "Ten Essentials" list for hikes or outdoor expedition. Variations of this list abound, and ready-made kits are available, but you can easily make your own. Try to have these items when you venture out in the Gorge. The equipment to include has changed over the years, but the basic idea has not. www.mountaineers.org*

## ***Be Prepared: Ten Essentials to Carry***

(1) *Navigation* (map and compass, GPS, etc.)

(2) *Illumination* (flashlight, headlamp, etc.)

(3) *Water* (always carry at least 1 quart per person, more if on a longer hike, and a water filter or purifier)

(4) *Extra Clothes* (depending on your walk and the season/weather; could be a vest, a raincoat or a jacket)

(5) *First Aid* (at least some band aids, antibiotic cream, etc.; several good pre-made kits available)

(6) *Fire* (a lighter or matches, flint and steel)

(7) *Knife* (folding knife or multi-tool is fine, has many uses)

(8) *Shelter* (could be a raincoat or a space blanket; more if needed)

(9) *Food* (at least some snacks, with both protein and carbs), and

(10) *Rain/Sun Protection* (again, could be a raincoat, and/or a hat, sunglasses, sunscreen, etc.)

Seasoned wilderness (and Gorge) travelers always have these items on hand when they venture out. You should too. And as the Mountaineers website says: "Better than the 10 essentials, pack plenty of knowledge on your next hike!"

# GLOSSARY

*acrocarpous & pleurocarpus*: the two primary types of moss

*anadromous*: fish born in fresh water that migrate to the ocean for growth, then return to their native freshwater streams to spawn and die; includes salmon, steelhead, euchalon, lamprey and shad

*Anthropocene*: what some geologists are calling our current geologic epoch, due to the major impacts to the planet caused by humans; tentatively pegged as beginning around 1950

*anticline*: a geologic fold that is convex, presenting like a peak or "A"

*basalt columns or columnar basalt*: when basalt lava cools it typically forms hexagonal shapes in columns; long columns are referred to as colonnade, while less organized material is called entablature or pillow basalt

*basalt lava floods*: a series of large extrusions of basalt that flooded much of eastern Washington and Oregon over a 12-million-year period; each flood left a layer of basalt columns in the Gorge, presenting in a layer cake fashion

*binomial nomenclature*: the formal system of naming plants and animals developed by Linnaeus in 1735, by which an organism is identified as part of a genus that shares certain features with other organisms, then classified by a species name unique to that specific plant or animal

*Boldt decision*: following the 1969 "fair share doctrine" articulated in an Oregon federal court by Judge Belloni, Judge Hugo Boldt of the U.S. District Court for the Western District of Washington held in 1974 that there should be an equal sharing of fish resources between Treaty tribes and non-Indians; the decision led to the further development of fishery management plans, which are under continual review

*Cascadia Subduction Zone*: the roughly 600 mile stretch of an overthrust fault off the Pacific Coast between northern California and Vancouver, British Columbia, where the San Juan oceanic tectonic plate is moving under the North American continental tectonic plate, causing earthquakes and volcanoes; the last Cascadia Subduction zone earthquake occurred in January 1700 and is estimated to have been a 9.2 event on the Richter scale

*channeled scablands*: term coined by the geologist J Harlen Bretz to describe the highly eroded and braided terrain of eastern Washington, caused by the glacial floods occurring between 15,000 and 18,000 years ago

*climax community*: an ecological community where plants and animals remain stable (unless or until physically disturbed by wind, insect, disease or human activity); the final stage of succession

*confine, contain, control*: wildfire response strategies first used by the federal government in the 1970s as alternatives to full suppression mandated by the "10 a.m. policy," which was adopted by the Forest Service in 1935 to control all wildfires by 10 a.m. the after discovery

*coniferous*: trees and shrubs that retain needles year-round and typically produce cones

*crustal plates*: large tectonic plates that cover the earth's crust (both oceanic and continental) and collide, causing earthquakes and volcanoes

*crustose, foliose & fruticose*: the three major types of lichen

*cryptogamic soil*: soil with a crust-like surface, comprised of interwoven filaments of cyanobacteria

*dalles*: term used by French-Canadian voyageurs and trappers to describe the layered rock underlying (and creating) the major rapids in the Gorge

*deciduous*: trees or shrubs that shed leaves annually

*deciduous evergreen*: trees or shrubs that have needles but shed them annually, such as larch trees

*defensible space or defensible fire perimeter*: recommended or mandated zones extending outward from homes or structures that eliminate or reduce flammable material, shrubs or trees (typically extending out to 100 feet from structures)

*dendrochronology*: the science of analyzing growth rings in trees to date events and past environmental conditions; can be extended back in time by overlapping trees of different age (or fossils)

*diversity*: the number of different species of plants or animals in a given community

*Doctrine of Discovery*: the concept that allowed European (and other) colonial powers to claim title to foreign lands simply by being the first non-natives to visit ("discover") the slightest edge of such lands; first used in the 1400s by the Pope to grant title to Portuguese explorers in Africa; used by both Captain Robert Gray to claim the Columbia River watershed for the U.S. in 1792 and then by Captain George Vancouver to make the same claim a few months later for Great Britain; invoked by the U.S. Supreme Court in 1823 to retroactively validate dispossession of native peoples in *Sherrill v. Oneida Nation*

*East Wind*: the foehn wind that develops when high pressure systems build east of the Cascade Mountains with low pressure systems to the west; gradient flow from east to west results in high winds through the Gorge and at mountain passes

*endemic*: plants or animals restricted to a certain place

*entablature*: irregular blocks of basalt lava flows, caused by extrusion of lava into a water or wet environment

*estivate*: the practice of some animals, such as Marmots, to sleep during periods of high heat or drought to conserve energy (distinguished from hibernation, which is longer and in winter)

*evenness*: the relative abundance of species in a diverse plant or animal community

*extirpated*: plants or animals that once lived in a given area but are no longer present (distinguished from extinction, where a species no longer exists at any location)

*fair share doctrine*: the legal decision from Judge Robert Belloni of the U.S. District Court for Oregon in 1969 that interpreted the 1855 Treaties' language guaranteeing the treaty tribes the right to continue to fish at "usual and accustomed places in common with others"; the decision was upheld by the Ninth Circuit U.S. Court of Appeals, then remanded for the parties to work cooperatively in developing management plans to fairly share the fish resources

*fixing carbon*: the process where photosynthesis converts carbon dioxide from the air into carbohydrates that plants use as food

*flag or banner trees*: where branches extend downwind from repeated exposure to high winds (a variation of the krummholz effect, but without the stunted vertical growth that results from more extreme cold and icy wind); occurs at low elevation in the Gorge

*foehn winds*: dry and gusty winds that descend from the leeward slopes of mountains

*Fungi*: the taxonomical kingdom that encompasses all mushrooms, yeasts, rusts, mildews, molds, etc. (more than 144,000 species)

*genus*: the taxonomical category above species and below family; a class of things that have common characteristics

*glacial or Bretz floods*: near the end of the last ice age, as glaciers melted in upper North America, the meltwater formed a giant body of water called Lake Missoula; the ice dams broke some 40 times over a 3,000-year period (from 15,000 to 18,000 years ago) and the resulting floods scoured out the channeled scablands of eastern Washington and the Columbia River Gorge; Harlen Bretz is the scientist who first described this phenomenon

*glacial erratics*: rocks that were entrained in the Bretz glacial floods, usually comprised of granite or quartz from the Rocky Mountains (Lake Missoula floods); such rocks settled out when the floodwaters backed up and melted, and can be found throughout the Gorge and lower Willamette Valley (called erratics because the type of rock is out of place where found)

*Holocene*: the most recent geologic period, from about 11,700 years ago (the last glaciation) to present (or to 1950, when some geologists believe we entered the Anthropocene geologic epoch, so named for the impact humans have caused to the planet)

*hydrology & geomorphology*: hydrology is the study of the distribution and movement of water on and below the earth's surface; geomorphology is the study of how topographic landforms are created by water and other actions

*jargon, pidgin and creole (Chinook Jargon/Chinuk WaWa)*: jargons or pidgin languages are typically developed when people create common words out of two or more languages; creole are those jargons that become more developed in both grammar and syntax and last for generations; "Chinook Jargon" (or Chinuk WaWa) was developed in the 1800s to create common words from Chinook, French, British and American words

*Key Viewing Areas*: a term used in the Gorge Commission rules to identify those roads, trails, recreational sites and other areas that offer significant scenic views to the public; more than 20 KVAs are identified; the rules require any new development or construction in the National Scenic Area (outside Urban Areas) to consider KVAs in project planning and site location. KVAs include I-84, the Historic Columbia River Highway, Washington Route 14, Crown Point, Rowena Crest, etc.

*keystone species*: an organism that helps define an entire ecosystem and is critical to maintenance of that system; first used by zoologist Robert Paine in 1969, analogizing some species to the role of a keystone in an arch (which is under little pressure relative to other stones, but without which the arch will collapse); examples in the Gorge include Whitebark Pine trees and Pacific Tree Frog

*krummholz*: a type of stunted tree shaped by continued exposure to high winds and limiting conditions, such as snow and ice; typically at elevation/timberline

*Lake Missoula*: the area of glacial melt water caused by ice dams on the Montana-Idaho border at the end of the last ice age; when the ice dams broke massive floodwaters coursed down the channeled scablands and through the Columbia River Gorge enroute to the sea

*lanceolate leaves*: leaves that are wider at the base than the midpoint, and that taper toward the apex end

*large fires and mega-fires*: federal fire management agencies currently define "large fires" as those that burn more than 100 acres in timber or 300 acres in grassland, and "mega-fires" as those burning more than 100,000 acres

*lenticular clouds or cloud caps*: stationary clouds that form over mountain peaks when high winds are aloft

*loam*: soil comprised of various material including organics from forest detritus, plant and animal remains

*loess*: soil comprised primarily of sand, silt and sediment (or volcanic ash)

*mesic*: an environment or habitat with a well-balanced amount of moisture, such as the west side of the Columbia River Gorge

*meteorology*: the study of climate and weather

*Miocene geologic epoch*: the geologic period from about 5 million years ago to 23 million years ago, during which time numerous basalt lava floods spread across the area that is now the Gorge (the floods occurred from 5 million to 17 million years ago)

*montane*: habitats in higher elevations

*morphology*: the study of form and structure in living things (distinct from function)

*mycorrhizas*: fungi that form a close symbiotic relationship with roots of vascular plants

*Ouragon*: word first known to be used in a 1765 written report by a British military officer who referred to "the great river of the West" (the Columbia River) as a potential Northwest Passage between the Mississippi River and the Pacific Ocean (the officer claimed to have heard the name from unspecified Indians); the word came to apply first to the Territory then the State of Oregon; other possible origins of the word exist

*Pangea (or Super Continent)*: Greek word meaning Whole Earth, used first in 1915 by German geologist Alfred Wegener to refer to the theory that at one time in the past there was a single land mass on earth, that split apart and separated into continents through plate tectonics

*pillow basalt*: irregular basalt formed when lava is extruded completely under water

*Plantae*: the taxonomical Kingdom that encompasses all plants on land, including moss, ferns, conifers, deciduous trees and flowering plants (more than 250,000 species included)

*polar easterlies*: prevailing winds that blow toward the east at the north and south poles; prevailing wind directions alternate with: there are easterly winds from the equator to about 35 degrees north (trade winds), then westerly from about 35 degrees to 65 degrees north; then turning easterly again up to the north pole

*prevailing winds*: wind that blows predominantly from a particular direction in a given region

*raptors*: carnivorous birds of prey, usually with large bills, strong talons and exceptional flight capabilities

*refugia or unburned islands*: unburned areas of vegetation within a larger burned area that provide important ecological functions, such as habitat for surviving animals and a source for seed dispersal

*rhizoids*: filaments or hairs that grow under mosses and some other plants that help give the plant structure or support (distinguished from roots which provide water and nutrients to vascular plants)

*richness*: the relative number of various species present in a diverse plant or animal community

*riparian*: habitats adjacent to rivers or streams

*roe – fry – smolt*: stages of growth for anadromous salmonid fish: the eggs are referred to as roe, which then become fry once they hatch and smolt (or just juvenile fish) when they grow large enough to migrate to the ocean

*sea floor spreading & subduction*: the geologic process where tectonic plates move over or under one another, pushing the earth's crust material down to the mantle of the earth

*species*: the taxonomical category that defines those organisms that can produce fertile offspring

*successional or seral*: the process of change in plant communities where plant composition changes over time, each stage building on the prior stage

*syncline*: a geologic fold that is concave, presenting like a valley or "V"

*topographic or orographic wind*: the process where wind is formed by constricted geographic features, such as the Gorge or mountain passes

*trade winds*: easterly winds that develop between 35 degrees north latitude and the equator

*versant*: a region of land sloping in one general direction

*water or hydrologic cycle*: the continuous circulation of water in the earth-atmosphere system

*waterfalls:* defined for purposes of this book as one of the following: *perennial* – year-round waterfalls fed by rainwater and snowmelt; *seasonal* – waterfalls that only appear during major rainfall or snowmelt events but follow predictable paths; *ephemeral* – waterfalls that occur only after heavy rainfall or snowmelt events and follow varying pathways that change from season to season and year to year; *inundated* – waterfalls now inundated (covered by water) from the impoundments behind dams

*wildland-urban interface*: transition zone between forested or wooded areas and land developed by human activity

*xeric*: an environment or habitat containing very little moisture, such as the east end of the Columbia River Gorge

# INDEX

## C

## D

## H



## I



## J



## K



## L

## M



## N

## O



## P

## R



## S

## T



## U

## V



## W

## X



## Y

Printed in the United States
by Baker & Taylor Publisher Services